THRESHOLD
EDITIONS

RADIO'S GREATEST
of ALL TIME

RUSH LIMBAUGH

with KATHRYN ADAMS LIMBAUGH
and DAVID LIMBAUGH

Threshold Editions

New York   London   Toronto   Sydney   New Delhi

Threshold Editions
An Imprint of Simon & Schuster, Inc.
1230 Avenue of the Americas
New York, NY 10020

First Threshold Editions hardcover edition October 2022

THRESHOLD EDITIONS and colophon are trademarks of Simon & Schuster, Inc.

For information about special discounts for bulk purchases, please contact Simon
& Schuster Special Sales at 1-866-506-1949 or business@simonandschuster.com.

The Simon & Schuster Speakers Bureau can bring authors to your live event. For
more information or to book an event, contact the Simon & Schuster Speakers
Bureau at 1-866-248-3049 or visit our website at www.simonspeakers.com.

Manufactured in the United States of America

1 3 5 7 9 10 8 6 4 2

Library of Congress Cataloging-in-Publication Data has been applied for.

ISBN 978-1-6680-0184-4
ISBN 978-1-6680-0186-8 (ebook)

*This book is dedicated to Rush and Mildred "Millie" Limbaugh,
who shared their wonderful son with our country.*

*To the loyal audience, thank you for your continued
support over the years.*

God bless you all.

CONTENTS

RADIO'S GREATEST
of ALL TIME

Rush Limbaugh
1992 Network/Syndicated
Personality of the Year

Rush Limbaugh
1995 Network/Syndicated
Personality of the Year

Rush Limbaugh
Network/Syndicated
Personality of the Year

INTRODUCTION

Kathryn Adams Limbaugh

I know so many of you are deeply missing your friend on the radio, the unwavering, optimistic voice of Rush. There are no words to fill the void—he is simply irreplaceable. However, I hope this look back at Rush's extraordinary life will make you smile, remembering the special moments you shared. Rush loved this country—and you, his wonderful audience—with all of his heart. He lived the American Dream and wanted us all to know it is never time to panic. No matter what challenges we face, our best days are always ahead.

Rush was the definition of courage and kindness. Despite his profound success, he always remained humble, never considering himself to be the incredible man that he was. One of the blessings that came after enduring a terrible diagnosis was that Rush was able to hear how important he was to so many and about the tremendous positive impact he had on our country.

A few years ago, when we began this book together, Rush thought it would be an overwhelming task to select individual transcripts from countless words said on and off the air. He would say with a memorable grin, "After all, they are all pearls of wisdom, right?"

Once Rush began to reflect on his life, the memories flowed naturally, and he enjoyed the process very much. He had the most amazing mind that could recollect details from even the earliest days of his career brilliantly.

As Rush told stories, often during treatments or at home in the library, we would take advantage of his love of technology and record his reflections on his iPhone. No matter what was happening around us, Rush was always a broadcaster at heart. The moment the Record button was pressed, he would speak flawlessly, just as if he were behind the Golden Microphone.

On these pages, inspired by our conversations, you will find a collection of Rush's timeless words from more than thirty years on the radio.

RUSH REFLECTS ON EARLY YEARS IN RADIO
Personal Recording in the Hospital with Kathryn, January 12, 2021

So, I just had this doughnut you brought me for my birthday. It reminded me of my first job in radio. This was 1966, what they called internships. It wasn't on the air—I didn't have a show. I just had a guy who worked there quote-unquote take me under his wing and show me the ropes—how it works, how to run the control board and all that stuff.

And he would pick me up every morning at home. And the first thing—this is around five o'clock in the morning—we'd stop by the doughnut shop and get a gigantic box of assorted doughnuts. This was not a chain, there was no Dunkin' Donuts or any other shop—this was 1966. It was just a guy and his wife, they had a doughnut shop, and I don't know what time they had to get there, because the doughnuts when we got there at five o'clock were ready. You could see them being made—it was the first time I knew doughnuts were actually fried. I had no idea they were fried.

The job was to get them and take them back to the radio station and have them there for the rest of the day for anybody who wanted doughnuts. The guy at the doughnut shop knew us and got to know me after one or two trips. That one doughnut reminded me. I don't think I've ever recounted that aspect of my early radio days to anybody . . .

Then when we got back to the radio station, the first hour we sign on—we were off overnight, on air sunrise to sunset . . . the first thing was an hour's worth of country music from the Grand Ole Opry. . . . I sat there and watched it and made sure the record didn't skip. . . . I was fifteen.

So, the summer of 1966 I show up every morning to be trained being a deejay and keeping the radio station on the air—meaning if the transmitter goes ker-plunk or whatever.

I fell in love with it, and I stayed at the radio station as often as I could. I learned and absorbed everything that I could. Everybody there was at least five or six years older than I was.

———— ❖ ————

RUSH HUDSON LIMBAUGH III

The Extraordinary Career of a National Treasure

At its peak, *The Rush Limbaugh Show* was heard on more than 650 radio stations across the country by over thirty million weekly listeners. For more than thirty-two years, the program was consistently ranked number one, making Rush Limbaugh the most-listened-to radio talk show host in history. The nationally syndicated broadcast debuted in New York City on August 1, 1988, with fifty-six total stations and a limited number of sponsors.

In just a few years *The Rush Limbaugh Show* gained a tremendous following, and hundreds more stations were added. Sponsors experienced sales spikes like never before. By the early 1990s, Rush Limbaugh had become the most powerful voice in talk radio, breaking up the mainstream media monopoly and paving the way for future conservative broadcasters. For decades, Rush and the Excellence In Broadcasting (EIB) Network dominated the 12:00 p.m.–3:00 p.m. eastern time slot on AM radio.

Rush was awarded the Marconi Award for Syndicated Radio Personality of the Year five times by the National Association of Broadcasters. He was inducted into the Radio Hall of Fame in 1993, the National Broadcasters Hall of Fame in 1998, and the Missouri Hall of Fame in 2012. In 2020, he was presented with the Presidential Medal of Freedom, the nation's highest civilian honor.

Rush thought of you in his audience as extended family and credited you for much of his lifetime success. He truly was Radio's Greatest, and had an exceptional gift that he shared with all of us.

Career Timeline

On January 12, 1951, Rush Hudson Limbaugh III is born.

At eleven years old, Rush uses a Remco Caravelle, a toy radio he received for Christmas from his mother in 1962, for his first family broadcast.

At thirteen, he shines shoes at a local barbershop.

At sixteen, Rush lands his first job in radio as an intern at KGMO in his hometown of Cape Girardeau, Missouri.

In 1969, he graduates from Cape Central High School (where he returns in 1989 to deliver the commencement address).

Never one to conform, Rush fails speech class at Southeast Missouri State University in 1971 for not outlining his speech correctly. He decides then that traditional university studies are not for him and leaves college to pursue his passion.

In 1971, much to his father's chagrin, he moves to McKeesport, Pennsylvania, to work at WIXZ-AM radio as an up-and-coming deejay using the stage name "Bachelor Jeff Christie" (he also uses the stage name "Rusty Sharpe").

In 1973, as a deejay at KQV radio in Pittsburgh, Rush coins familiar phrases like "all across the fruited plain."

Throughout his early radio career, he is fired seven times for a variety of reasons, including economic downturns hurting the radio industry and, as Rush called it, "not following orders."

In 1979, after his deejay stint comes to a halt, Rush accepts a position in sales and marketing in Kansas City, Missouri, with the Kansas City Royals baseball team. There, he meets lifelong friends and people he "otherwise never would have met," but longs to get back into radio. "Corporate life was not for me," he says at the time.

In 1984, he is recruited by Norm Woodruff, a well-known radio consultant, to replace Morton Downey Jr. at KFBK in Sacramento, California. Within a year Rush becomes the top radio host in the city. This is the first time that Rush can put his opinions into the program and run the show as he wishes. He affectionately calls Sacramento his "adopted hometown."

The famous intro music of *The Rush Limbaugh Show*, "My City Was Gone" by the Pretenders, is first played on air in Sacramento in 1984 and remains the opening music through the life of the program.

Rush first hears Mannheim Steamroller in 1985. His playing of their version of "Silent Night" on the program becomes an annual holiday tradition.

In 1988, Ed McLaughlin, a top executive at ABC and a powerhouse within the broadcasting industry, asks Rush to come to New York. He is offered a two-year contract for the 10:00 a.m.–12:00 p.m. eastern time slot.

On August 1, 1988, the first nationally syndicated episode of *The Rush Limbaugh Show* is broadcast from the flagship WABC station in New York City. Rush's studio is located on the top floors of the famous Rockefeller Center in Midtown Manhattan.

In 1989, the first issue of the *Limbaugh Letter* is published; it will become the most widely read political newsmagazine in the country.

In 1990, in order to personally meet fans and promote the show, Rush begins the very popular Rush to Excellence Tours. He completes forty-five personal appearances in that year alone.

From 1992–1996, he hosts the popular *Rush Limbaugh* television show.

In 1992, Rush writes his first book, *The Way Things Ought to Be*, which sells millions of copies worldwide. (He will later write a second best-seller, *See, I Told You So*.) That same year, Rush is invited by President George H. W. Bush and First Lady Barbara Bush to visit the White House and stay in the Lincoln Bedroom.

In 1993, Rush is featured on the cover of the *National Review* with the headline "Leader of the Opposition."

In 1994, he is saluted as the "majority maker" and made an honorary member of the House of Representatives' incoming Republican class. He is credited with helping the Republican Party take back the House for the first time in forty years. Around this time, Rush visits Israel and is welcomed as a foreign dignitary by then prime minister Yitzhak Rabin and past and future prime ministers Shimon Peres, Ariel Sharon, and Benjamin Netanyahu.

In 1997, Rush escapes New York City taxes and opens the "Southern Command" studio in Palm Beach, Florida. He exchanges suits and ties for golf polos and shorts as part of a more relaxed lifestyle in a warm climate.

On October 7, 2001, he announces to listeners that he has lost his hearing and is almost 100 percent deaf. Later that year, he undergoes his first cochlear implant surgery at the House Institute Hearing Health Center in Los Angeles, California. For over a month, while healing from surgery, he remarkably hosts the radio program without being able to hear his own voice. He will undergo a second cochlear implant surgery years later.

In 2005, Rush visits American service members in Afghanistan and meets with world leaders, including Hamid Karzai.

In 2008, he signs a $400 million contract with Clear Channel Communications (which later becomes iHeartMedia). His contract is later renewed to run through 2024 with national syndication partner Premiere Networks.

The radio program grows through the use of innovative technology, including the early adoption of the RushLimbaugh.com website, the Dittocam studio camera feed for visual broadcasts, and the Rush Limbaugh app.

In 2009, Rush delivers the nationally televised keynote address at the Conservative Political Action Conference (CPAC) in Washington, DC. He calls this speech his first "public address to the nation" and the "speech that inspired a movement."

In 2013, he and his wife, Kathryn Adams Limbaugh, create the Adventures of Rush Revere series of children's books in order to combat the inaccurate American history being taught in many schools. Beginning with *Rush Revere and the Brave Pilgrims*, the series of five books skyrockets to number one on the *New York Times* bestseller list, and Rush wins Author of the Year at the Children's Choice Book

Awards. Millions of copies are sold, making Rush Revere and Liberty the Horse household names.

Throughout his career, Rush is incredibly generous, donating hundreds of millions of dollars and countless hours of personal time to charitable organizations around the world. In 2009, he is named one of the most generous celebrities in the country by *Forbes* magazine.

In 2020, he is honored with the Presidential Medal of Freedom, America's highest civilian honor, during the State of the Union address. That year, millions of listeners tune in live to the Largest Radio Rally in History.

The Rush Limbaugh Show remains the number one most-listened-to radio show for more than thirty-two years, through Rush's last show on February 2, 2021.

• • •

I would listen every day, and it felt like Rush was sitting right next to me saying everything that I was already thinking. He always gave us so much hope. I remember when he used to say he would let us know when to panic. . . . He never did. Love and miss you every day. —Kathy, longtime listener

• • •

Chapter 1

THE NUMBER ONE VOICE FOR CONSERVATISM

TRIBUTE
by Governor Ron DeSantis

Rush Limbaugh, in my judgment, is one of the top five conservatives of the past seventy-five years. I would put him in the same league as William F. Buckley Jr., Clarence Thomas, Ronald Reagan, and Antonin Scalia. Rush had a profound influence on tens of millions of Americans, and I always joked with Rush, "Rush, please give me a degree from the Limbaugh Institute of Advanced Conservative Studies, so I can hang it up in my office in the governor's mansion." Rush said the learning never stops, and so that wasn't something he could do, but he did say I'm the closest thing that he ever had to an honorary member.

But I can tell you Rush had a huge impact on conservatism and on our country. I was proud to be governor of the state that was home to Rush Limbaugh. We're gonna miss him dearly. There's going to be someone that will ultimately succeed him at twelve o'clock as the most-listened-to radio person at that hour. But there's no one that's ever going to replace him. God bless the memory of Rush Limbaugh, great American and the greatest broadcaster that ever lived.

In February 2021, Governor Ron DeSantis ordered US and state flags in Florida lowered to half-staff in honor of Rush Limbaugh.

G reetings to you, music lovers, thrill seekers, conversational-ists all across the fruited plain. Time for yet another excursion into broadcast excellence hosted by me, America's Real Anchorman, Rush Limbaugh, here at the Excellence in Broadcasting Network. It is great to have you here today. Great to be with you."

Every day at exactly 12:06 p.m. eastern time, Rush's iconic voice would come on the air, giving us all reassurance that it "is not time to panic." For many years, he was a part of our daily lives, and so many of you remember the first time you started listening to the program. For three hours a day, he would make us all laugh uproariously while he tackled important issues in the most brilliant way. Rush was an extraordinarily captivating man and storyteller, who would always say that life is show prep. He was able to make the most complex topics relatable. Rush spoke to all of us personally and respectfully while encouraging us to think for ourselves. He became "a father figure," "a brother," "a best friend you've never met," and made an incredible impact on the country and on all of our lives. Rush will forever be our American hero—Radio's Greatest of All Time.

From a young age, Rush was incredibly unique with a mind of his own. At just eight years old, he knew he wanted to be on the radio. He had a genius-level IQ and loved to learn, but was never interested in traditional classroom education, considering elementary school to be a torturous "form of prison." Rush never liked the idea of conformity and thought the hours spent in a first-grade classroom learning to paint were a waste of time. He began his budding radio career from his bedroom in the family home in Cape Girardeau, Missouri. There, Rush would imitate his favorite sports broadcasters while playing on his Remco Caravelle toy radio, showing, even then, his "talent on loan from God."

At sixteen, Rush started an internship at the local radio station in his hometown. He used to joke that he would quit everything he tried—to the great dismay of his parents—but never radio. In his early twenties, as an up-and-coming deejay, he moved to McKeesport, Pennsylvania, to begin working at WIXZ, taking the stage names "Bachelor Jeff Christie" and "Rusty Sharp." After a few years spinning records, Rush left radio for a short time to work in sales and marketing for the Kansas City Royals baseball team. He said of this period, "I met people I otherwise never would have met but realized the corporate world was not for me." Rush longed to get back into radio in some form.

RUSH DESCRIBES HIS "BIG BREAK" — 1984
Personal Recording in the Hospital with Kathryn, Fall 2020

I spent five years with the Royals, 1979 to 1983. A great five years—met people I would have never otherwise met—but I also learned that I'm not cut out for corporate life. I'm not a conformist. I can't just do everything everybody else is doing when told.

So, I wanted to get back into radio; it's what I loved most. I went back to spoken-word-format radio in Kansas City, KMBZ, and loved it. That station, unbeknownst to me at the time, was being consulted by a guy from San Francisco–Sacramento—Norm Woodruff—and after, I guess, about a year, I got fired at KMBZ because I was putting my opinion in the news.

I said, "Peter Jennings does that every night; why can't I?" "No he doesn't." Anyway, I got fired. . . . I was the most eager-beaver employee; it was just strictly 'cause of controversy, and they didn't like controversy.

So, this consultant, Norman Woodruff, calls me two weeks after I've been fired, says, "How would you like to come to California and be a star?" I said,

"Well, where?" He said, "No, I'm not telling you. Tell me that you'll come." That told me right away it wasn't Los Angeles or San Francisco.

So I say okay. . . . He said Sacramento, and my heart sank. Sacramento, state capital, I mean, good grief—big-market Kansas City—Sacramento. But I went, because it was the only job offer I had after two weeks, and I found out again how much I loved radio.

So I went, and it turned out to be the biggest break of my life, because two weeks after I got there, they hired a new morning team at this station—KFBK Sacramento—and morning drive is prime time in radio. I was 9:00 a.m. to noon. They totally forgot about me; they paid all attention to this new morning team they'd hired. It allowed me to do a radio show the way I'd always wanted to do it for the first time since I was sixteen years old! And it took off, and it dominated the whole market—became the number one show in the market— and that is what then led to my show in New York, national show, 1988.

That turned out to be the absolute best career move I have ever been offered, and ever made.

* * *

I'd get up in the morning, get ready to go to school, and I would dread it. I hated it. My mother would have the radio on. And the guy on the radio sounded like he was having so much fun. And I knew, when his program was over, he wasn't going to go to school. —Rush Limbaugh

* * *

On August 1, 1988, the first nationally syndicated *Rush Limbaugh Show* aired on WABC in New York City. Rush soon became a household name heard by millions on hundreds of stations nationwide. As we look back on Rush's incredible career, it is clear that his words transcend time and will always be relevant.

Rush worked tirelessly to perfect his broadcasting skills and develop an encyclopedic mind. Always mentally engaged, he read feverishly and learned from everything around him, mastering topics from politics to pop culture and economics. Rush also had an unwavering work ethic, devoting every single day to delivering the best possible program. Rush did not have a producer or a large group of people telling him what to say on the air. Instead, he relied on his printed "stack of stuff" method. "I never know how I am going to start the program," he would say, "I organize this stack of stories in front of me and see where it goes." Amazingly, the show flowed naturally and flawlessly as if he had planned the hours to the minute.

Every day after the program, Rush would return to the quiet beauty of his home library. There he was surrounded by a combination of high-level modern technology and a large volume of books, including historical biographies of conservative greats, American generals, Founding Fathers, and early patriots. Among the heroes he admired most were conservative legends William F. Buckley Jr., Ronald Reagan, and Margaret Thatcher. Rush learned from the conservative greats he admired and became the greatest voice for conservatism the world has ever known.

PART 1 — RUSH'S MENTOR WILLIAM F. BUCKLEY JR.

RUSH RECALLS MEETING WILLIAM F. BUCKLEY JR. IN 1990

I will never forget the first time I met Bill Buckley. It was at his legendary maisonette on Park Avenue in Manhattan. It has to be 1990, seventeen years ago. He had invited me to attend an editors' meeting of *National Review*. They did this once or twice a month, and they always did it—it was a tradition—at his home. I had my driver go around the block a couple times while I built up the courage to actually enter this place.

The important thing at this event, though, this evening was how Mr. Buckley and his editors, everybody there that night, welcomed me into their world. They had no idea who I was. I was just some whippersnapper on the radio. They were intrigued. "What's all this about?" They were very gracious; they were very accommodating, and it was that night—and you know, meeting your idol and having your idol interested in what you do and then end up being supportive and encouraging—it's one of the memories that I will cherish, one of the highlights of my life that I will cherish for the rest of my life.

That was the first night that I had a sense, if you can understand this, of belonging to the "movement." And here's one of the things that I think is, in a way, a little sad. As the movement has grown, it has become more and more competitive, and new arrivals in media and publishing and so forth are often viewed as threats now, or as interlopers.

Everybody is competing to be the "leader" of the conservative movement, the smartest guy in the room, the brainiest guy, the one who's inspiring all the thought. Everybody today, or a lot of people, [all] out trying to be the next William F. Buckley.

This creates jealousy and creates guarded personalities and people who become protective of their turf and so forth, and none of that existed when I walked into that *National Review* editors' meeting at Mr. Buckley's home. They weren't threatened. They weren't jealous. They wanted to find out what I

● ● ●

Liberals claim to want to give a hearing to other views,
but then are shocked and offended to discover that
there are other views. —William F. Buckley Jr.

● ● ●

was made of, who I was—and when they discovered that I shared the same passions and the same desires that had formulated the founding of [the] *National Review* and its ongoing efforts to spread conservatism, they welcomed me into their world.

REMEMBRANCES OF MR. BUCKLEY
The Rush Limbaugh Show, February 27, 2008

RUSH: For me to trace my knowledge of William Buckley, I have to go back to when I was thirteen, fourteen years old and hated school. I felt like school was prison. I felt like I was being controlled and dominated. When I feel like I'm being controlled, I'm outta there. I just revolt, I leave, don't want any part of it from anybody anyhow. So, school was not a particularly productive place for me. I did absorb a lot there, but only because I had to be there.

My desire to learn actually came from outside the classroom. It came from my father, perhaps the most brilliant man I ever knew intimately, and my grandfather, of course, and many members of my family, and tossed into the mix was Mr. Buckley, who had a newspaper column. I remember at age twelve or thirteen it was published in the *St. Louis Globe-Democrat*, which was the morning paper in St. Louis at the time [and] was conservative, for the most part. No longer publishes, of course. But I remember at age thirteen, fourteen, all the way up through high school just being mesmerized.

It was the things that Buckley wrote in those columns that literally created my desire to learn. Of course, listening to my father just rant on about a number of things constantly, regarding politics, cultural things—we were a very active family in that regard, and, you know, the old image of families sitting around the dinner table and talking about stuff was true at our house. For me it was a listening experience, and, of course, peppered with questions and so forth. The single greatest motivation I had to learn to read, write, speak the English language the best I could, to expand my vocabulary, came from Bill Buckley.

Bill Buckley is indescribable. He's irreplaceable. There will not be another one like him. And although that's true of all of us, once you take the

* * *

Idealism is fine, but as it approaches reality, the costs become prohibitive. —William F. Buckley Jr.

* * *

time to learn about Buckley and his life and look at what all he did with it—he did not waste a moment, did not waste a moment. . . . He was prolific in output, but it was his intellect and it was his good humor that [were] literally inspiring to me. Even after I went through one year of college and I was having trouble, flunked speech, should have called the course Outline 101.

Flunked speech, did every speech, showed up at every class and still flunked it. I said, "This is not for me." And one morning I was sitting in the house at twenty years old and I said, "I'm quitting." I told my dad, "I'm quitting. I can't handle this. I'm leaving. I've got a job offer in Pittsburgh, and I'm going to go there." And, of course, he came from the Great Depression, and that was the worst news he could hear. The formative years of his life were the Great Depression and World War II. You go through the Great Depression, and if you didn't have a college degree, you had no chance of getting a job.

He had great fears. I'm the only member of my family, I think, that doesn't have a college degree. He was very concerned he was a failure as a father, and I remember telling him, "Well, I want to be like Bill Buckley." He said, "What do you mean?" "Well, I want to be able to sit around and write and think and speak," and so forth, and my dad blew up at me. "What are you talking about?" He gave me a two-hour lecture on "Where do you think Bill Buckley went to become what he is? Do you think Bill Buckley just sits around and writes and thinks and speaks, and people like you have this reaction to him?"

I got a serious lecture on how hard and time-consuming achievement is. When you see the output of someone's work but you don't see what goes into it, you can make the mistake of assuming it comes easy to them, especially those who are great at what they do. They make it look so easy that you think you could do it, too. And you form impressions of how they do it, and you

see these people on television and so forth, [but] you really don't see any of the prep or any of the hard work that goes into the final product, and my dad was right about that.

So, it wasn't until I left the formal academic setting at age twenty that I got serious about education above and beyond what I'd learned at home. I'm not just talking about politics and political things; I'd absorbed a lot of that. But I started working on my vocabulary, all of these things, trying to acquire just as much knowledge as I could. I did it in trying to imitate Mr. Buckley, thinking he would say something like this. I was reading omnivorously and voluminously, meaning anything I could get my hands on that was of interest to me. So, one thing leads to another, my career spawns, it starts and stops, but eventually I got my break in Sacramento in 1984, which led to moving to Sacramento in 1984, which led to moving to New York in 1988.

WILLIAM F. BUCKLEY JR. DISCUSSES RUSH LIMBAUGH
on the *Firing Line* Television Program, September 16, 1992

Rush Limbaugh is by everyone's reckoning a phenomenon—the most spectacular media success in recent years. His preeminent medium is a culture almost ignored by American critics, even the most beady-eyed. It's because it's assumed that nobody who really counts spends time listening to people talk over the radio.

We should have taken more seriously the polls, that for a couple of decades that told us that one-third of the American people get all their news from the radio. It isn't news that Rush Limbaugh sets out to give, although he could not perform as he does without reading the scores of daily newspapers and weekly magazines he chews up. His medium is opinion. Advise him that the moon yesterday was caught blinking at the sun, and he will run that through his cosmology and come up with a meaning for it all.

What astonishes is that no one is surprised, and only the humorless are really offended. In this sense it's fair to say, I suppose, that he gets away with his scams as no one since Norman Lear got away with his, in his series *All in the Family*, done at the expense of every conservative position ever held, and glorious entertainment it was. *Veni, vidi, vici*, they said about Julius Caesar: he came, he saw, he conquered.

Rush was tremendously honored to receive the William F. Buckley Jr. Prize for Leadership in Political Thought. He shared his appreciation in the following remarks in front of an excited audience at the Breakers Hotel in Palm Beach, Florida.

RUSH LIMBAUGH'S ACCEPTANCE SPEECH

for the 2019 William F. Buckley Jr. Prize for Leadership in Political Thought

NATIONAL REVIEW ANNOUNCER: For his influence and accomplishment, this year's William F. Buckley Jr. Prize for Leadership in Political Thought goes to Rush Limbaugh.

NATIONAL REVIEW EDITOR RICH LOWRY: When the history of conservatism and of media in this era is written, Rush Limbaugh will loom as a giant. Rush is more talented than most and has used every single ounce of that talent to try to support and preserve this country, this Republic, and this last best hope on earth. Ladies and gentlemen, I give you Rush Limbaugh. *[Applause]*

RUSH LIMBAUGH: Thank you all. Thank you, thank you all very much. This means really a lot to me. Growing up, my father was a profound positive influence on me, but William F. Buckley was a close second in terms of inspiration, education. I never thought I would meet him. I wished that I had his brain. I wished I had the chance to get to know people that knew him. I wanted to know what it was that he had done throughout his life to become what he had become. Folks, I was so naive and from such a different part of the country. When I first heard about the *National Review*, the way I heard about it, it made me think that you had to be a special, select member of a club to get it. I'm thirty years old thinking this. *[Laughter]*

And one day I got the courage to call the *National Review* office in New York. A woman answered the phone. "Can I subscribe?" *[Laughter]*

"Yes . . ."

It was like Christmas Day. "I can?" *[Laughter]*

Yes, [and] she told me how to do it, and I became a subscriber and started reading it. The radio program took off and it took me to New York, and not to belabor the point, but I got the chance to meet Mr. Buckley at his invitation to an editors' meeting at his maisonette. You know what a maisonette is? It's not a condo; it's not an apartment. A maisonette was his Seventy-Third and Park Avenue apartment, with an entrance on both sides—makes it a maisonette. I drove around the block three times trying to get up the courage to go in. *[Laughter]*

Thing about Bill Buckley, I was telling some people at the table at dinner, Bill Buckley had this unique ability about him. He knew what he was to people. He was not arrogant, but he was very confident. He knew how to make whoever he was meeting feel very comfortable meeting him. And that's how he met me the night that I attended that editors' meeting, and it was a lifelong dream that I realized, and I can't tell you how much I miss him.

Folks, he was he was such a resource. I would love to have—just in the past three years, I would have loved to have been able to ask Bill Buckley, "What do you think of this? What's your reaction to that?" It was just a real gold mine for me, improving my life and extending his life to me.

I really, deeply appreciate an award with his name on it. To have my name in the same name of an award with William F. Buckley, I can't tell you how much that means to me. It's a deep honor, and I thank you all very much for it. *[Applause]*

When you meet people that you admire, people that you have almost an idol relationship with, it's one of the greatest things in the world when you meet them and they are exactly who you want them to be, exactly what you expect them to be. It's kind of like the way people are when they meet me. *[Laughter]*

* * *

The most terrifying words in the English language are "I'm from the government and I'm here to help." —President Ronald Reagan

* * *

PART 2 — RUSH'S HEROES: REAGAN AND THATCHER

President Ronald Reagan and Prime Minister Margaret Thatcher were in office during Rush's rise to national fame. He deeply admired both leaders for their strength and commitment to advocating for conservative values, and throughout his career, Rush often referenced their incredible accomplishments on the world stage and their leadership styles. He thought President Reagan and Prime Minister Thatcher shared a remarkable way of disarming critics with humor and fearlessness.

Some of Rush's fondest memories included visits with Prime Minister Thatcher and her husband, Denis, including the time he and Lady Thatcher rode around in a golf cart as he gave her a tour of the course. Rush would laugh, recounting the story of golfers staring and saying to one another in disbelief, "I could have sworn I just saw Prime Minister Thatcher and Rush Limbaugh riding in a golf cart!"

AFTER FORTY-FIVE YEARS, CONSERVATIVES STILL HAVE A "RENDEZVOUS WITH DESTINY"
The Rush Limbaugh Show, May 19, 2011

RUSH: We are now fighting to save our own country from itself. We are fighting within our own country to preserve our freedom. Reagan was exactly right. This is why the era of Reagan will never be over, because it is the era of our founding. It is the era of individual freedom, American exceptionalism. These are crucial times, and we are in an ascendancy here in winning this battle, at least in the hearts and minds of the American people, which I've always believed is where it starts. . . .

The era of Reagan is the era of our founding. It is never over. Ronald Reagan is not being held up as somebody whom every candidate must be like. That's not possible. People like me, who love and appreciate Ronald Reagan, have no cultlike appreciation for Reagan. This is not an attachment to a personality. It's an attachment to leadership and ideals and principles, ideals and principles [that] will never die, because freedom will never die. Therefore, the era of Reagan will never be over.

REMEMBERING PRESIDENT RONALD REAGAN
The Rush Limbaugh Show, June 7, 2004

RUSH: He was optimistic and happy. He was infectious. He dared to embrace big ideas. He dared to do big things to overcome huge obstacles in the midst of all kinds of experts telling him it couldn't be done, in the midst of all kinds of criticism, in the midst of all kinds of personal insults. . . . Along came Ronald Reagan, and there's no doom and gloom in Ronald Reagan. He's the optimist, eternally so, shining city on a hill. He would have none of this doom and gloom. He rejected Washington elitism, and he had since 1964 and before. Talk about core values; talk about sticking to them.

He rejected Washington elitism and connected directly with the American people who adored him. He didn't need the press. He didn't need the press to spin what he was or what he said. He had the ability to connect individually with each American who saw him. That is an incredible—I don't even want to say "talent." It's a characteristic that so few Americans have, so few people have, but he was able to do it.

He brought confidence, he brought vigor, and he brought humility to the presidency, which had been missing for years; and this profoundly upset his political and media adversaries to no end, and Reagan enjoyed that. Ronald Reagan rejected socialism; he rejected big government. He insisted on returning as much government back to the people as was possible. He cut taxes so deeply that even some on his own staff became disbelievers and wrote books about it. They were wrong. He was right.

Our lives today are a testament to how right Ronald Reagan was. . . . This has been a staple of this program since its inception in 1988—actually, '84 in

Sacramento, my adopted hometown, and that is that you are the ones who make this country great. . . . I'm trying to celebrate Reagan. Reagan knew because of his unbridled love for the American people, coupled with our God-given freedom, our natural yearning to be free.

Reagan knew that all he had to do was unleash that, and it was "Katie, bar the doors," and he was right. He was right then; he is right today. He will be right for as long as there is America. Those who choose to follow his footsteps will also be right. Those who choose to follow in his footsteps will experience the optimism and the good cheer and the love of country that he always had. There are many who will carry on in his tradition. I'm honored to be one of them. I wouldn't be sitting here were it not for Ronald Reagan, and I never met him.

You know, Ronald not only rejected socialism and big government but he also rejected communism. He defeated it ultimately. . . . Those of you who weren't around during all of this, the era of the Cold War and Soviet expansionism, it is imperative you find out. It is imperative you understand what this man did. It is imperative you understand how he did it. It's not just that he did it without firing a shot. He did it because he refused to accept it, all alone amongst those at his leadership level. So he set us out on a course to win, not "manage," the Cold War, and I consider that to be the final battle of the Second World War. He freed tens of millions of people who had been imprisoned behind the Iron Curtain for nearly five decades. Those people survive Ronald Reagan today. . . .

He knew America and the American people better than anyone, especially those who sought to govern from inside the Beltway. I'll never forget—it was, I think, 1990, and I was at the 21 Club in New York for dinner with some friends. I had been doing this show for two years. I don't want to over-personalize this, but Ronald Reagan believed things happened for a reason, so he wasn't worried about little details and the ups and downs of things, because he [took] the long view, saw the far-off distance, and just had faith that it was going to be okay—as long as America remained America.

Now, two years into this program and I'm being criticized, having things said about me that have never been said about me before, and I don't know how to deal with it. I'm getting advice from people. Should I respond to this stuff, or should I ignore it? People said, "Well, if you respond to it, you're sort of validating it. You're letting them know it bothers you. Just blow it off. Don't react to it."

I said, "Yeah, but then people are going to think it's true if I don't respond to it." This was one of the early frustrations that I experienced during this program: people saying things about you that aren't true. The instinct is to fix it and change the record. But I never knew what. I mean, for those two years, there was nobody who could tell me what to do. I was with no one who had been through it, and I really had no instinct myself what to do.

One night I'm at dinner, 21, and I had to go to the bathroom, so I walked into the restroom. The restroom attendant in there recognized me and came up, shook my hand. He was just ebullient. He started talking. He knew who I was. He started talking to me about the one time he met President Reagan, and he just was as effusive, full of love and excitement, exuberance, as anybody I can recall, just happy to be telling me this.

And after he went through describing what his meeting with Reagan was like, and it had been fairly recently, he looked at me, he cocked his head, his eyes got wide, and he said, "You know, Mr. Limbaugh, he never got mad at 'em. He never got mad at 'em once. He just laughed at 'em." I said, "Bingo. There's my answer." In the restroom at the 21 Club, from an attendant whose biggest thrill in life was having met Ronald Reagan. That man is a preacher today, that attendant. . . .

Throughout the early years of this program it was an objective of mine to keep the Reagan legacy alive. I was a product of it. It's not even enough to say I believed it. I felt like I was part of it, that I would not have had the life I have were it not for Reagan.

• • •

If my critics saw me walking over the Thames, they would say it was because I couldn't swim. —Prime Minister Margaret Thatcher

• • •

THE RULE OF LAW MUST BE RESPECTED, ESPECIALLY BY OUR ELECTED OFFICIALS
The Rush Limbaugh Show, July 6, 2016

I drove Margaret Thatcher around a golf course one day out in Colorado, a golf course called Eagle Springs. We nicknamed it "Ego Springs" because the membership is largely Wall Street billionaires who helicoptered in.

But anyway, we were out in Vail for a celebratory social weekend. She decided she wanted to see the golf course, but she doesn't play golf. So, it was suggested to me that the next day I take her, drive her around in a cart. "Would you do that, Rush?" *[laughing]* "Yes, I'll do that."

She left dressed to the nines, typical Margaret Thatcher in a dress. She sits on the passenger side of the golf cart and we go tooling around the cart path. People are out playing golf, and as we would approach tee boxes or players about to hit shots, we would stop so as not to be a distraction, using proper golf course etiquette. She was wearing an Easter-type bonnet hat. It was windy. But that didn't stop people from noticing her.

And you should have seen the double-takes and the open-mouthed stares. 'Cause it's Margaret Thatcher being driven around a golf course, just seeing it; she wants to see the beauty, the vistas and so forth. And there were several dinners that took place, and I remember at each dinner, she held court. Whatever she introduced as subject matter was what we all discussed.

. . .

Ronald Reagan and Margaret Thatcher did more to liberate people by defeating the Soviet Union and freeing Eastern Europe than the Obamas, the Clintons, and Kerrys of this world ever have. They were all on the wrong side of that debate. —Rush Limbaugh

. . .

IN HONOR OF PRIME MINISTER MARGARET THATCHER
The Rush Limbaugh Show, April 8, 2013

Lady Thatcher I was very fortunate to know. Because of some friends of mine who knew her, I was often invited to social occasions with her. I must have spent quality time with Lady Thatcher on ten to fifteen different occasions, all in the 1990s. I've regaled you with some of the stories.

In every one of those instances—every one—she was identically the same. She was purely formal and sophisticated. I don't mean boring and dull and old-fashioned. She carried herself with a dignity and a self-respect and a seriousness that led no one to question who she really was. If you ever had the chance to be around her, you would know that she was in person as you saw her on television. She was committed; she was serious. She was formal. She was a great woman, a great human being.

Some people call it a coincidence—I think it's more than that—that at the same time in the world we had Ronald Reagan, Pope John Paul II, and Margaret Thatcher. During those years were the only times in my lifetime [when] the left was actually turned back. Not just stopped but defeated and turned back. It was the only time in my life. Poland, Berlin, Moscow, the United States. Wherever. Those three leaders on the political stage, the world stage at the same time, did more for freedom and liberty for people all over this world than any three people since the founding of this country—and they all served at the same time, overlapping.

Lady Thatcher is the only one of the three that I met, and I got to know her very well.

* * *

Here's a little trivia question: Does anybody out there know who it was that decided to call Margaret Thatcher "the Iron Lady"? Any idea who it was? It was not Neil Kinnock, and therefore not Joe Biden. It was not a British politician. It was not an American politician. It was no one in the media, at least in the Western media. It was the Soviet news agency Tass that called her, that dubbed Margaret Thatcher the Iron Lady, and the West's Drive-by Media gleefully picked up on that.

Rush with Prime Minister Margaret Thatcher and former Supreme Court Justice Anthony Kennedy.

Tass did not mean it to be a compliment—neither did the American Drive-by Media—but of course it turned out to be one. Margaret Thatcher reminded me of my grandfather. My grandfather was serious all the time. He wore a jacket and tie every day of the year—Saturday, Sunday, no matter what—because he worked every day.

Lady Thatcher was serious. She was funny, but she was serious. Everything mattered. One of the many things she said that I've never forgotten—and there were a lot of them, but this one has always stuck with me—was "Consensus is the absence of leadership."

Consensus is now the objective in this country.

To her, it meant no leadership. . . .

* * *

Lady Thatcher really was transformative in the true sense of the word. She transformed the UK, during her time, from socialist left to a free market, wealth-creating free society—and she is hated and reviled today in her own country by the media, much as conservatives in this country are, but there's no denying what she accomplished, what she achieved, and how she did it. . . .

I remember one particular evening, it was the end of the week, it had been a long week for me, and I showed up, cocktail party, dinner. I sit down at dinner and Gay [Gaines] immediately says, "Okay, Rush, what's the latest in . . ."

I said, "Gay, I'm tired. I just don't want to talk about politics right now." Of course the table looked. "You don't want to talk politics? Do you understand who's sitting here?" She was seated next to me. And I said, "No." At the time I just didn't want to be on stage. I was exhausted, I was worn out, and I just wanted to listen. And Gay kept trying to urge me, and Lady Thatcher said, "Gay, he doesn't wish to speak about politics. So let's talk of the rule of law," and bam, there we are off on a discussion, the rule of law. She loved the Founders. She absolutely thought they were the most brilliant people, 'cause they were Brits, don't forget. Our Founders were British. She loved them.

She loved Thomas Jefferson. Thomas Jefferson was it. But she loved them all. She knew the history of this country better than most people in this country do, and she revered it. She was one of the greatest Americans, quote unquote, that I've ever met.

· · ·

It is well known that my husband and Lady Thatcher enjoyed a very special relationship as leaders of their respective countries during one of the most difficult and pivotal periods in modern history. Ronnie and Margaret were political soul mates, committed to freedom and resolved to end Communism. —First Lady Nancy Reagan

· · ·

PART 3 — THE EARLY PATRIOTS

Like all of us, Rush revered the Founding Fathers and early patriots. He wanted all Americans to know how phenomenal it was that a small group of underdogs could escape the tyranny of a king's rule to create a free nation. He felt that these early patriots were inspired by God, with the foresight to create a nation like no other in the world, run for and by the people. Rush said, "We must never forget the story of our founding and the bravery of the early Pilgrims."

GEORGE WASHINGTON GIVES THANKS TO GOD FOR AMERICA
The Rush Limbaugh Show, November 25, 2009

George Washington's Thanksgiving address. Now, before I read this to you, I've read it just a very few times on this program. Before I do, I want you to try to understand. This is in 1789, and I want you to understand: They knew. They knew what they had done, these Founders. They knew that they had participated in a miracle in creating and founding this country.

> *Whereas it is the duty of all Nations to acknowledge the providence of Almighty God, to obey His will, to be grateful for His benefits, and humbly to implore His protection and favor—and whereas both Houses of Congress have by their joint Committee requested me "to recommend to the People of the United States a day of public thanksgiving and prayer to be observed by acknowledging with grateful hearts the many signal favors of Almighty God especially by affording them an opportunity peaceably to establish a form of government for their safety and happiness. . . ."*

Given under my hand at the City of New York
the third day of October in the year of our Lord 1789
George Washington

As we celebrate Thanksgiving this week, folks . . . remember and appreciate all the freedoms that we enjoy in this country. Freedom is why the Pilgrims came to America in the first place. They were in search of freedom of religion, freedom of speech, press, assembly, and a freedom of enterprise.

America had the kind of freedom the world had never seen before. That was what was exceptional about America. We still have it, though it's under assault. . . .

Now, ladies and gentlemen: Thanksgiving. This is traditionally the beginning of the, quote unquote, "Christmas season," holiday season, which is one of my favorite times of year. We're just days away from starting our Mannheim Steamroller Christmas bump music rotation, and I get choked up at this time of year when I think of the blessings that have been bestowed upon me and my family, and it's all because of all of you. I say it every year.

I have people thanking me all day long for doing this show. You have no idea what you have meant to me. There's no way I could properly express my gratitude, other than to thank you from the bottom of my heart and wish you and your family a happy Thanksgiving as well, as well as all uniformed military personnel in the theaters of battle overseas.

THE ROLE OF GOVERNMENT IS TO SECURE OUR LIBERTY, NOT TO SEIZE IT
The Rush Limbaugh Show, June 26, 2009

James Madison, the speech delivered in 1788 in favor of the federal constitution, said: "Since the general civilization of mankind, I believe there are more instances of the abridgments of the freedom of the people by gradual and silent encroachment of those in power than by violent or sudden usurpations." It's amazing. Every time you go back and consult Founding Fathers, you find that their wisdom was timeless. Their ability to foresee the future was incomparable. Liberty is the birthright of every American. The usurpation of liberty—whether it be by nationalized health care or taxing the energy we need to live—that's a seizure of liberty. That's a usurpation of liberty under the false pretense of providing security or "saving the planet."

* * *

The Founding Fathers were highly suspicious of government because they understood human nature. And they understood the human quest for power. They were fleeing what they thought were the worst aspects of the human quest for power. They were fleeing a monarch. They were fleeing a tyrannical king in Britain. They founded something completely opposite.

—Rush Limbaugh

* * *

HOW JOHN ADAMS GOT HIS UNITY
The Rush Limbaugh Show, March 19, 2008

How many of you are taking the time to watch the series on HBO called *John Adams*? It started Sunday night. There are seven episodes in total. They ran the first two. It's about John Adams, the first vice president of the United States, about his life; his wife, Abigail; and their children. . . . What happened in that room [the Philadelphia Convention of 1787, at which the US Constitution was created] for all of those months was a miracle. It was a miracle that it happened. . . .

But there were elements from Pennsylvania and New York and New Jersey who had no desire for independence. To listen to them speak, "No, this is the time for caution," while the Redcoats are firing and murdering innocent people. Essentially the war had already broken out in Boston, and these people from Pennsylvania . . . they're all saying, "This is the time for caution. This is the time for restraint," and I'm watching the screen, and I'm just smiling. We've got those same kind of pansies today, and they wanted to send a proclamation to King George demanding that King George stop taxing their tea and stop taxing them exorbitantly on a number of things, to basically stop squishing them and squeezing them.

So, Adams says, "All right. If you want to do that, go ahead. I'm going to still try to convince you, but you do what you want to do. It's going to be months before we hear back, and I can tell you what we're going to hear back, but if it will make you feel better, go ahead and do it."

So they did it. All the while, Adams continues to try to arm-twist and persuade. Finally they get the answer from King George, and King George says, "How dare you ask me this! Now you guys are really in for it. We're going to kick your butts." So the moderates say, "Oh, further caution is required here," and then we got eloquent speeches about "We don't need bloodshed and we don't need warfare, and this is not the way to go about this," because some of these people did not want independence. They were Englishmen. . . .

This thing shows how difficult it was, how almost impossible it was. It's why it was a miracle for John Adams to craft unanimity from thirteen colonies who had thirteen different special interests. . . . It took a lot of time. It took a lot of persuasion. It took strategy. It took negotiation. It took manipulation to get the necessary unanimity. But how did he get it? His objective was independence—pure, 100 percent independence. . . .

He never compromised what he wanted at all, and they ended up with unification, unanimity. You could call it unity, but he did it in a way that was not at all weakening of his desire and passion—and, of course, George Washington is portrayed here, too. Colonel Washington becomes General Washington. . . . Gosh, it sent tingles up my spine to watch how this country actually came together. It's why I think what happened there is a miracle.

* * *

Abigail Adams was a force of nature in her own right.
—Rush Limbaugh

* * *

THE TRUE NATURE OF LIBERTY AND THOMAS JEFFERSON
The Rush Limbaugh Show, February 13, 2015

Thomas Jefferson said, "God, who gave us life, gave us liberty. Can the liberties of a nation be secure when we have removed a conviction that these liberties are the gift of God?"

Now, to me that makes perfect sense. To some it might be confusing. But Jefferson is a Founding Father. Jefferson is one who acknowledged and agreed that we are all created equal and endowed by our Creator with certain unalienable rights, among them life, liberty, and the pursuit of happiness.

Jefferson was one of those who acknowledged that God is the source. Jefferson was obsessed—well, I won't say obsessed. Jefferson was really concerned about making sure that this freedom and liberty [was] maintained, even to the point of throwing the government over now and then if necessary. He called it the tree of liberty. Sometimes blood has to be shed. The point is, Jefferson thought about all this a lot, and he said, among other things, God, who gave us life, gave us liberty.

"Can the liberties of a nation be secure when we have removed a conviction that these liberties are the gift of God?" In other words, how secure is the nation when people like Chris Cuomo are running around thinking that freedom is a gift of Obama or a gift of a human being? How damn secure? We're not very secure, because if our freedom comes from the good graces of a human being, what happens if we elect a bad guy who takes our freedom away? Oh, my God, that would be horrible.

How secure could our freedom be if a country believes that its freedom comes from other men—human beings? I don't mean to leave women out here, but I'm talking in the generic sense. How can this be? But if your freedom comes from God, that's who you are. The only thing that can happen to that is evil men come along and encroach on it.

Replica of Missouri Hall of Fame bust proudly displayed in the Limbaughs' home.

JOHN ADAMS'S PROPHECY ON THE CONSTITUTION AND MORALITY

The Rush Limbaugh Show, February 17, 2009

RUSH: This is Joe in Allentown, Pennsylvania. Great to have you here, sir. Thank you.

CALLER: Hi, Rush. How you doing?

RUSH: Just well, just fine . . .

CALLER: I think that the greatness of our nation was always in our God. . . . When you have to have the government say that I am free, you are not really dependent on God. But I think the greatness of our nation is our God, and I think the more people like us are really crying out to our God, I think we'll bring change. I think that's the greatness of our nation more than anything. . . .

RUSH: I want to go through this little quote from John Adams, one of the Founding Fathers, once again . . . "Our Constitution was made only for a moral and religious people. It is wholly inadequate to the government of any other." That's John Adams, one of the Founders. Now, of course, people who are unbridled by morality—or the immoral, if you will—and the people who are not truly religious, this Constitution—and he's dead right—this Constitution is a restriction to them. I mean it is punitive to them. And he said this Constitution cannot deal with people like that.

⁕ ⁕ ⁕

*The great part of our happiness or misery
depends on our dispositions and not our
circumstances.* —First Lady Martha Washington

⁕ ⁕ ⁕

THE ALEXANDER HAMILTON OF RADIO
The Rush Limbaugh Show, November 21, 2007

RUSH: Here is Don in Flat Rock, North Carolina. I'm glad you waited, sir. Welcome to the program.

CALLER: I equate you to Alexander Hamilton, who was instrumental, as you probably know, in starting this country.

RUSH: Yes, except he lost a duel, and I hope the comparison ends there.

THE GEORGE WASHINGTON OF TALK RADIO
The Rush Limbaugh Show, July 19, 2007

RUSH: Marisa in Sappington, Missouri, welcome to the EIB Network. It's nice to have you with us.

CALLER: Well, thank you, Rush. . . . I think you're practically perfect, so I think that you and George Washington are practically the same. You could be brothers, because you've built a whole war, if you will, a whole army of people to hold together to a conservative ideal by yourself. You started with nothing, and you built it, and it is what it is today, and George Washington enabled the country to win the Revolutionary War by holding together a pathetic army through thick and thin when everything was going terribly, and he really, almost by himself, had the magnetism and the trust and the belief of all the people. . . .

RUSH: Yeah, but you know what? He was the only one who could be the president and hold this country together. They offered to make him king.

CALLER: Well, I know. That's my point.

RUSH: Right.

CALLER: . . . I think, you know, if you got on the air Monday (since you won't be here tomorrow) and said, "I'm going to run for president in '08," that's all you'd have to do, and you would be elected—

RUSH: *[Laughing]*

CALLER: —and you would save our country.

RUSH: That's awfully nice of you to say, but no.

CALLER: You would.

RUSH: It's awfully nice of you, but really, this is embarrassing for me to say, because I can't do anything about it. I've gotta go, because I'm way long in this segment. I have to go to the next profit center time-out.

CALLER: Well, think about it when you're playing golf.

RUSH: All right, I'll think about it. But thank you. I appreciate it more than you know. I continually am stunned when I hear these kinds of things. The only difference between me and George Washington is if somebody wanted to make me king, I'd take it.

● ● ●

My first time on Nightline *with Ted Koppel, I'm debating Al Gore on the environment. I'm in New York, don't know where Gore is, with Koppel. My dad and mom are watching from their little house in Missouri. And my mom told me the story. [My dad] watched it, didn't say a word. Just stared at the TV, was in stunned disbelief. And my mom said he looked at her and said, "Millie, where did he learn all that?" And she said to him, "From you, silly." Which was true. I think he was proud.*

—Rush Limbaugh

● ● ●

Chapter 2

Our Founding
Principles

TRIBUTE
by President Ronald Reagan

Ronald Reagan
December 11, 1992

Dear Rush:

Thanks for all you're doing to promote Republican and conservative principles. Now that I've retired from active politics, I don't mind that you've become the number one voice for conservatism in our country.

I know the liberals call you the "the most dangerous man in America," but don't worry about it; they used to say the same thing about me. Keep up the good work! America needs to hear "the way things ought to be."

Sincerely,

Ron

Mr. Rush Limbaugh
New York, New York

PART 1 — FOUNDING DOCUMENTS AND VALUES

One of the most memorable times in Rush's life was when he was asked to be the keynote speaker at the Conservative Political Action Committee Conference in 2009. When we arrived in Washington, DC, for the event that evening, Rush had no outline or plan for what he was going to say as the main speaker. Surprisingly, despite being the number one broadcaster of all time, he was not a fan of public speaking in front of large crowds. Rush was always his own worst critic and would berate himself for (in his mind) boring the audience. There are many adjectives that can be used to describe Rush, but "boring" is certainly not one of them!

On this night at CPAC, Rush was extraordinary, as always, and the crowd cheered uproariously at almost every syllable. He spoke from the heart without a teleprompter and without notes. Rush termed this speech his "first national address," as it was televised live nationwide. That evening, Rush rallied Americans to cherish and protect our nation's founding and the rights enshrined in our Constitution and Bill of Rights. His words were delivered with passion, brilliance, and humor, and the speech is widely regarded as the greatest at CPAC of all time.

* * *

We hold these truths to be self-evident, that all men are created equal, that they are endowed by their Creator with certain unalienable Rights, that among these are Life, Liberty and the pursuit of Happiness.

—Preamble to the Declaration of Independence

* * *

RUSH LIMBAUGH KEYNOTE ADDRESS
Conservative Political Action Committee Conference, 2009

Thank you so much. Thank you. Thank you all very, very much. Thank you all. I can't tell you how wonderful that makes me feel. It happens everywhere I go, but it's still special here. *[Laughter]* If you all will indulge me, I learned something, I guess it's early Friday morning, that I didn't know. Friday morning is when I learned this. I learned that Fox, God love them, is televising this speech on the Fox News Channel, which means, ladies and gentlemen, this is my first ever address to the nation. . . . *[Applause]*

I want to tell you who we all are in this room. I want to tell you who conservatives are. We conservatives have not done a good enough job of just laying out basically who we are, because we make the mistake of assuming people know. What they know is largely incorrect based on the way we are portrayed in pop culture, in the Drive-by Media, by the Democrat Party.

Let me tell you who we conservatives are: We love people. *[Applause]* When we look out over the United States of America, when we are anywhere, when we see a group of people, such as this or anywhere, we see Americans. We see human beings. We don't see groups. We don't see victims. We don't see people we want to exploit. What we see—what we see is potential. We do not look out across the country and see the average American, the person that makes this country work. We do not see that person with contempt. We don't think that person doesn't have what it takes. We believe that person can be the best he or she wants to be if certain things are just removed from their path, like onerous taxes, regulations, and too much government. *[Applause]*

We want every American to be the best he or she chooses to be. We recognize that we are all individuals. We love and revere our founding documents, the Constitution and the Declaration of Independence. *[Applause]* We believe that the preamble to the Constitution contains an inarguable truth that we are all endowed by our Creator with certain inalienable rights, among them life *[Applause]*, liberty, freedom *[Applause]*, and the pursuit of happiness. *[Applause]* Those of you watching at home may wonder why this is being applauded. We conservatives think all three are under assault. *[Applause]* Thank you. Thank you.

We don't want to tell anybody how to live. That's up to you. If you want to make the best of yourself, feel free. If you want to ruin your life, we'll try to stop it, but it's a waste. We look over the country as it is today, we see so much waste, human potential that's been destroyed by fifty years of a welfare state. By a failed war on poverty. *[Applause]*

We love the people of this country. And we want this to be the greatest country it can be, but we do understand, as people created and endowed by our Creator, we're all individuals. We resist the effort to group us. We resist the effort to make us feel that we're all the same, that we're no different than anybody else. We're all different. There are no two things or people in this world who are created in a way that they end up with equal outcomes. That's up to them. They are created equal, given the chance . . . *[Applause]*

We don't hate anybody. . . .

We want the country to succeed, and for the country to succeed, its people—its individuals—must succeed. Everyone among us must be pursuing his ambition or her desire, whatever, with excellence. Trying to be the best they can be.

• • •

Folks, don't doubt me.

—Rush Limbaugh

• • •

RECALLING THE CPAC SPEECH
The Rush Limbaugh Show, February 10, 2011

RUSH: Here's Bobby from the New Jersey Turnpike. You're next on the Rush Limbaugh program. Hello, sir.

CALLER: Hey, Rush. What a pleasure to talk to you again.

RUSH: Thank you, sir.

CALLER: But I just wanted to congratulate and thank you for your speech at CPAC in 2009. I watched it in its entirety again last night, and it was incredible to watch your sense of confidence and your prescience in reaffirming what conservatism is and what it should be and what it could mean, and how that speech really laid the foundation for what has transpired over the last two years.

RUSH: That CPAC speech, that was given within three weeks or two weeks of Obama's immaculation.

CALLER: That's correct.

RUSH: And at that time there wasn't a dry eye in conservatism. Everybody was in tears, and everybody's heads were hung low, and everybody thought we were destined for the wilderness for generations.

CALLER: You really couldn't tell that from watching you, though.

RUSH: Well, it's my point.

CALLER: You had confidence, and everything was tremendous.

RUSH: Well, I'm glad you liked it. Thank you very much.

CALLER: You're welcome.

RUSH: That was a fun day. That went on for an hour and twenty minutes. It was supposed to go for forty-five minutes, and during one of the sustained periods of applause, the CPAC people said, "Look, can you keep going? Another forty-five minutes would be fine." I said, "Sure," so we did. We had the room all night. *[Laughs]* They said we didn't have to get outta here 'til ten o'clock. So I'm glad you mentioned it, because CPAC's convention is happening now. What prompted you to go back and watch it?

CALLER: The fact that CPAC was coming on again and I remember watching that and sort of applauding to myself and my family at home at the time, and really sort of getting a charge from it, because it was darkness for the times for everybody that believes like we do, and it really was the start of how things turned around.

RUSH: Thank you very much.

CALLER: No teleprompter. No teleprompter, of course, as well.

RUSH: No.

CALLER: Your first address to the nation.

RUSH: That's right. *[Laughing]* My first national address.

CALLER: That's right.

RUSH: My first address to the nation—without a teleprompter to boot; exactly right. Thank you very much. You have made my day.

CALLER: Thank you, Rush.

Rush is an American original. It is said that some originals,
that if you didn't have them, you'd have to invent them. Yet no
one could have invented Rush, because he was inconceivable.

—Andrew McCarthy, *The American Spectator*

IRISH CALLER AND RUSH AGREE: BELIEVE IN FREEDOM!
The Rush Limbaugh Show, June 11, 2013

RUSH: We go to Atlanta. John, I'm glad you waited. Great to have you on the EIB Network. Hi.

CALLER: Hi, Rush. Thank you very much for taking my call. I was listening to your show from the start—I listen most days—and the letter you read out from your subscriber really hit a chord with me. I actually don't live in America; I'm Irish. . . .

RUSH: Hey, John, I need you to slow down a little bit so that I, with my hearing disability, can understand what you're saying. I got you're from Ireland . . .

CALLER: Yes, sir.

RUSH: Okay.

CALLER: . . . One thing I've noticed is something similar to what that person e-mailed you in. And it's greatly upsetting to me, because as someone who loves this country so much and admires everything you've done, the founding principles, the first three words in your Constitution are "We, the people." And the fact the people are saying that what can you do, we can't do anything; they seem to be almost paralyzed. . . .

RUSH: You know, you're singing my song in one sense, in the sense that I have constantly told people they have much more influence over people just by living their lives than they possibly will ever even know. But you're hitting on something, and I want to ask you if maybe I'm interpreting you incorrectly. . . . It sounds to me like what you're saying is, "Hey, guys, stop waiting on somebody else to do it and join the crowd and try to help make change yourself."

CALLER: Exactly. Because this is what American was founded on: individualism. . . .

RUSH: John, you're hitting on a number of things here. One of the themes that you're talking about is individualism—rugged individualism, I call it. This is one of the aspects of life in America today that has so many people frustrated. People are willing to throw away their individuality in exchange

60

● ● ●

I have said over the course of many years that I've been hosting the program, the purpose of the Constitution is to limit government. The Constitution does not limit us. I'm a constitutionalist. The Constitution does not limit us. The Constitution does not spell out how government gets big, doesn't spell out how government can usurp power. It's all about how government shouldn't and can't!

—Rush Limbaugh

● ● ●

for being accepted by some community, whatever community it is; not just the town but a group of people, like-minded thinkers, conformists. Americans, way too many of 'em, are way too interested in conformity and what people think of them and getting along and letting Washington make decisions for them. You know the old adage about trading a little freedom for security here, trading some there. The individual is under assault in this country as a selfish, mean-spirited, you fill in the blank. And so ignorance is rewarded, conformity is rewarded, and I think that's a great point of frustration that many people that you're talking about sense and think in this country, that way too many others are just blindly accepting of what's happening without being concerned about it in any way, shape, manner, or form. . . .

CALLER: Freedom is priceless. . . .

RUSH: Today, the way you're speaking about America gets laughed at by a lot of people in different parts of the country. You're talking about freedom and the Founders and liberty. Nobody thinks their freedom's up for grabs. Nobody thinks their liberty is being lost. Not nobody. A lot of people don't think any of this is at risk. . . . You're great, John, I'm glad that you got through. Thanks so much.

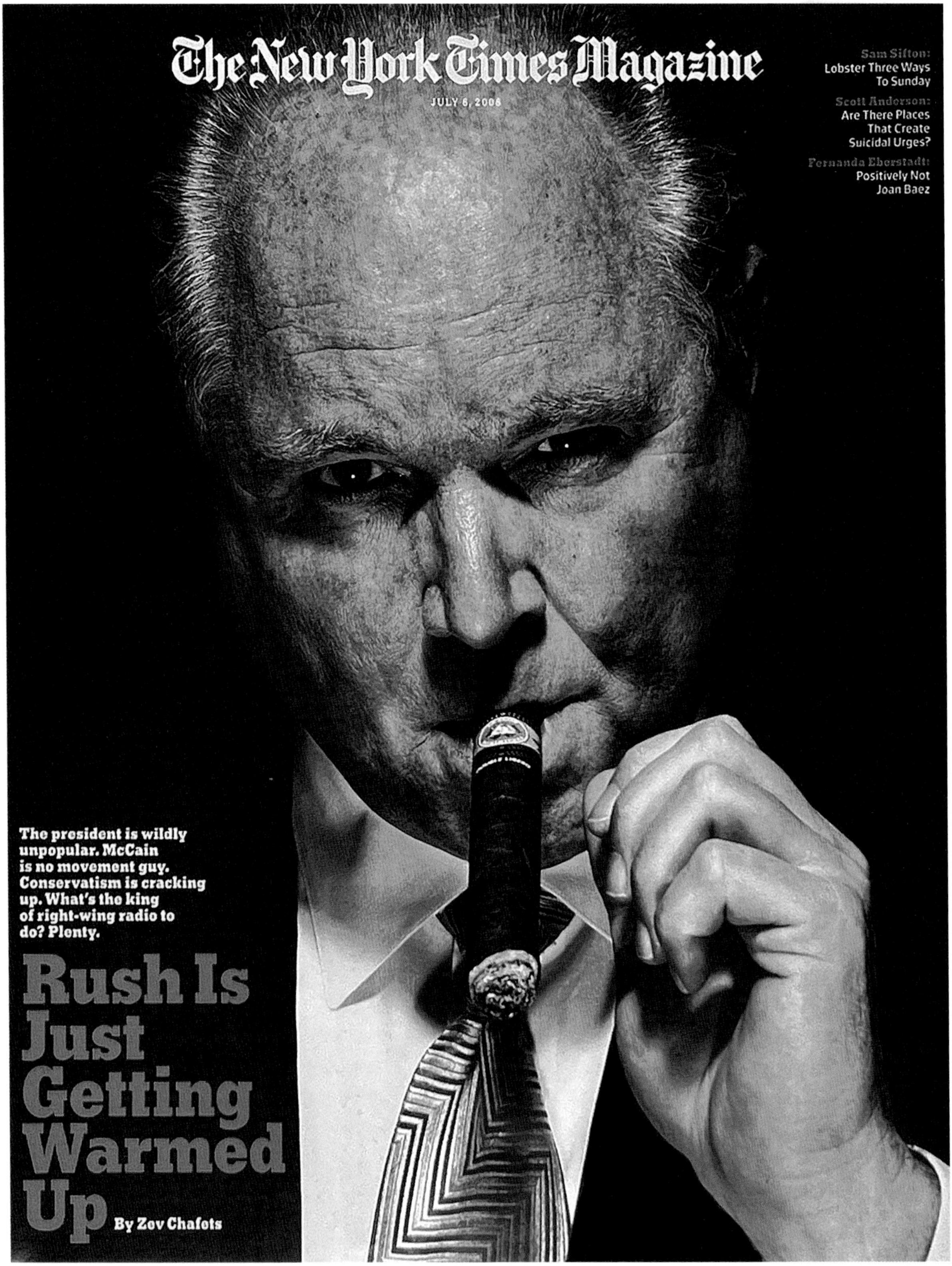

The New York Times Magazine
JULY 6, 2008
Sam Sifton:
Lobster Three Ways To Sunday
Scott Anderson:
Are There Places That Create Suicidal Urges?
Fernanda Eberstadt:
Positively Not Joan Baez
The president is wildly unpopular. McCain is no movement guy. Conservatism is cracking up. What's the king of right-wing radio to do? Plenty.
Rush Is Just Getting Warmed Up
By Zev Chafets

• • •

A Bill of Rights that means what the majority wants it to mean is worthless. —Justice Antonin Scalia

• • •

WHAT MAKES AMERICA GREAT AND WHY WE MUST PROTECT IT

The Rush Limbaugh Show, September 7, 2007

RUSH: You know, what happened in Philadelphia in 1776 was a miracle. Divine inspiration had to have been there. The principles may be bigger than the men who wrote 'em down, but they did write them, and they were not racists, and they were not bigots, whatever else the PC crowd teaches today. . . .

Have you read the Declaration of Independence? "One nation under God . . . Creator." The Pledge of Allegiance? Clearly the founders of this country believed in God and believed that we were all created and that we were all created equal. "Certain unalienable rights, among them life, liberty, the pursuit of happiness." Life, liberty, pursuit; these words mean things.

You say that the principles are bigger than the people that wrote 'em down, but it took people to write them down. Where did they get the inspiration? Where did they get the intelligence? They were great people that put this country together, a country that stood the test of time like no other country in the history of civilization. Today's liberals are none of the Founding Fathers. Today's liberals are not capitalists as constituted today. They are socialists. . . .

I'm right, and the future of our country depends on maintaining the institutions and traditions that built this country, and in order to preserve these traditions and institutions, we've got to understand their origin. We must admit and be honest about what they are. Today's liberals do, and they are trying to tear them down. Today's liberals want to tear down these traditions and institutions and then remake the country in their own image. . . . If there is to be a demise of our country, it is because we will lose control of

• • •

I totally reject and have rejected throughout my entire career the proposition that the end justifies the means or that a judge should decide cases based on a desire to reach a certain outcome. —Justice Amy Coney Barrett

• • •

maintaining the traditions and institutions that made this a great country, a great culture, a great society, a great population. . . . It's all happening from within. . . .

What it is that makes this country unique . . . is two things.

Our founding documents—and what's in the founding documents? The documented recognition that we are all created by God and that we all have certain inalienable rights. That means it's part of our yearning spirit. It's part of our creation. That is liberty, a yearning to be free. We don't want to be bound up. We don't want to be shut up. We don't want to be constrained. We are human beings. We're explorers. We're researchers. We're pioneers. We don't want to be caged, and they understood this.

Pursuit of happiness. Life is to be maximized and pursued in its full, and people are to get as much out of it as they are able, and they can't do it with shackles around their ankles. They can't do it with governments that hold them in contempt. They can't do it with leaders that think they have no brains. People are going to be constrained by people who think they have no ability to do things, so they're going to want to do everything for them. The right to life. We're all created equal. Right to life.

Those definitions of our creation and our freedom are what set us apart from virtually every nation on the face of the earth. I don't know if you know this or not: Nothing against the Brits—they don't even have a constitution. They do not have one. The European Union, they're trying to write one, but it's a bunch of commie libs. It's a disaster. Nothing but a PC manual and digest, and that is how we've stood the test of time.

It is those three things that are under assault by today's left. The right to life, the pursuit of happiness. You're not supposed to be happy, because if you're happy while somebody's not happy, it's not fair. And if your pursuit of happiness offends somebody or robs somebody else of their happiness, we can't have that. No, because the liberals today want misery equally because that's the only way we can all be equal.

So we have to spread misery as equally as possible. We can't humiliate anybody. This is why the country's under assault. . . . Not the war on terror, not the fact that the rest of the world hates us. The fact the rest of the world hates us is bogus, but it's irrelevant anyway if it were the case, because it's their problem; because we're a great nation. If we're going to run around and try to remake ourselves to satisfy every little slimeball dictator or every Western European socialist who for some reason is unhappy with us, then we're going to cease to exist as we've known it—and that's part of what today's left wants.

OBAMA AND LIBERALS LIKE HIM SEE THE US CONSTITUTION AS A CONSTRAINT
The Rush Limbaugh Show, April 21, 2009

RUSH: I want to go back to this Obama sound bite at the CIA yesterday afternoon. Listen to just the first part of this.

OBAMA: *I understand that it's hard when you are asked to protect the American people against people who have no scruples—*

RUSH: Yeah, you try it.

OBAMA: *—and would willingly and gladly kill innocents.*

RUSH: Now, listen here.

OBAMA: *Al-Qaeda is not constrained by a constitution—*

RUSH: Stop the tape. Al-Qaeda is not "constrained" by a constitution. Your president, our president, Barack Obama, looks at the Constitution as a constraint, and we know this because President Obama is also the kind of man who has legal people around him who look at the Bill of Rights, who see it as a set of what is called negative rights. I know a lot of people, "Negative rights, how can the Bill of Rights be negative rights?" Because, folks, to liberals, the

Bill of Rights is horrible, the Bill of Rights grants citizens freedom. It tells the citizens what the government cannot do to them. The Bill of Rights limits the federal government, and that's negative to a socialist like Obama; that's negative to an elitist like Obama. The Constitution is negative. So he's got constraints. The Constitution tells him he's got things he can't do that he wants to do. That's not his job. He is there to defend and protect it, not unilaterally change it.

LIBERALS SAY CONSERVATIVES HAVE A "FETISH" FOR THE US CONSTITUTION
The Rush Limbaugh Show, May 19, 2011

Washington Post, by Jason Horowitz: "And the Founders said: Let there be a constitution. And the Founders looked at the articles and clauses and saw that it was good." That's how this story begins. "And the Founders said: Let there be a constitution. And the Founders looked at the articles and clauses and saw that it was good. For more than two hundred years, Americans have revered the Constitution as the law of the land, but the GOP and Tea Party heralding of the document in recent months—and the planned recitation on the House floor Thursday"—actually, Wednesday—"has caused some Democrats to worry that the charter is being misconstrued as the immutable word of God. New York Rep. Jerrold Nadler"—these people have such contempt for the Constitution, these Democrats—"'They are reading it like a sacred text,' said New York Rep. Jerrold Nadler (D-NY), the outgoing chairman of the House Judiciary Subcommittee on the Constitution, Civil Rights, and Civil Liberties." By the way *[laughing],* this is great. As they quote this clown, "They're reading it like a sacred text." That's Nadler talking about the Republicans in a critical way. "They're reading it like a sacred text." Now, listen to this, listen to how the *Post* describes this guy Nadler.

"Chairman, House Judiciary Subcommittee on the Constitution, Civil Rights, and Civil Liberties, who has studied and memorized the Constitution with talmudic"—or Talmudic, the Talmud, Jewish Talmud—"intensity." So here's a guy who'd looked at it as his Bible, they say, accusing the Republicans of looking at the Constitution as a sacred text. "Nadler called the 'ritualistic reading' on the floor 'total nonsense' and 'propaganda' intended to claim the document for Republicans. 'You read the Torah, you read the Bible, you build a worship service around it,' said Nadler, who argued that the Founders were not 'demigods' and that the document's need for amendments to abolish slavery and other injustices showed it was 'highly imperfect.' 'You are not supposed to worship your constitution. You are supposed to govern your government by it,' he said." Nobody's worshiping it, you fool. What we're doing is trying to reestablish it, because it's under assault from people like you! Pardon my yelling. I get passionate about this.

Individual liberty, the Constitution, freedom, are all under assault. They have been since the founding of this country. The change is that a large element of that assault now comes domestically from people like Jerrold Nadler and courts like the Ninth Circus, who just found another cross in a public place unconstitutional. The Democrats so hate this document, leftists so hate this document, they read it and tell us it means the opposite of what it says. A couple fascinating stories I want to share with you today about Justice Scalia answering some questions about the Constitution, specifically the Fourteenth Amendment and how that just sent Democrats practically needing straitjackets and ambulances to the home. But here are a few sound bites on this Republican fetish with the Constitution. Last night on PMS MS—whatever it is, the stupid Mess NBC—Slate.com senior editor and legal correspondent Dahlia Lithwick about the Republican plan to read the Constitution. The question: "Is there an historical precedent for the Constitution fetish on the right?"

LITHWICK: I think so. I think the way some people rub Buddha and they think the magic will come off, I think there's a long-standing tradition in this country. We're awfully religious about the Constitution. I think there is a sort of fetishization here that is of a piece with the sort of need for a religious document that's immutable and perfect in every way.

RUSH: Miss Lithwick, you'll never understand it, but all this is simply because health care is unconstitutional, Obamacare is. So much of Obama's agenda is unconstitutional. So much of what has come out of Congress in the form of legislation, unconstitutional. It's only the foundation for our existence,

Now, Clarence Thomas and Antonin Scalia have remained rock solid. I talked to Justice Scalia on the phone twice. Both times I've told him: If I didn't have my own brain, I would want his. —Rush Limbaugh

Miss Lithwick, and it's under assault. So what if it's revered. It's the most brilliant governing, founding document ever in the history of mankind. What is there about it that so threatens you, that you have to characterize people who love it, believe it, admire it as somehow having a fetish? All these people are doing, again, as I say, is showing their contempt. This is Chris Hayes. He's the guest host on this Mess NBC show, and he responded to Dahlia Lithwick and her notion of a fetish here by saying this:

HAYES: They kind of fetishize the Constitution, and they had to give it this sort of biblical textual status. You know, what's wrong with that? Is this sort of harmless, or is there something kind of insidious underneath that?

LITHWICK: Part of what's a little bit fraudulent about this conversation is that the same people who are fetishizing the document as written, as framed by the Framers and, you know, bracket the idea that there wasn't one Framer, and there was no—

HAYES: Right.

LITHWICK: —one agenda embodied in this, but even if you bracket that idea, I think there's a real problem with the idea that we're trying to sort of fetishize the document at the same moment that we're falling over ourselves to amend and change the parts we don't like.

RUSH: Well, that's part of the process, is changing and amending it. But you guys don't do that because your changes and amendments would never see the light of day if voted on legislatively, so you've ginned up the courts to do it for you, and that's what's under assault here. They're simply defenders and protectors. And people are going to swear an oath today on the floor of the House to the Constitution and to God, to defend and protect the Constitution. A piece of propaganda, the left says. And, of course, the template having been established, Maud Behar had to get in on the act on her show last night on the headline, whatever it is—

BEHAR: Do you think this Constitution loving is getting out of hand? I mean, is it a nod to the Tea Party?

MAN: I think—

BEHAR: For the first time a lot of congressmen will have heard about it, read it.

RUSH: Just to show you how the template gets started and the privates, the buck privates in the army start falling in place.

THE TRUE NATURE OF LIBERTY
The Rush Limbaugh Show, February 13, 2015

Did I ever tell you the story about Natan Sharansky? I interviewed him for a long-ago issue of the *Limbaugh Letter*. He was in prison, a Soviet Jew, and he was imprisoned in a Soviet jail. And he loved to tell the story of taunting his guards by telling them that he was more free than they were. Every time he got a new guard, he'd get into a conversation: "You know, I'm more free than you are," and the guard would look at him like he's an idiot. "What do you mean? You're behind bars. I'm on the free side here. You have to do what I tell you. You're the prisoner."

And Sharansky said, "Yeah, but I can sit in here and I can tell jokes about Brezhnev and Andropov and Khrushchev and all those guys all day long, and I can sit here and laugh at them. You can't, or they'll throw you outta here."

It was a brilliant point about what is really freedom and what's liberty, and how freedom exists in prison. You know, I don't mean to get too deep with this, but it's important, 'cause it isn't taught anymore. . . .

Now, my question about where do you go to buy your freedom, it's not as simple as you may think. You might say, "Nowhere. I wake up in America and I'm free." Yeah, that's true, as far as it goes. But the point is if you wake up in Cuba, you are not. And you can't buy your freedom in Cuba, unless you have what no Cuban has—either a lot of money and can become part of the regime, in which case you're still not really free, or enough money to get out of there. . . .

The same with any oppressive socialist or communist country: you can't go anywhere to buy your freedom. You're born with it, but if you live in a regime that tyrannizes people and you're not allowed to exercise it, you still have it; it's just being denied you. But when it comes to where do you go to buy your food, well, McDonald's, grocery store, whatever. The point is, you have to go buy it. It's not given to you. You're not born with an endless supply of food in the cupboard. You have to go buy that.

But, you know, your freedom is actually not free. You may not get up every day and have to go buy it, but there have been people from the beginning of time who've given their lives or put their lives on the line for your freedom and mine. They're paying the price. They're called the US military, and other similar types of organizations. There are all kinds of people that would buy our freedom for us. But it's not something you have to go to the store and buy every day. You're born with it.

• • •

When the people fear the government there is tyranny; when the government fears the people there is liberty. —Thomas Jefferson

• • •

FAITH IN SOMETHING BIGGER THAN GOVERNMENT
The Rush Limbaugh Show, May 9, 2011

The problem is that we have people in office who are rejecting the country as founded, rejecting the foundation principles—including limited government, the rule of law, individual liberty, and faith. Faith not in big government, by the way. Faith in something bigger than big government. Faith in something bigger than ourselves. Our founding principles are based on morality. They are based on common sense. Individual human behavior. You can't separate the fiscal and social issues, really, 'cause they are the result of a common morality—and I know that makes people uncomfortable, but it doesn't bother me to say it in the least.

You know, I have to ask some of these Republicans: "What do you mean by 'moderate'? Moderate what? What do you want us to moderate? Do you want us to be less forceful about our faith? Do you want us to dial back our passion on our liberty and freedom? Should we be less enthusiastic for the Constitution, the Declaration of Independence? What are we supposed to moderate? What are we supposed to dial back? What of our passions are we supposed to apologize for by saying that we're moderates?"

I fully understand that there's compromising in legislating, just as long as the compromises don't compromise core beliefs and our way of life.

Fine. But why would we compromise on legislation that would, in fact, change the country in ways that we oppose? That's not moderation. That's capitulation! That's cowardice! It's shortsightedness! It is fear! Why would we do that? We cannot begin to turn things around in this country by pandering, by ducking, by excusing, by confusing—and we certainly can't get where we want to go by making a requirement at the top that we be liked in the process.

GLENN BECK WRITES ABOUT RUSH MAKING *TIME* MAGAZINE'S TOP 100 MOST INFLUENTIAL PEOPLE IN THE WORLD, 2009

For some of us, being a media personality just isn't as easy as it used to be. The theory goes that to build a large audience in this age of iPhones, podcasts, and whatever the latest buzzword is, you have to do everything at once—and that means simultaneously host a radio program, host a TV show, write books, and tour the country. Even Barack Obama had to hold a press conference, go on *60 Minutes*, talk to Jay Leno, and post clips on YouTube within the span of one week just to get people to pay attention to his budget.

But not Rush Limbaugh. When Rush wants to talk to America, all he has to do is grab his microphone.

He attracts more listeners with just his voice than the rest of us could ever imagine. He is simply on another level.

No matter how many new technologies pop up, nothing will ever surpass the intimacy of radio. And nobody will ever be better at utilizing it than Rush. His consistency, insight, and honesty have earned him a level of trust with his listeners that politicians can only dream of. And that is why the more irrelevant critics try to make him, the more relevant he becomes.

Rush, fifty-eight, saved the spoken-word radio format from obscurity and paved the way for thousands of broadcasters, including myself. His career serves as the most successful stimulus package in radio history. All without a government dime.

Knowing firsthand just how hard it is to hold an audience's attention for a few hours makes it that much more amazing to have seen Rush do it for more than twenty years. To say that he has set the standard for success in broadcasting would truly be an understatement.

* * *

When this program started in 1988, the liberals, it took 'em a couple years to realize what was actually happening, and it took a while for them to really gin up this whole notion that you were just a bunch of mind-numbed robots and I'm the Pied Piper. The fact of the matter is, you've always been who you are—other than you converts, and we have made a lot of those, but for the most part the vast majority of people in this audience have always been conservative. They just finally had somebody come along in the national media that validated what they believed. —Rush Limbaugh

* * *

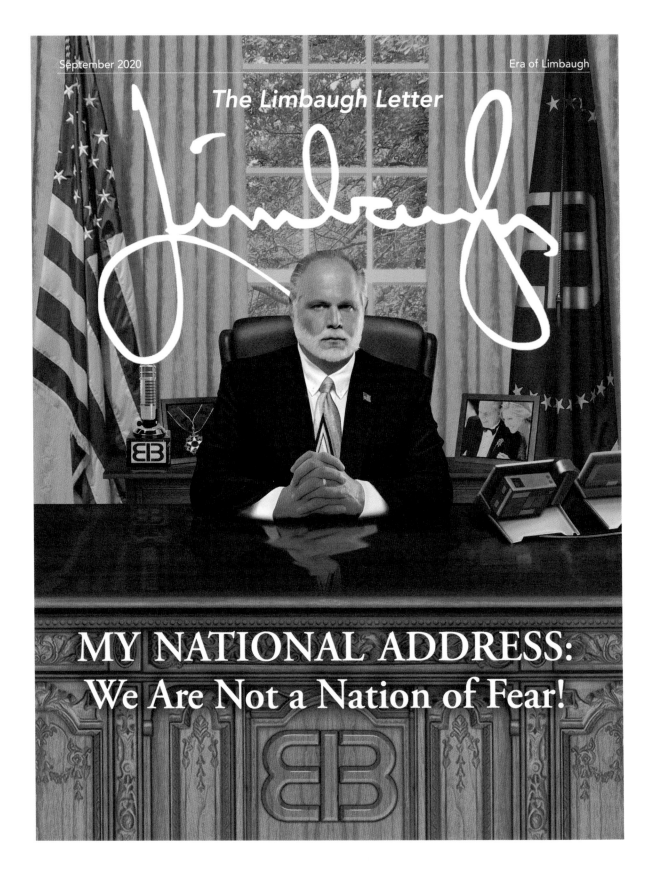

The Limbaugh Letter

MY NATIONAL ADDRESS:
We Are Not a Nation of Fear!

PART 2 — AMERICAN EXCEPTIONALISM

Rush believed with the core of his being that we are all extremely fortunate to be Americans and to live in the greatest country on earth. He recognized that our country has flaws and our history is not perfect. However, he knew that with our eternal optimism for the future, we will always be striving toward a "more perfect union."

OUR MISSION STATEMENT: LIFE, LIBERTY, AND PURSUIT OF HAPPINESS
The Rush Limbaugh Show, February 17, 2010

You know, my friends, it's very simple—and I have used this phrase consistently over the course of my twenty-plus years behind the Golden EIB Microphone—what I believe has made the country great. I've addressed this. When I do my rare, overwhelmingly popular public appearances, I challenge the audience to think about something: "Do you ever wonder how it is, and why it became so, that a population at any one time of less than three hundred million people created the highest standard of living? Progress—economic, political, education, by any standard you want to measure—the United States of America has been the greatest collection [or] population of human beings in the history of the world."

There have been civilizations, countries, and populations long before us that were the trademark of their day, their standard-bearers of their day. They can't compare to us, and they've been around thousands of years. Now, what was it? What is it? What is it that makes three hundred million people special? Our DNA is no different than the ChiCom DNA. I'm talking about in terms of humanity. Our DNA is no different than any other human being anywhere on earth or has ever been on earth.

What is it about this two hundred, three hundred million people that have created by far—there's no comparison—the greatest country and collection of human beings on the face of the earth for good? We feed the world, we relieve the world, we repair the world. We defend the world. We have liberated hundreds of millions of people who have lived in bondage and slavery. What is it about us? We're not born special in terms of our DNA. What is it? I asked people to think about this, 'cause I don't think they do.

This is part and parcel of what I call American exceptionalism. What is American exceptionalism? It's not that we're better people. It's not that we're smarter. It's not that we have the advantage because of our geography, because we clearly don't. So what is it that sets us apart? There's one answer, and it's found in the Declaration of Independence: "We are all endowed by our Creator."

So, we acknowledge God as a country. When we were founded, we acknowledged God: We were all created. We are all endowed by our Creator with certain inalienable rights. Undeniable. They're just there. And they come from the Creator. Among them, but not just, life, liberty, pursuit of happiness. That's pretty simple to me. Those three things, the acknowledgment of our creation by God—a loving God—that our spirit has this natural yearning to be free and to be happy, and that there's nothing wrong with either of those.

There's nothing wrong with being created, nothing wrong with being happy, or trying to be, and there's certainly nothing wrong with living. It was that codification that made one crucial thing possible—and that is for ordinary people to accomplish extraordinary things. Not the smartest, not the brightest, not the wellborn, not the richest. Ordinary.

This is a nation that became the greatest nation in human history—in however many hundreds of thousands, billions, whatever years you want to say we've been plodding the earth—because of ordinary people accomplishing extraordinary things, made possible by the fact that our country was founded acknowledging that our freedom comes from God.

Not from a government and not from some other man or some other woman. It does not come from a demagogue. It does not come from somebody promising to take care of us. It inspired people to produce, to take care of themselves and anybody else that needed it in their community via their church or whatever neighborhood organization they happened to belong to.

That's what's been lost. Too many people think that without government doing the right things, we can't succeed—and the government, when run by people like are running it now, gets in the way and makes it impossible for ordinary people to do anything extraordinary.

● ● ●

Mr. Limbaugh, I consider you a part of my family. I look forward to hearing you every day. You are an eternal beacon of hope, wisdom, knowledge, humor, optimism. You are a national treasure. Rush, I love you. Thank you for everything. —John, member of the audience

● ● ●

AMERICAN EXCEPTIONALISM IS ENSHRINED IN OUR VALUES
The Rush Limbaugh Show, September 12, 2013

RUSH: So just to review, what is American exceptionalism? The core of American exceptionalism is that we are the first country to enshrine in law, via our founding documents, that the individual has rights and liberties that cannot be taken away from them, especially by government.

And it is this that has helped us otherwise ordinary people to achieve extraordinary things, because it has resulted in the removal of shackles that allow everybody in this country, whether they know it or not—it's a shame that too many don't—to set out on a path to get whatever they want. It's nothing more complicated than that. To be whatever they want, to do whatever they want.

Now, we understand there's a common morality and framework of law within these behaviors that take place. I don't need to specify. It doesn't mean you can do whatever you want outside the law. You know what I'm talking about here. Any normal, sensible person does. American exceptionalism. America, the first country to enshrine in law that the individual has rights, liberties, and freedoms that cannot be taken away, because we are born with them. They are part of our creation.

They cannot be taken away even by the government. It's written. And that's what the Democrat Party objects to and doesn't like. And it is this, primarily, that has allowed everybody in this country to do what they want, to get what they want, to be what they want, applying themselves to whatever degree they wish.

*   *   *

America will never be destroyed from the outside. If we falter and lose our freedoms, it will be because we destroyed ourselves. —Abraham Lincoln

*   *   *

HIGH SCHOOL CLASS COMPARES FOUNDING FATHERS TO TERRORISTS
The Rush Limbaugh Show, October 6, 2009

RUSH: Sherwood, Wisconsin, Josh, welcome to the EIB Network, sir. Hello, sir.

CALLER: How are you, Mr. Limbaugh? I've been listening to you since I was just big enough to walk. It's a pleasure to talk to you. I went to public school all my life, and when I was a junior in high school, I had a teacher that had us read an article that compared our Founding Fathers to terrorists in Afghanistan and Iraq. I just wanted to call to, first of all, thank you for helping me in my conservative view, but to also thank my teacher for strengthening my conservative views.

RUSH: Thank you very much. You're not the first person that I have heard— I've heard parents say that they have kids going to school being taught that the Founding Fathers were terrorists. Look, it dovetails precisely with how the radical left views the country: unjust, immoral, Eurocentric, white supremacist, racist, sexist, bigoted, homophobic, brought syphilis in, took the land away from the Indians who are at one with it. They got us the multicultural curriculum in schools. They hate the country as it was constituted. They've always been fringes; they've always been out there; they've been telling us who they are for years. The thing is now they got elected. They finally got elected.

CALLER: Exactly. But again, thank you very much. I appreciate everything you've done for me. I know you've opened up my eyes very widely to what's happening.

RUSH: Well, thank you, sir, very much. I have to tell you, though, you couldn't have done it without yourself. You hung in there.

CALLER: And my mother and my father, they're another one that really helped me in my belief.

RUSH: That's right, you had a—

CALLER: The Catholic view and the conservative view is all basically one, in my eyes.

RUSH: Well, excellent, thanks so much, very nice of you to say.

* * *

RUSH: All right. We did one of our famous Google searches here. We searched the keywords "Founding Fathers were terrorists." We Google searched "Founding Fathers were terrorists." It returned 11,200 pages for "Founding Fathers were terrorists." That's how mainstream it is, at least out there on the Internet.

• • •

Rush Limbaugh, in essence, became the Founding Father of national talk radio when his Sacramento show went national in 1988. —Jeffrey Lord, *American Spectator*

• • •

David and Rush Limbaugh, early stars!

RUSH EXPLAINS THE MEANING OF DITTOS
The Rush Limbaugh Show, December 16, 2016

RUSH: Melissa in New Orleans, great to have you. Welcome to Open Line Friday.

CALLER: Well, hello, Rush, and mega dittos.

RUSH: Thank you very much.

CALLER: *[Chuckles]* I guess I show my age when I tell you mega dittos, right?

RUSH: Well, no. "Mega dittos" is timeless.

CALLER: You're right. Just as you are.

RUSH: It predates probably the first six months of the program. It wasn't part of the original program. Do you know what the meaning of "dittos" is?

CALLER: No!

RUSH: What do you think? When people call here and say, "Mega dittos," what do you think they are actually saying? Just "Hear, hear, Rush! I agree. You're really right. I just hope you keep saying it because I really agree with you," something like that?

CALLER: Something like that, yeah.

RUSH: That's not what it means.

CALLER: Agreeing with you wholeheartedly.

RUSH: That's not what it means.

CALLER: No, huh?

RUSH: No. You know what it means?

CALLER: What?

RUSH: I had a call from a guy—this is like in the first year of the program—and he was going on and on and on about how wonderful the show is and how much he loved it because there wasn't anything like it in 1988 and '89 in all of the rest of national media, the networks and the newspapers. There wasn't anything like this back then, and he just kept praising it effusively. So I thanked him and went on to the next call, and the first words out of that next caller's mouth—it was a woman—were, "Ditto to what that guy just said." So "ditto" actually means "I love the show. Please don't ever go away.

It's too important. It's too crucial." And then part of it also means "And you're always right, and don't stop being." But it really is more an expression of gratitude for the existence of the show, which I'm sure you meant as well.

CALLER: That is exactly what I mean.

RUSH: Okay, cool. So there you go.

CALLER: All right.

RUSH: But now you have the exact meaning of it.

CALLER: I do. Thank you. And you're always informing us, as always.

RUSH EXPLAINS RIO LINDA

The Rush Limbaugh Show, June 15, 2007

RUSH: Here's Brett in Lancaster, Pennsylvania. Brett, it's nice to have you on the EIB Network. Hello, sir.

CALLER: Hey, good afternoon, Rush.

RUSH: Yes.

CALLER: Very proud father in Lancaster, Pennsylvania. The point of my call is, for the last four and a half years, including today, you've had me incredibly confused on your Rio Linda comments.

RUSH: Yeah?

CALLER: I was hoping you could give me a history and summary on that.

RUSH: Yes, I'd be happy to. Now, those of you that know this, please indulge me here. This is an example of the constant new tune-in factor that occurs on this program, due to the ever-increasing size of our audience. When I moved to Sacramento in 1984, I was driving around town because I wanted to get familiar with it and be familiar with the place I was now living and working. I'm driving around and I came to this place called Rio Linda. You know, they had the city sign but no indication of who lived there, no population number. I have never seen that before. I've always seen population numbers on the sign of the city. So I drove through this place, and it was like going to the Twilight Zone. On the main drag, there were cars on concrete blocks in the front yards, washing machines and dryers and washboards on the porch, and I said, "Whoa! This is a depressed area, and it needs my help."

So one of the bits that I did when I went on the air was to offer to move there if they would change the name to "Limbaugh, California," and just by moving there, I would increase property values. Of course, the idea was rejected and so forth. So I decided, "Well, I'm just going to tease these people." Anytime I say something I think is remotely, just remotely complicated, I will try to translate it for Rio Lindans so that they can understand it. The Rio Linda population and I have a great, great, great relationship. It has put them on the map; they're very good-spirited about it. But it's just a little town, not far from Sacramento. They don't like being called a suburb, and, frankly, Sacramento wouldn't like for people to think Rio Linda is a suburb of Sacramento. It's sort of its own little pocket there. It's amazing.

CALLER: All right, well, I was close. I always figured you were talking about Detroit.

RUSH: *[Laughing]* You've been waiting all this time for that line?

CALLER: Yes.

RUSH: *[Laughing]*

CALLER: You said the cars are on cinder blocks, so . . .

RUSH: No, no, no, no. I've been to Detroit. I've not seen that in Detroit. I've been to a lot of places, but Rio Linda stands out. That's why there's never been a substitute, an addition, or a replacement.

CALLER: It's an honor to talk to you, sir. I've been listening since they had Rush Rooms in 1989 here in Orlando.

RUSH: Hey. Yes, yes. I remember those.

*　　*　　*

The views expressed by the host on this program are documented to be almost always right 99.8 percent of the time. This is according to the latest opinion audit that's in from the Sullivan Group. It came in last week. I actually was happy to see that it had not changed. —Rush Limbaugh

*　　*　　*

PART 3 — FREEDOM OF SPEECH

Some might think it was always easy for Rush. After all, he was incredibly successful with on-air bravado that made him appear invincible. The truth is that Rush experienced many lows and challenges throughout his life, and worked extremely hard to overcome them, earning everything he achieved.

In 1988, when Rush appeared on the national scene, there was a total liberal media monopoly, and no one was publicly saying the things he said. Rush provided a voice for millions of hardworking Americans who cherished conservative values, and he soon became known as "America's Anchorman" and the "Doctor of Democracy." The show created a tremendous buzz, with people asking, "Who is this Limbaugh guy?" and Rush "listening rooms" started popping up all over the country. As Rush's popularity grew, so did the mischaracterizations and attempts to force him off the air.

At first, it frustrated Rush to be routinely taken out of context, but he came to the realization that "being hated is a measure of success." He began to take pride in "tweaking the media" and proving naysayers wrong. He used satire and humor like no other to "annoy the left, simply by showing up." Rush would smile from ear to ear and say, "Folks, I am just a lovable little fuzzball. Just sitting here, bothering no one."

Rush never backed down from stressing the value of free speech. No matter if he agreed with someone or not, he would say, "The moment our basic right of free speech is silenced, the country we know will never be the same."

• • •

Congress shall make no law respecting an establishment of religion, or prohibiting the free exercise thereof; or abridging the freedom of speech, or of the press; or the right of the people peaceably to assemble, and to petition the Government for a redress of grievances. —US Constitution, First Amendment

• • •

AN ARMENIAN IMMIGRANT ON FREE SPEECH
The Rush Limbaugh Show, May 11, 2012

RUSH: Livingston, New Jersey. Hi, Lucy. Great to have you on the program.

CALLER: Hi, Rush. Thank you for accepting my call.

RUSH: You are welcome.

CALLER: It's a great honor to speak with you.

RUSH: Thank you very much.

CALLER: You know, I came to United States in August of last year. I got married and now I live in New Jersey.

RUSH: Where did you come from?

CALLER: I came from Armenia—Yerevan.

RUSH: Yes.

CALLER: You know what? I love United States. I love a lot of things about United States. But what I'm impressed and amazed very much, it's like freedom of speech, you know. Before, when I was living in Yerevan, you know, I have heard about the freedom of speech, about how USA is great, but right now I'm starting to understand it more and more. Americans are very lucky just because they have freedom of speech. Second, because they have Rush Limbaugh, who provides them the truth all about the political and economic situation here.

RUSH: I think many people take that for granted. You are wise to understand that.

CALLER: You know, I understand because I have things to compare with, because in country from where I am, freedom of speech is like very dangerous thing. You are gonna pay a high price for that, and I—

RUSH: I have to tell you something, Lucy. There are many people in this country who have a great fear that we are headed in that direction. By no means are we there, but there are people in this country who are afraid right now to be overheard—

CALLER: Yeah.

RUSH: —saying certain things. Afraid it will be reported to somebody or afraid that they'll be condemned. And there are attacks. I mean, I'm attacked for what I say, and a lot of people are, and other people are not. But that's part of the political process in my case. But freedom of speech is still alive and well in this country, but censorship is all over the place. It's called political correctness, or in some cases flat-out censorship. Intimidation is constant to try to get people to shut up.

CALLER: But, you know, in Armenia, it's just dangerous. Journalists can be killed there just because they are speaking truth, as you do now.

RUSH: Well, we don't know of any instances of that, journalists being killed.

CALLER: You know what, I want to say that as long as United States has freedom of speech, and as long as here nobody's above the law, even the president, as long as the elections here are free and fair, the future, I can see the future of United States very bright, you know what I mean?

RUSH: I understand totally what you mean. What I find fascinating about this is that you are a recent arrival from a very oppressive place, so your point of reference—we are the freest anyone could imagine, and we are. There's no question we are, but people in this country have a different frame of reference or point of reference, and they see the erosion of freedom of speech that you see as something wide open. Is there a National Organization for Women chapter in your country?

CALLER: No.

RUSH: I didn't think so. Sadly, yeah. Afraid of that.

* * *

The United States government's purpose is to secure our unalienable rights, not to seize them. —Rush Limbaugh

* * *

• • •

You have enemies? Good. That means you've stood up
for something in your life. —Winston Churchill

• • •

WE STAND FOR FREE SPEECH AND THAT'S WHAT
THREATENS THE LEFT
The Rush Limbaugh Show, April 12, 2007

All right, this is now about racial politics, folks. The Reverend Sharpton is out there saying, "This is only the beginning. This must be a walk that CBS now does. It must be a walk that others will do; then we must have a broad discussion on what's permitted and what's not permitted," and the Reverend Jackson and the Reverend Sharpton have been empowered as the final arbiters on this in the United States of America. How absurd and ridiculous.

But they exist for one reason: liberal, white plantation-owner racists have created these two figures and have granted them power and authority as Democrats, and now guess who have become the targets of the wrath of Sharpton and Jackson? For now it's the white liberal executives at CBS and NBC. So it's about racial politics. It's about racial politics, and when it comes to the lack of minority reputation of the big three networks, MSNBC as well as CNN, I have to agree that Reverend Jackson [and] Reverend Sharpton are right. On to something now that's the practical reality of all this. If it's about racial politics, then what shall be the ideal percentage? This argument we've been having since the first affirmative action argument came up, the whole quota argument.

I made the point back in the early eighties, mid-eighties, when this all started, "Affirmative action is about making sure that the race wars never end." You won't get 'em to come. That's why they hate the quota business. Because when you start saying, "Yeah, there should be quotas," then they're willing to put a finite number on the number of minorities in any job, and that's not what this is about. This is about shakedowns.

Of course, censorship, that's also here. I want to say something for the record here, folks, and I want it to be recorded. Today, April the twelfth, the day of the cigar dinner, let it be recorded that we conservatives are the ones standing for free speech.

We conservatives are the ones standing for diversity of thought and honest communication. You do not hear a conservative anywhere suggest that anybody be taken off any radio station, television station, movies, or what have you. We do not urge censorship because we are not afraid of the free flow of ideas. Liberals are. . . .

They want to shut down anybody who doesn't embrace their ideology, and they want to criminalize those who don't embrace their ideology. Today it's the race baiters. Tomorrow it's going to be some other cause, but liberalism is what it is, and it exists to silence people who don't agree. They can't win the debate, which they admit by their own actions. They don't want debate. They can't compete in the open marketplace of ideas because their ideas are flawed, and airing those ideas makes it clear that they are flawed.

• • •

Long before I became President, I used Rush Limbaugh as my true north for decades. I've been listening to his show since the very beginning. I even remember going to the dedicated Rush Rooms in restaurants where you could listen to the show on your lunch hour. In his first few years with a nationally syndicated show, I always marveled at how people could call him up and say, "Thank you for speaking up like you do. I thought I was the only one who had those beliefs." The fact is, Rush helped bring the conservative movement together three hours a day for a family meeting.
—Kay C. James, President of the Heritage Foundation

• • •

A FAIRNESS DOCTRINE FOR THE INTERNET?
The Rush Limbaugh Show, March 16, 2010

RUSH: To Bucks County, Pennsylvania, we start with John. Great to have you on the program, sir. Hello.

CALLER: Rush, it's an honor, sir.

RUSH: Thank you.

CALLER: *USA Today,* the sixteenth, front page, small story, it seems insignificant. The FCC wants more fast lanes to the Internet.

RUSH: Well, it's actually much more hideous than this. This story that you're quoting is just talking about the spectrum, the frequency spectrum, and they want more broadband spectrum for higher-speed access for everybody that uses the Internet. In getting this, one of the areas they're looking at is asking over-the-air television stations to stop broadcasting over the air, since it's all cable or satellite now and they want to take that spectrum and apply it to Internet. Now, you can say that they want to take over the Internet, but they already have. I mean they regulate all broadcasting. They don't regulate cable or satellite but they regular over-the-air broadcasting, like radio. You have to go through, every five or ten years, whatever it is now, for license renewal, community ascertain, you have to run out and talk to librarians, a bunch of people, ask them what their big issues in the community are, okay, document that, send it in with your license renewal, they say you're paying attention to local issues, blah, blah, blah, blah, blah. What's coming way beyond this, what's coming in the fall is the deceptively named net neutrality. The easiest way to understand this is to think of a Fairness Doctrine for the Internet. Now, how would this work? Let's say that you want to go Google or Bing, you want to search the mating habits of the Australian rabbit bat. Net neutrality would require that every search engine produce an equal number of results that satisfy every disagreement about the issue. Yep. And that's going to happen. That pretty much is going to happen. And the White House is in bed with Google. The White House and Google are bedmates. Google, largest search engine. Already, if you do a search of me on Google and you look at the crap that comes up, it's by design and on purpose. It's literal crap—I mean, the most obscure places you never knew existed with comments about what happened on this program every day. It took a long time, but we had to really work hard at getting our website to pop up in a search of Google. Our own website. So in the era of net neutrality—and this is where the Google–White House partnership comes into play—the results of any search—let's say you want to search abortion, or you want to search the health care bill—they want to control what you see. They want to control what your options are. They can't really control the content; it's too massive and it's too big. What they want to try to do is limit your access to it and have that access flavored toward whatever particular point of view the administration wants supported. Now, that is coming. That's why they want all this new broadband. That's why they want all this new speed. That's why they want all this new access. It's not to own it; it's to control the content as best they can. Just think of it as a Fairness Doctrine for the Internet. I'm not making this up. I guarantee you that's what's coming. I think this is a fait accompli. I think it practically has been voted on, done deal.

* * *

Government, even in its best state, is but a necessary evil; in its worst state, an intolerable one. –Thomas Paine

* * *

SENATOR DICK DURBIN INTRODUCES BACKDOOR ATTEMPT AT THE FAIRNESS DOCTRINE
The Rush Limbaugh Show, February 26, 2009

In the Senate this afternoon, ladies and gentlemen, the Senate today is voting on two versions of the Fairness Doctrine, starting in twenty-four minutes, if they're on time. The first bill in the Senate on the Fairness Doctrine is authored by Dick Durbin of Illinois. His bill proposes these contrivances that I wrote about in the *Wall Street Journal* op-ed.

"Localism," meaning local content, a notice to broadcasters they must ratchet up and increase the local content on their radio stations. Other guidelines for programming and diversity and advisory boards overseeing

Rush Limbaugh was an icon, patriot, and American hero.
No one fought harder for freedom and liberty. The greatest
radio host of all time. —US Representative Jim Jordan of
Ohio, Tribute to Rush, 2021

radio stations, "making sure that the laws," the requirements in the Durbin bill, "are monitored and upheld." The second vote is the anti–Fairness Doctrine bill offered by Senator Jim DeMint. It's an amendment, actually, that would forever close off the Fairness Doctrine as something that could be voted on in the Senate.

The conventional wisdom is that Durbin will win and DeMint will lose, because there are more Democrats than there are Republicans in the Senate. Now, of course, this is just the Senate. It'd then have to go to the House, and it's interesting.

Obama has said that he's not in favor of the Fairness Doctrine, but I don't think this is the Fairness Doctrine. They're not calling it the Fairness Doctrine. These are new guidelines, new restrictions: "local content," "diversity in ownership," that kind of thing. So don't let anybody tell you they're not going for it. They certainly are, and it's happening in the Senate even as we speak.

⋆ ⋆ ⋆

RUSH: Dick Durbin on the floor of the Senate this afternoon.

DURBIN: Section 307(b) of the Communications Act requires that the FCC ensure license ownership be spread among diverse communities. It's there already. I don't think this is socialistic, communistic, or unconstitutional. It's in the law. So to say we're going to promote what the law already says is hardly a denial of basic constitutional freedoms. Second, the Communications Act requires the FCC eliminate market entry barriers for small businesses to increase the diversity of media voices. That's Section 257. So to argue that what I'm putting in here is a dramatic change of the law, is going to somehow muzzle Rush Limbaugh, it's not the case. What we're suggesting is that it is best that we follow the guidelines already in the law to promote and encourage diversity in media ownership.

RUSH: All right, folks, I've been in this business all my life. I understand the Communications Acts of 1934, 1944, 1995, 2003, '04, I know it all. Let me first ask you a question: Senator Durbin, if it isn't about changing things, why do this? If the law is already the law, why do this? Why throw my name in here? The Fairness Doctrine will never be used, and they're voting on this today in the Senate. The very idea, he says, that something in the law is going to muzzle Rush Limbaugh is not the case. Then why do it? Obviously I'm not

You can never replace Babe Ruth, but I'd take it a step further. Rush Limbaugh was Babe Ruth, Lou Gehrig, Hank Aaron, Derek Jeter, and everyone in between. You want to talk about the greatest in radio of all time, the GOAT? It is definitely Rush. —Sean Hannity

being muzzled by the current law, which you say is already the current law, Senator "Turban," so there's something different here. When somebody goes to the floor of the Senate and says, "I'm not trying to muzzle Rush Limbaugh," yes, you are. It's like when somebody says, "Look, it's not the money," it's always the money.

> In the Southern Command studio, Rush had two large television screens positioned on the wall in front of him. He kept various news programs on all day in the background. One afternoon, during a commercial break, he happened to glance up at one of the televisions and saw an ESPN anchor commenting on whether the United States should consider an exchange program with China. He thought in disbelief, "What is this?"

ESPN ANALYST: WE HAVE TO IMPORT CHICOM CENSORSHIP
The Rush Limbaugh Show, October 9, 2019

RUSH: Yesterday toward the end of the program I told you I was watching somebody on TV who said that relationships with China require an exchange program. It was the most convoluted, crazy thing I'd ever heard. Well, we dug it up. Cookie went out there and found it in all of the audio and video that had been broadcast yesterday. It turned out to be infobabe Brooke Baldwin interviewing ESPN jock sniffer "LZ" Granderson. Well, they're all groupies.

All of these reporters at ESPN, sports people, they're all groupies. "Jock sniffer" is just another name for groupie. LZ Granderson, the question: "Do you think that there is a benefit to have this connection with China that, you know, an American presence in a country such as this and our American values perhaps seep into the culture, and how we roll?" She basically said, "LZ, is it a good thing that we're in China? Maybe American values can find a way to be intertwined there?"

GRANDERSON: Well, it's an exchange, and this is what not just the NBA's dealing with but American culture in general. Yes, we are exporting a certain degree of freedom of expression.

BALDWIN: Mmm-hmm.

GRANDERSON: But we also are importing communist censorship. That is, there's only gonna be so much of our freedom in which [*sic*] China's gonna allow in, and if we want to do business with them, we may have to consider some censorship of our own. So, it's an exchange. It's not a one-way street here.

BALDWIN: [*Dramatic pause*] LZ Granderson, you wise man.

GRANDERSON: [*Chuckles*]

BALDWIN: Thank you so much for your opinion.

RUSH: [*Laughing*] Did you hear this? It's an exchange program! The ChiComs are going to have to allow some of our freedom in. But in exchange, we're gonna have to consider importing some of their censorship. We're gonna have to import censorship. We're going to have to use censorship in America if we're gonna expect the ChiComs to dole out some freedom. Good. . . . No wonder Millennials don't know what the hell is happening in the world today!

* * *

We don't forget anything here and nothing gets past us. In fact, if you listen regularly you will hear about things long before they become mainstream pop culture. —Rush Limbaugh

* * *

CIVILITY IS THE NEW CENSORSHIP
The Rush Limbaugh Show, January 13, 2011

RUSH: This is Kathy in Potomac, Maryland. It's great to have you here.

CALLER: Oh, thanks, Rush. Happy New Year, and happy belated birthday to you.

RUSH: Thank you very much.

CALLER: Before I get to the reason for my call, I would like to make a very brief linguistic observation, and that is that "civility" is the new word for "censorship."

RUSH: I think you're right. It's a great point. "Civility" is the new word for "shut the heck up."

* * *

RUSH: We keep hearing about "uncivil," and I love our previous caller's comment that this civility equals censorship. That's exactly what Obama and the left mean when they start talking about civility. "We need to bring civility back to our discourse"—that means shut us up! Censorship. Now, if politicians are uncivil to us—if they are dismissive of the last election, for example. They lost. They got shellacked. But if they are dismissive of that election, if they are dismissive of the Constitution (as they were the other week, when it was read on the floor of the House) how are we to react to them?

Say we disagree but do it quietly, without passion, in hushed tones, with words [like] "please" and "thank you." How are we supposed to react when they are uncivil to us? I've actually been thinking about doing a program the way they would like to hear this program done. *[Laughing]* I think it would be fun to try, you know, to do an hour of civility as they mean it. Don't get scared, Snerdley. There's no reason to fear this. No, there's not. No, there's not. It's like every other illustration we do on this program: to make the point of how silly and stifling it would be. Well, no, I could be boring. I could very easily be boring. I'd just have to be myself. *[Laughing]*

● ● ●

I'm just a harmless, lovable little fuzzball.

—Rush Limbaugh

● ● ●

THE INFAMOUS HARRY REID SMEAR LETTER

Rush laughed out loud when Senator Harry Reid wrote a letter to the then CEO of Clear Channel Radio, Mark Mays, signed by forty-one Democrat senators that said Rush should be pulled off the airwaves for being critical of our United States military personnel. "This is absurd!" Rush said, and in his typical fashion, he decided to illustrate the absurdity. He announced publicly that not only was he going to put the infamous Harry Reid Smear Letter up for auction, he was going to match the funds raised and donate all proceeds to the Marine Corps–Law Enforcement Foundation. The letter was purchased on eBay by Betty Casey for $2.1 million, and the money was matched by Rush to make a total donation of $4.2 million to support the families of fallen heroes.

EBAY BIDDING UPDATE
The Rush Limbaugh Show, October 16, 2007

This is a historic document in that you have forty-one US senators who willfully and knowingly lied to slander a US citizen in an effort to discredit and/or impede his free speech rights. That is a direct violation of their sworn oath of office to defend and protect the Constitution of the United States of America.

Our Founding Fathers crafted such language to protect citizens from exactly this kind of behavior. Hopefully the highest bidder will get some media time to explain just that. And to think at least one of these oath violators [the forty-one Democrat senators, including Barack Obama and Hillary Clinton] wants to become president.

The United States Congress is supposed to protect innocent citizens by protecting and defending the Constitution. These guys are shredding it and trying to get my corporate partner in the syndication side of the program to condemn me, to make me apologize. This is an effort to harm my ability to do business, and it's backfired on them big-time.

We're at fifty-one one, $51,100, on the eBay auction. It will go through Friday at one p.m., and it's going to really start percolating here toward the end of the week. You know the big money is holding out so as not to bid this up. But it will get fast and furious. All the money goes to the Marine Corps–Law Enforcement Foundation. I'm going to match whatever the final donation is with a donation of my own to the Marine Corps–Law Enforcement Foundation.

United States Senate

OFFICE OF THE MAJORITY LEADER
WASHINGTON, D.C. 20510

October 2, 2007

Mr. Mark P. Mays
CEO, Clear Channel Communications Inc.
200 East Basse Road
San Antonio, TX 78209

Dear Mr. Mays,

At the time we sign this letter, 3,808 American soldiers have been killed in Iraq, and another 28,009 have been wounded. 160,000 others awoke this morning on foreign sand, far from home, to face the danger and uncertainty of another day at war.

Although Americans of goodwill debate the merits of this war, we can all agree that those who serve with such great courage deserve our deepest respect and gratitude. That is why Rush Limbaugh's recent characterization of troops who oppose the war as "phony soldiers" is such an outrage.

Our troops are fighting and dying to bring to others the freedoms that many take for granted. It is unconscionable that Mr. Limbaugh would criticize them for exercising the fundamentally American right to free speech. Mr. Limbaugh has made outrageous remarks before, but this affront to our soldiers is beyond the pale.

The military, like any community within the United States, includes members both for and against the war. Senior generals, such as General John Batiste and Paul Eaton, have come out against the war while others have publicly supported it. A December 2006 poll conducted by the *Military Times* found just 35 percent of service members approved of President Bush's handling of the war in Iraq, compared to 42 percent who disapproved. From this figure alone, it is clear that Mr. Limbaugh's insult is directed at thousands of American service members.

Active and retired members of our armed forces have a unique perspective on the war and offer a valuable contribution to our national debate. In August, seven soldiers wrote an op-ed expressing their concern with the current strategy in Iraq. Tragically, since then, two of those seven soldiers have made the ultimate sacrifice in Iraq.

Thousands of active troops and veterans were subjected to Mr. Limbaugh's unpatriotic and indefensible comments on your broadcast. We trust you will agree that not a single one of our sons, daughters, neighbors and friends serving overseas is a "phony soldier." We call on you to publicly repudiate these comments that call into question their service and sacrifice and to ask Mr. Limbaugh to apologize for his comments.

Sincerely,

Senator Harry Reid
Majority Leader

Senator Richard Durbin
Assistant Majority Leader

Senator Charles Schumer
Vice Chairman
Democratic Conference

Senator Patty Murray
Secretary
Democratic Conference

GOYA FOODS CEO MAKES ALEXANDRIA OCASIO-CORTEZ (AOC) EMPLOYEE OF THE MONTH

The Rush Limbaugh Show, December 8, 2020

Did you hear what the Goya Foods CEO did? This is clever. It's a feel-good story where a successful businessman, who happens to be a capitalist, turns lemons into lemonade. You see, Alexandria Ocasio-Cortez called for a boycott of his company.

The Goya Foods president and CEO, Bob Unanue, revealed that after she echoed a call for a boycott of Goya products back in July because this guy supports Trump, his company has named her employee of the month because sales rose so dramatically after she demanded the boycott.

Unanue had visited the White House, where he stated: "We're all truly blessed at the same time to have a leader like President Trump, who is a builder." That prompted Julian Castro, former Housing and Urban Development secretary of the Obama Regime, to tweet that: "Goya Foods has been a staple of so many Latino households for generations. Now their CEO, Bob Unanue, is praising a president who villainizes and maliciously attacks Latinos for political gain. Americans should think twice before buying their products."

Then Ocasio-Cortez chimed in, saying, "Oh look, it's the sound of me Googling 'how to make your own Adobo.'" So she ends up, along with Julian Castro, demanding that Americans boycott Goya, and their sales go through the roof; so he makes her employee of the month. I love people that think that way. I love people that react that way. It's just absolutely fabulous.

———— ❖ ————

• • •

So, I'm just sitting here in the library minding my own business bothering no one. According to Cookie, I'm causing a storm out there. —Rush Limbaugh

• • •

Over the years, Rush developed his own language, coining terms that will go down in history. We all remember them well!

- El Rushbo

- Environmentalist Wacko

- Feminazi

- Mayor of Realville

- All-Knowing, All-Sensing, All-Everything Maha Rushie

- The Doctor of Democracy

- Annoying the left, simply by showing up

- For those of you in Rio Linda

- America's Real Anchorman

- The Big Voice on the Right

- America's Truth Detector

- Zip, Zero, Nada

- The most dangerous man in America

- Harmless, lovable little fuzzball

- Annoying the left, simply by showing up

- Having more fun than a human being should be allowed to have!

- King of Talk Radio

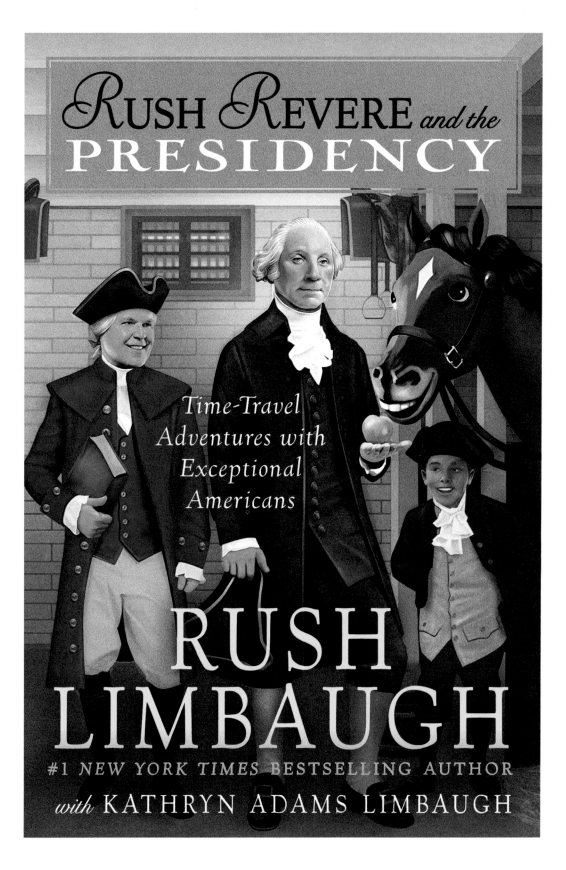

RUSH REVERE and the PRESIDENCY

Time-Travel
Adventures with
Exceptional
Americans

RUSH LIMBAUGH

with KATHRYN ADAMS LIMBAUGH

PART 4 — AMERICAN HISTORY IS FUN WITH RUSH REVERE!

Rush was always keenly aware of time. If we were leaving for the airport, he would say that we should be ready at 12:42 p.m. on the dot. Not 12:30 or around quarter to one but the very specific 12:42 p.m. As an exceptional broadcaster, Rush spent the majority of his life making sure he rarely "ran long." He would be wrapped up in an opening monologue and, without skipping a beat, would know precisely what word he needed to end his thought on in order to make the hard commercial break. He made talking for three hours a day (rarely with guests) look easy. It most certainly was not.

Our favorite way to disengage was to say to each other, "No clocks!" But this plan usually did not come to fruition, because it was virtually impossible for either of us to fully disconnect our minds. One year, in the midst of an attempt at "no clocks" during a Christmas vacation in Honolulu, we started talking about the nonsense being taught in many schools. Before arriving back in Florida, we were immersed in a new challenge and about to embark on one of the greatest experiences of Rush's life—writing the Adventures of Rush Revere series.

Through the magic of time travel, young readers are taken back in time with substitute history teacher Rush Revere, his hilarious sidekick Liberty, and a group of middle schoolers. They witness key events like the Boston Tea Party while meeting early patriots George Washington, Ben Franklin, and Abigail Adams. Rush loved the challenge of making history come alive for young patriots in an accurate, patriotic, and fun way. The first book in the series, *Rush Revere and the Brave Pilgrims*, quickly rose to number one on the *New York Times* bestseller list. The next four books in the series followed the same trajectory.

When eight- and ten-year-olds started calling into the program on Open Line Fridays and sending in photos of themselves dressed as Rush Revere by the thousands, Rush would light up. So many callers would say that they enjoyed reading for the first time, and of course everyone loved Liberty the talking horse!

. . .

We are so blessed, Kathryn and I and everybody on the Rush Revere Time-Travel Adventures with Exceptional Americans team. We just published our fifth book in the series, Rush Revere and the Presidency. *It's the fifth book in three years. These books are for young people, to teach them the glorious truth of the founding of the greatest nation on earth, the United States of America, precisely because it's not being taught in enough places in America anymore.* —Rush Limbaugh

. . .

IT'S MY NEW BOOK! *RUSH REVERE AND THE BRAVE PILGRIMS: TIME-TRAVEL ADVENTURES WITH EXCEPTIONAL AMERICANS*
The Rush Limbaugh Show, September 5, 2013

My friends, I am so excited. I have been waiting for this day to be able to tell you something. I have been waiting with bated breath. I have been champing at the bit. I've almost let it slip out of the bag a couple of times, and now I don't have to worry about it slipping out of the bag because today I can announce it.

Now, I don't want to give away the book. Remember, it's a kids' book, but you get the book and you read it with them or you read it to them or you have them read it. It's for everybody. I don't want to give an age group here because I don't want to exclude anybody, 'cause the book is for everybody, but it's written for young people, and it's written honestly, and it does not have an agenda. It's just the truthful history of the Pilgrims—who they were, where they came from, why they came here, what happened when they got here. The true story of Thanksgiving. There's no politics in this. Ages ten to thirteen is the targeted age group it's written for, but it's for everybody.

The book is a way, folks, of teaching what isn't being taught. People ask me all the time what they can do beyond voting to effect change in the country. And I ask myself that, too—what can I do besides the radio show? And when Kathryn had this idea—I mean, for twenty years people have been urging me to write a book. "Nah, I don't want to." And Vince, "You know, put together a compilation of your monologues." "Nah, I don't really want to." When she mentioned this to me, that lit the fire. That was something I hadn't done. That was an area that I hadn't targeted. I talk about it all the time. I lament what's going on in schools all the time. But this is my way of doing more than what I'm doing now. It is a way of teaching what isn't being taught. This isn't being taught.

We live in an amazing, free country, founded by people with unwavering spirit and determination to triumph, regardless of the hardships and obstacles they faced. Way too many people believe that prosperity, success, or whatever is an exception now, that it really is impossible—and it's not, folks.

And times are tough for a lot of people today, but they're not tougher than they were for the people that founded this country. It's an amazing, amazing story. It's a miraculous story, the blessings of God and any number of other things that led to the founding of this country. But exceptional Americans are not few and far between. It's quite the opposite. You start from the early days, people like William Bradford, who was the grand poohbah of the Pilgrims on the *Mayflower* and who set up their first settlement.

This country is made up of exceptional people and stories of rags to riches. They made it with hard work, determination, a little luck, and God's grace. So, in *Rush Revere and the Brave Pilgrims*, we have brought to life our loving character from *Two If by Tea*, Rush Revere. We've given him a horse. We've given him a talking horse! Liberty talks. Liberty has the ability to time travel. So, in this book, Rush Revere and Liberty will go to the *Mayflower* and talk to the Pilgrims aboard the *Mayflower* as they're sailing to what will become America.

Rush Revere is a substitute school teacher at a middle school anywhere in America, and he will take a couple of students with him to the first Thanksgiving, and they will learn all about it. Again, it is a unique way of reaching the target audience here, which is America's young people—who are, sadly, not being taught what is in this book. And what's in this book is

the historical record, accurate historical record of the Pilgrims. It's who they were, why they existed, where they were, how they got here, what they did when they got here, and what they did and why it mattered and [how it was] related to the founding of this country.

It's fun, and when you establish the premise that your lead character can go anywhere in history with his talking horse . . . I mean, I don't want to spoil it. *[Laughing]* I'm so excited.

REVERE SCHOLARSHIP RECIPIENT INTERVIEW

My name is Saadyah, and I'm nine years old. I think the Adventures of Rush Revere is amazing! I love the American history. I love all the jokes. I really love this series.

My favorite character is Liberty! I love Liberty! He is a very unique horse. He can freeze time, travel through time, and he thinks about food. I love food! We both love food. We also love to do pranks!

I love the book about the brave Pilgrims; how they got through all of their hardships. The Pilgrims had to travel on the Mayflower *on rough seas, many people died, and they had to suffer through the winter, and then Squanto helped them and they were all happy again.*

They all had their first Thanksgiving together. I really love the Rush Revere series that he made. I thought history was boring at first, but now American history is so much fun with Rush Revere and his horse, Liberty—and his students.

—Saadyah

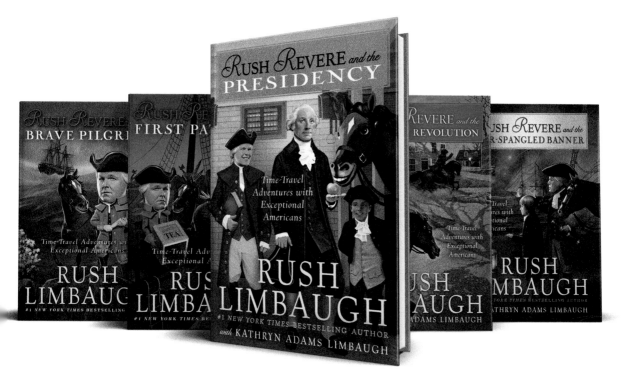

· · ·

TEN-YEAR-OLD CALLER: (laughing) Is it really true,
are you really a harmless, lovable fuzzball?

RUSH: Totally. Totally. I'm one of the nicest, sweetest,
quietest people you would ever meet. I'm one of the most
humble people that you would ever run into, Riley.

CALLER: (laughing)

RUSH: She's laughing, but it happens to be the truth.
You asked, and I wouldn't lie to you about it.

CALLER: Yep.

RUSH: If I were a mean person, I would tell you,
and then I'd hang up on you.

· · ·

THANK YOU TO EVERYONE FOR MAKING ME THE CHILDREN'S CHOICE BOOK AWARDS AUTHOR OF THE YEAR

The Rush Limbaugh Show, May 15, 2014

Ladies and gentlemen, you are listening to your harmless, lovable little fuzz-ball host, Rush Limbaugh, well-known radio raconteur bon vivant, and now children's book Author of the Year. The awards were handed out last night by the Children's Book Council, and I want to take a moment here to thank everyone in the audience, particularly the young people who voted. This is an award where the readers determine the winners.

Kathryn and I flew up after the program yesterday to New York for the awards banquet, the event. This is the seventh annual. It's relatively new, and it's combined with the Children's Literacy Project, and what a great evening. It was a wonderful event, and I had, honestly, to make sure you understand, no expectation of winning this thing.

When they announced my name, I was momentarily frozen. We were sitting in the front row with a couple people from Simon & Schuster, the well-known publishing house. It was just a really, really nice event. I have to tell you, there were so many immigrants that came up to me before the event started, when everybody was being seated and during the event, and they were telling me what coming to America meant to them.

One of them was the photographer, one of the official photographers for the event. There were a lot of people that were working the event that came up and wanted me to understand how much America had meant to them, and it was really great.

I love America. I wish everybody did. I hope everybody will. It's one of the most fascinating stories of human history, this country and what it has meant to the world and what it means to citizens who live here. And it's a delight and it's an opportunity to try to share that story with young people so that they can grow and learn to love and appreciate the country in which they're growing up and will someday run and lead and inherit.

Rush and Millie   *May 19, 1984*

• • •

Our mother was a comic, a singer, a natural ham, and an entertainer; our dad was unusually brilliant, the small-college national debate champion, a lawyer's lawyer, and the guy who would hold court in our living room to the fascination of our friends. But he never had the national platform that Rush would carve out for himself. Rush did our parents proud in a way that is indescribably gratifying to me. —David Limbaugh

• • •

Rush would often tell stories about his father and mother, Rush and Millie. Rush's father was a World War II pilot in the Pacific and known for his legendary talks on politics at their family home in Cape Girardeau, Missouri. Rush described his mother as a wonderful lady who lit up the room and cared for everyone she met. When Rush became extremely well-known throughout the country, Millie was thrilled to share her boy with the world—at times to Rush's amused embarrassment!

A TRIP DOWN MEMORY LANE WITH MILLIE LIMBAUGH!
The Rush Limbaugh Show, August 1, 2008

MRS. MILLIE LIMBAUGH: One day, the teacher had me in for conference, like she did all the parents. She said, "If Rush doesn't change his ways, he'll never grow to be the man his grandfather is, or his father." *[Laughing]*

I've always said he got his smarts from his dad and, I will say, silliness from me. *[Laughing]* . . .

We had four- and five-year-old kindergarten here at the college. You know, the "training school," they called it. And one day the teacher, who is now gone, had me in for conference, like she did all the parents.

RUSH: I was a hell-raiser and causing problems even at four and five years old, when I had to be stashed away in prison in school. Well, I don't know, I was probably throwing spitballs, harassing the other kids, probably not taking a nap when I was supposed to take a nap.

All I know is, I didn't want to be there, and when you don't want to be someplace, you're letting the people know that you think they are your captors, that you [don't] want to be there. I didn't want to drink the Kool-Aid. I didn't like anything about it.

* * *

RUSH: Those of you who have been listening to this program since the beginning will no doubt remember my mother and her numerous appearances on this program and on the television show. She was the queen of the Blue-Haired Bloody Mary Gang, as I called her and her friends. We grew up in a little town in Missouri, and when this program first started and it was just building, and it was kind of white-hot, popular, associated-with-something-new, unique, everybody glomming on to it.

And people driving through southeast Missouri would pull off I-55, drive into Cape Girardeau, and look up my mother. And they'd go by the house—and she'd let 'em in! Thankfully, every one of 'em was a solid, upstanding citizen fan. Folks, I'll tell you, I got so mad one day. It got to the point, I'd go home to visit my mother and I'd get there and there'd be 150 books stacked up on the table in the dining room that she'd collected from people who had been sending 'em in.

I said, "Mother, I'm coming here to get away from this."

"No, son. These people love you. They sent me those books, and you've gotta sign 'em so I can send them back."

I said, "I'm not gonna have time to talk to you."

"That's okay. You have to pay attention to these people."

The fact that people all over the country loved her little boy just was the greatest thing that ever happened to her. Yeah, and everybody who met Millie loved her, too. Folks, my mother invited the *National Enquirer* in to have coffee when they came by! "Son, we don't have any secrets. We're Limbaughs. We've got nothing to hide. If they want to see your draft records, I'll be glad to show 'em to them."

She did that!

The *Enquirer* reporter said, "I can't believe this."

Of course, I don't know about any of this until it's over, and I said, "Mother, look, this is my business. You can't be injecting yourself."

"No, no, son. You, you don't . . ."

I was always the son. I never knew what was good for me. I never knew the right thing to do. I was . . . I was . . . I remember I got so mad one day when I finally had to start flying privately just for the privacy and the security of it, she'd pick me up at the airport and I'd spend the weekend. And on Sunday, she'd take me back to the airport. One Sunday, she was behaving extremely differently, eager for me to leave. Normally, that wasn't the case. She kept reminding me I had to get to the airport.

I said, "Well, I'm just standing by at noon."

"No, no. You really should get there a little earlier, 'cause you never know the weather."

"No, the weather's fine, I've checked it."

"Well, you still, you should," she said. "By the way, I'll meet you out there. I've gotta go do some things, so I'll just meet you at the airport. David can take you."

"Oh, okay."

So David came and picked me up. We drive to the airport, we drive up to the airplane, and I can see immediately, there's her car, and there's another car, and I look in the windows of the airplane; there's a bunch of people in there! I got on the airplane, and she had four people she didn't know who had stopped in the week prior to say hello, and she'd invited 'em back to meet me and hadn't told me!

They're big fans, and she hadn't told me any of this, and they're on the airplane. But she was just so proud that the people of this country loved her little boy. If they called her or if they wrote her a letter, or if they sent her a book of mine to sign, they were king and queen, and she wanted to make sure that they knew that our family appreciated 'em.

⊛　⊛　⊛

I've described my dad as passionate, opinionated, and fearless. And in junior high—even high school—there were many Friday nights that my friends said, "Let's go to your place and get your dad riled up instead of going out and trying to find a keg of beer or going to the teen town hall dance," or whatever it was. And so they'd come over, and somebody would come up with some comment about anything in the news, and he was off and running. –Rush Limbaugh

⊛　⊛　⊛

Chapter 3

GOD BLESS AMERICA

TRIBUTE
by David Limbaugh

Everyone who ever listened to Rush knew he was a super patriot. This didn't stem from some blind, uninformed loyalty to the country of our birth. It was a passionate love for the United States, intentionally instilled by our father in the beginning. Our father was a World War II fighter pilot, a lawyer, a student of America's founding, and an ardent defender of the Constitution and the rule of law. He taught us early on about America's tradition of liberty, that our freedoms are God-given rights, and that the Constitution was designed to preserve those rights against internal and external threats. When we were very young, he talked to us about limited government, federalism, the separation of powers, the Bill of Rights, and the indispensability of an independent, nonpolitical judiciary, and the impartial administration of justice. He also taught us about the menace of Communism and how it represented both a foreign and domestic threat to the United States. He was forthright about the deceptive lies of godless Marxism and explained how capitalism—a free, robust economic system—maximized prosperity and was essential to political liberty.

Some may not realize that before he became a consummate talker, Rush was a superb listener. He absorbed our dad's lessons, and when he moved away from home to begin his life in radio, he continued what would be a lifelong study in political science. Whereas our dad would hold forth at our kitchen table, to larger groups of our friends, and in speeches to service clubs in our local area, my brother would take it to a national level, becoming a tutor to everyday Americans hungry for someone in the national media to articulate and validate their conservative beliefs and their unwavering love of country.

One reason that Rush can never be replaced is that he didn't just lecture didactically from his then New York–based microphone. He used his combination of talents and personality traits—wit, wisdom, insight, approachability—to begin a national conversation with everyday Americans. He was in the living rooms and cars of millions of Americans every day, discussing things that mattered to them while simultaneously entertaining them and restoring their hope and confidence that the American dream was still alive.

After Rush died, I can't tell you how many messages I received via email, Twitter, text, phone, and personal letter expressing the same moving idea: Rush was the best friend they'd never personally met. He was their lunch companion. He was their lifeline to hope in the preservation of American liberty. He made them feel good and reassured, not with empty platitudes but with substantive discussions of current and historical events. He inspired them—us—with his irrepressible love for America and his fervent belief in the American people, who he was convinced were committed to maintaining America's freedoms and greatness.

As you read the excerpts in this chapter, please do so with an abiding awareness that Rush loved this country with every fiber of his being, and that it mattered deeply to him that we share his passion. We all know that he loved life and that he was enthusiastic about things he cared about—and boy, did he care about this country. Rush's listeners—his friends he never personally met—will always be his (and our) extended family, and Kathryn and I love you for loving him.

American flags line the streets on Veterans Day in Cape Girardeau, Missouri.

PART 1 — OUR AMERICAN FLAG

Like you, Rush loved our American flag deeply. It infuriated him to see the flag disrespected in any way. It was vitally important to Rush that our flag always be protected and remain a beacon of strength, hope, and peace around the world. American flags were proudly displayed throughout our home and in Rush's studio.

THE AMERICAN FLAG IS STILL THE SYMBOL OF FREEDOM FOR THE WORLD
The Rush Limbaugh Show, August 13, 2019

RUSH: I just watched something amazing. While all this was going on, there are massive protests at the Hong Kong airport. The ChiComs have been threatening to impose ChiCom government policies on Hong Kong. And the people of Hong Kong don't want any part of it, because they know it's going to add up to a massive loss of freedom and independence.

I mean, Hong Kong, before the ChiComs regained control of it, Hong Kong was maybe one of the classic illustrations of raw capitalism that you could find. It worked, and it worked like a charm. And then the Brits, when they're getting rid of their empire, they're turning [it] back over to the ChiComs.

Now, watching the live footage, there are people protesting. They've shut down the Hong Kong Airport. This new Hong Kong airport is huge, folks, and they've shut it down for two days in a row. Live footage of the police clashing with the protesters.

And you know what the Hong Kong protesters are holding and waving around? The American flag. The protesters in Hong Kong protesting the incursion planned by the ChiComs are hoisting and waving proudly the

American flag. There aren't any of them taking a knee. There aren't any of them scraping that flag along the floor.

In Hong Kong today—tonight; they're twelve hours ahead—the American flag is still the symbol of hope and freedom for oppressed people around the world. In Hong Kong, the American flag is part of the weaponry that the protesters are hoisting with great pride.

PILOTS IN AFGHANISTAN FLY AMERICAN FLAGS IN RUSH'S HONOR

The Rush Limbaugh Show, November 6, 2017

It's May of 2003. A couple of months earlier, we began the invasion of Iraq, one of the first acts in the War on Terror. This was the war that was to remove and eliminate Saddam Hussein. George W. Bush had spent a year and a half traveling the country explaining it, gearing up support for it. It was a major, major conflict in the War on Terror and our response to it.

And it had become controversial, of course. The Democrats, the unity after 9/11, 2001, lasted about two weeks, and then that became politicized. And on that day in May, early May of 2003, I went home. Well, I'd gotten a note before I got home. "You have got to come straight home. You won't believe what just arrived [via] FedEx."

I said, "What is it? Just tell me."

They said, "No, you have to see this." So I got home, and I looked at what I had received, and I was floored. I was stunned. I'd never seen anything like it. I didn't know these things happened. I was moved. I was blown away. I felt small. I ran through all kinds of emotions—I mean, in lickety-split fashion. What it was was an American flag, properly folded inside a Ziploc bag. And there were certificates stating that flag had flown on the following aircraft. And each aircraft had a—well, you would frame it. It's like an official notification of the date that the aircraft flew that flag on a mission.

There were five different aircraft and a tanker. And all the pilots of the five different aircraft and the tanker had signed the documents certifying that that flag had flown. The tanker pilot was the originator, the mastermind of this, and he included a handwritten note on yellow legal paper explaining

This flag proudly representing the

United States of America

Belonging Rush H. Limbaugh

Was flown on
KC-10A aircraft 86-0032
"Sonic Boom"

Call Sign: Taint 45

On the the night of, 14 April 2003
in support of

Operation IRAQI FREEDOM

Prince Sultan Air Base, Kingdom of Saudi Arabia

1. Solomon, Maj, USAF	D. Horn, Capt, USAF	B. Reed, MSgt, USAF	R. Upton, TSgt, USAF
ilot, KC-10	Pilot, KC-10	Flight Engineer, KC-10	Boom Operator, KC-10

that these five crew members had flown that flag in my honor on the initial bombing runs, the first bombing runs in the war against Iraq, the Shock and Awe portion. And, as their missions were completed and as they were all refueled by this tanker pilot, that flag was put in the Ziploc bag and the pilots all signed these certifications, and they were FedExed to me. And they did nothing more than that.

I received this and was floored. As I say, I went through a mixture of emotions, including humility and smallness. And I'm asking myself what have I done—'cause this was an honor, I mean, it was clearly an honor. I didn't know things like this happened. Just not enough experience in actual military combat circumstances to know that time was taken for this kind of ceremonial or memorial-type event.

Well, we took that flag, and we unfolded it, and it's now framed, and the certificates with all those signatures and the picture of each of the aircraft—and there's fighters, there's bombers, and the tanker—they surround the flag. And we had an actual golden eagle carved to stand, and it's about five feet tall once it's on its pedestal. It's huge. And we put this in a niche, big niche in a room right outside my library so you can't miss this when you're walking into the library.

People who don't know about this ask, "What in the world is that?" And I get to regale them with the story. I said, "Yeah, these guys flew that flag in my honor on the initial bombing run of Iraq." Well, the ringleader of this operation was Lieutenant Colonel Mark Hasara. He flew the tanker. He flew KC-135s, which is the military version of the Boeing 707, and the KC-10, which is the military version of the DC-10.

He's the one that had written the note on yellow legal paper explaining why they did it. And it was filled with recognition and support and thanks for the support I had given the military over the years. As I say, I was blown away by it. It was an honor that I didn't even know existed, and I had no idea it was coming. And even now when I stop and think about the fact that it happened, it's one of those events that happens in your life or in your career that you never forget and that you're always going to be overwhelmingly and supremely proud of.

Well, over the years, Kathryn and I have gotten to know Lieutenant Colonel Hasara and his wife and his family, and we see them now and then. And, folks, these people that you never meet, they're just humble. When I talk about people who make the country work, these are the people I'm talking about. They're out there volunteering every day; they sign up to defend the country, to protect the Constitution, to carry out their orders. They're doing it because this is how they've decided they want to serve their country.

In Hasara's case, it's been his life, and most of these other pilots, they never really leave it even after their service ends. But they never seek any fame. They didn't send me this for fame. They didn't send this for notoriety or notification or anything else. They just sent it as a distinct honor.

I can't tell you—I mean, I'm sitting here, I'm looking at this package, and we're going through the process of getting this all framed, and I'm thinking, "Here these guys have their orders, they're part of the initial bombing run, and before they leave somebody organizes this tribute to me by having this flag fly in every one of these aircraft."

Now, they didn't all fly in one day, of course, because the aircraft have to land and the flag gets transferred to the next aircraft, so it takes maybe as many as two days, but the dates that the flag flew on each aircraft are specified. I later came to learn that it's something that's done with some regularity, so it was not unique, but that didn't matter. Just to be thought of, to be considered and thought about during a time like this, it just, to this day, still humbles me. It's the best word I can come up with to describe it.

LETTER FROM OPERATION IRAQI FREEDOM PILOT

Mr. Limbaugh,
Please accept this flag as a small token of our appreciation for your support of the troops currently in the Gulf, as well as in other conflicts. This flag flew on five different aircraft stationed at Prince Sultan Air Base in Saudi Arabia. . . .

We have flown this flag for you to show in some small way our appreciation for your support of the troops in Iraq. . . . From all of us to all of you at EIB, for all you do for the men and women in uniform, we salute you.

> *Lt. Colonel Mark Hasara*
> *Chief, Air Refueling Control Team*
> *Operation Iraqi Freedom*

Flag flown in Rush's honor by American military pilots, proudly displayed in the Limbaughs' home.

Rush admired many things about President Ronald Reagan, including his love of our American flag and all that it represents. He remembered this speech and visual very fondly: On June 4, 1983, President Ronald Reagan spoke in front of a stunning 210-foot-by-411-foot American flag laid out on the Ellipse on the South Lawn of the White House.

RONALD REAGAN REMARKS ON FLAG DAY
South Lawn of the White House, June 14, 1983

Who could stand before this scene, with Old Glory unfurled in all its majesty across the area of two football fields, and not feel their heart fill with pride? . . .

This giant flag is a testament to the unity and patriotism of our people and to the deep love and commitment we have for our country, our freedom, and our way of life. I'm reminded of a verse that I once read, written as if the flag were speaking to us now and for generations to come. It said, "I am whatever you make me, nothing more. I am your belief in yourself, your dream of what a people may become. I am the day's work of the weakest man and the largest dream of the most daring. I am the clutch of an idea and the reasoned purpose of resolution. I am no more than you believe me to be, and I am all that you believe I can be. I am whatever you make me, nothing more."

If you look out at that grand flag stretched behind us, you can see what we think of ourselves, our country, and our future. That flag was made by and for men and women who still know how to dream great dreams and who still believe they can make their dreams come true. That giant banner was not created by a timid nation but by a bold one. Not a stitch was sewn in confusion or doubt. We understand that those stars and stripes stand for freedom and the forces of good. We apologize to none for our ideals or our principles, nor the prosperity that we've made for ourselves and shared with the world. Let this grand flag forever be a symbol of the potential before us that free men and women can soar as high as their dreams and energy and ambitions will take them.

On behalf of all Americans, I would like to thank the Great American Flag Fund and all the men and women who've made this inspiring gift possible. I promise you your government will keep it and treasure it and use it as a reminder of the greatness that is America. And now, if you will all join me, I would like to lead you in the Pledge of Allegiance. . . .

I have to go now. I am leaving in that whirlybird for the Volunteer State, Tennessee. So, I'm looking forward to it for one reason, too. At the very start of the trip, I will get to see that magnificent flag from above, from the air. Thank you all very much. God bless you.

TWEAK THE LEFT BY BEING AS AMERICAN AS YOU CAN BE!
The Rush Limbaugh Show, July 3, 2018

Tomorrow's the Fourth of July. Yeah, I know. I know. Everybody knows, but here's what you may not remember: There was a Harvard study—I had this some years ago—by the way, greetings. I am America's Real Anchorman, and I'm here.

Remember that survey from Harvard that Fourth of July, just on its own, Independence Day celebrations tend to make people feel more Republican? And the same survey had the same data about the flag, that the flag flying, along with all the traditional social behavior that takes place on the Fourth of July, tends to promote feelings of the Republican Party. People obviously are motivated toward patriotic, love-of-country themes and ideas.

And it struck home with me, because it also had the counterpart that this kind of activity angered Democrats. Flying the flag, engaging in traditional Independence Day, Fourth of July behavior. And if you doubted it then, you should not doubt it now. I made a point on yesterday's program: What's wrong with America remaining America? And, of course, that's the objective of the people currently protesting, say, getting rid of ICE or whatever. They want to transform and change America.

So I would suggest everybody fly your flag tomorrow—be American. Go out and just do what you would normally be inclined to do, but don't be

intimidated in flying the flag, don't be intimidated by any patriotic activity, because you never know the impact it's gonna have on people. These effects on that Harvard survey were not just outward. Some of them were subliminal. You never know where this kind of influence could take place. . . .

* * *

I remember, growing up, I was not taught hateful things about America. I was not told I needed to feel guilty over being an American.

Steve Limbaugh Sr. and Rush enjoying Thanksgiving in Cape Girardeau, Missouri.

IMPACT OF EXPOSURE TO THE AMERICAN FLAG ON LIBERALS
The Rush Limbaugh Show, July 21, 2011

Well, get this now: This is from *U.S. News & World Report:* "US Flag Only Boosts GOP." The US flag makes people think and vote Republican, just like Fourth of July celebrations. No wonder Democrats and their leftists are always so eager to burn the American flag—because it tends to motivate people to vote and think Republican.

"Just a brief exposure to an image of the American flag shifts voters, even Democrats, to Republican beliefs, attitudes, and voting behavior, even though most don't believe it will impact their politics, according to a new two-year study just published in the scholarly [journal] *Psychological Science*." You ever heard of that? *Psychological Science* magazine. "What's more, according to three authors from the University of Chicago, Cornell University, and Hebrew University, the impact had staying power. 'A single exposure to an American flag resulted in a significant increase in participants' Republican voting intentions, voting behavior, political beliefs, and implicit and explicit attitudes, with some effects lasting eight months,' the study found."

Folks, go out and put a flag up in front of the house! Everybody get a flag out there, 'cause it's a double whammy. A, it'll tick off the Democrats. Your house might be at risk, but it will grow conservatism. Look at this study, two-year study, three universities, three scholars.

I read this to you again: "'A single exposure to an American flag resulted in a significant increase in participants' Republican voting intentions, voting behavior, political beliefs, and implicit and explicit attitudes, with some effects lasting eight months. These results constitute the first evidence that nonconscious priming effects from exposure to a national flag can bias the citizenry toward one political party and can have considerable durability.'" Oh, this explains so much. That's why the left is out there burning flags all day long, why they don't like the Fourth of July. This is just classic.

*   *   *

*My Aunt Anne, love of my uncle Steve Sr.'s life, used to
write me notes all the time encouraging me, applauding me.
She reminded me in the most humorous way, she was the
aunt and I was the nephew. 'Your dad was Rush and your
grandfather was Rush, you're Rusty.'"*
—Rush Limbaugh

*   *   *

RUSH REMEMBERS A FAMOUS PATRIOTIC MOMENT IN BASEBALL HISTORY: RICK MONDAY SAVES THE FLAG
The Rush Limbaugh Show, September 26, 2017

You know, folks, let me tell you something: I got a message from George Brett last night. You know what it was? His message says, "Boy, have things really changed." And it was a video of Rick Monday saving the flag from an anti-America protester at Dodger Stadium in—I think it was at Dodger Stadium in Los Angeles. Rick Monday became an overnight national hero, like Villanueva was on Sunday, because he saved the American flag. He ran out there and he picked it up and saved the flag, and he was heralded, and he was loved.

We've gone from an entire country celebrating Rick Monday saving the flag to a thrice-decorated Special Forces army man in Afghanistan apologizing for standing up for the national anthem.

STAND UP FOR BETSY ROSS

Rush always said that you are the most generous audience in the entire world. Through your support, the Stand Up for Betsy Ross campaign raised over $5 million in just a few months for the Tunnel to Towers Foundation, allowing for fifty homes to be provided to the families of injured and fallen service members or first responders. The campaign also created over one hundred American jobs to produce merchandise and fulfill orders.

Rush started the Stand Up for Betsy Ross Campaign to push back against attacks on Betsy Ross and the original American flag. Sales of this single T-shirt design skyrocketed following one on-air announcement. In minutes, there were sales in every state in the union, leading to hundreds of thousands of shirts sold and the creation of an entire line of merchandise. It blew Rush away!

• • •

What in the world did Betsy Ross do? What did Betsy Ross do to anybody? Why on earth does anybody want to trash and tarnish Betsy Ross—an American hero? —Rush Limbaugh

• • •

AMAZING! STAND UP FOR BETSY ROSS RAISES $5M FOR TUNNEL TO TOWERS
The Rush Limbaugh Show, December 6, 2019

The Stephen Siller Tunnel to Towers Foundation has . . . Because of you, they have paid off fifty mortgages for families, folks—because of you—since early July. They also build smart homes from scratch for surviving, terribly wounded military personnel. They manufacture and build houses that are made with kitchens, for example, that are specifically manufactured to help people who can only get around in wheelchairs, can't bend over, can't get down to lower shelves.

It's amazing what they've done. And this all started back in July, when, as you know, Nike came out with a new pair of tennis shoes for the Fourth of July with the Betsy Ross flag in the heel. And Colin Kaepernick, the former quarterback for the San Francisco 49ers, told Nike he didn't like the Betsy Ross flag and they should not start selling the shoes. So Nike said, "You know, Colin doesn't like them; we're not gonna sell the shoes."

And for me, I don't know. Maybe even prior to that was the last straw. I mean, here comes Colin Kaepernick, who starts kneeling during pregames and the anthem of National Football League games, ostensibly to protest police brutality against American minorities. But it wasn't that. He was protesting the country. And it clearly became obvious to everybody that he was doing so, protesting the anthem, protesting the flag, politicizing all these things that stand for unity.

The flag is about unity. The flag was created, designed by one of the first feminists in America, Betsy Ross. They're trying to politicize her. It was outrageous—and that's born of rage. That's born of hatred. Everything the left is doing today is because they hate and they hate and they hate—and their hate is primarily aimed at the fact that they are not winning, that they are losing. They hate it. They hate the people beating them, and they hate the fact that they have to put up with it.

Well, I got irritated—we got irritated—and said, "This needs something to push back. We're tired of people like Kaepernick, tired of people like Nike and others bashing the flag, bashing fundamental American values." I mean, the flag! No matter what side of the political aisle you're on, it stands for unity and freedom, liberty, perseverance.

You know, we want everyone to prosper. We want a great country. We want a nation of people pursuing excellence. We want a nation of people fulfilling their dreams and desires, and we don't care what color they are. This is a miraculous country. We wanted everybody who sees the flag to know just how lucky we are to be Americans, to be free. What incredible early patriots did to establish this country and preserve and protect freedom and guarantee it.

So we decided to start the Stand Up for Betsy Ross Campaign. People could purchase a Stand Up for Betsy Ross T-shirt while supporting our heroes. The Stand Up for Betsy Ross Campaign raised over $5 million for charity, with one of the most successful individual direct-to-customer T-shirt campaigns in history selling hundreds of thousands of shirts in a few months. One hundred and fifty jobs were created for Americans, and fifty homes were built for military members.

*   *   *

This week we are giving away three homes for Thanksgiving to the Gold Star families of Private First Class Billy Anderson in Tennessee, and Sergeant Aaron Blasjo, and Sergeant Terrence Hinton in Florida, who gave their lives for our country. Thank you to Rush and Kathryn Limbaugh and all of the generous listeners. It's just incredible—the goodness of America. —Frank Siller, Stephen Siller Tunnel to Towers Foundation

*   *   *

The Stand Up For Betsy Ross Campaign swept the nation and made it all the way to Mount Everest!

PART 2 — THE WHITE HOUSE

A common question Rush received over the years was, "What do you like most about being famous?" He would usually reply jokingly, "I don't." Laughing, he would go on to explain that he was never really interested in the fame aspect but accepted it as part of his career choice. He said that he would take back his anonymity in a minute if he could, joking about the "notice me" Hollywood types paying reporters to follow them around. Rush loved to say he was a "self-proclaimed hermit" who was very content reading tech blogs on his iPad and impersonating actors from television shows he was watching. He would often provide David with a list of television series recommendations. As with everything, Rush possessed a wealth of information on every genre, from "cop shows," as he called them, to subtitled period dramas.

But fame on the radio did bring some incredible moments for Rush, including being invited to the White House by presidents of the United States. Even though he intellectually understood that he was at the top of his field, Rush was always humble and considered himself to be just a boy from Missouri with incredible good fortune. When recounting stories of his visits, he would light up with childlike enthusiasm, saying, "I sometimes have to pinch myself. My father would never have believed my life."

PRESIDENT GEORGE H. W. BUSH AND FIRST LADY BARBARA BUSH INVITE RUSH TO THE WHITE HOUSE
The Rush Limbaugh Show, April 18, 2018

But yes, indeed, I was invited to overnight at the White House by George H. W. Bush. It was in 1992, in the middle of the Republican primary

campaign. It was the year Ross Perot looked like he was actually gonna secure the nomination. And that year I had gotten very close to endorsing Pat Buchanan in the New Hampshire primary simply because I thought there needed to be a strong conservative element in the Republican primary and in the Republican campaign.

And George H. W. Bush, when he ran for office in '88, promised that it would be the third term of Ronald Reagan, the third term of Ronaldus Magnus. But then some unfortunate things happened, such as the "Read my lips: no new taxes," and then we got taxes, and H. W. Bush thought that he could work cooperatively with Tom Foley, who was then the Speaker of the House. So, in the midst of all this, I was summoned. I was invited to the White House, and it was great. . . .

We were gonna go to dinner, go to the Kennedy Center with them for some musical performance, come back to the White House, talk politics, and sleep in the Lincoln Bedroom, which is what I did. I called my mom from the Lincoln Bedroom. She didn't believe it. But I did. . . .

We got to the White House. We went in the diplomatic entrance, and they escorted us up the elevator to the residence. And there's nobody there, other than the Secret Service and the White House staff guiding us. And out of nowhere, President Bush's voice is heard . . . he had just finished a jog, he'd gotten dressed, came and grabbed my bags, and started walking down the hallway toward the Lincoln Bedroom. And I am apoplectic. I cannot have this, cannot have the president of the United States carrying my luggage. So I said, "Mr. President, no, no, no, let me grab it."

"No, no, no, come, let me show you." He gave me the quick tour on the way down the hall, and then some brief historical information about the Lincoln Bedroom. So, after a little talking, we got into the presidential limo and sped over to the Kennedy Center, where there was a performance of something going on. The Bushes were gonna leave at intermission. At intermission we went down and met the cast and so forth. We went back to the White House and sat down and talked campaign when we got back in the president's study. . . .

Anyway, I then spent the night in the Lincoln Bedroom. I didn't sleep much, because I . . . I mean, who wants to be unconscious when you're in the White House? The Lincoln Bedroom, by the way, was never a bedroom. It was Lincoln's office when he was president. It's on the second floor with the residence. I got up the next day and flew back to New York for the radio program, and it wasn't long before the Drive-bys found out about it. . . .

I was a frequent visitor to the George W. Bush White House as well. The family's been amazingly helpful to me, and I will always remember it.

* * *

Never lose sight of the fact that the most important
yardstick of your success will be how you treat other people.
—First Lady Barbara Bush

* * *

RUSH VISITS THE WHITE HOUSE, STAYS IN THE LINCOLN BEDROOM

The Rush Limbaugh Show, August 26, 2010

One of the funny stories that I remember is that after my night—it was in 1992 in the summertime that I'd spent the night in the White House. George H. W. Bush was president. . . . I got to know the usher; they were all big fans. And it was like a hotel room—you could have a wake-up call. This was on the same floor that the president and his wife live. It's a big floor, obviously, but you could order coffee from, quote unquote, room service. A uniformed steward would bring it to you, and I got to know all these people. And when Clinton won the election, I remember Harry Thomason and his wife, Linda Bloodworth-Thomason, talking about how they couldn't wait to sleep in the Lincoln Bedroom after Clinton was inaugurated.

So, through channels I reached people that I had met in the White House: "Could I leave a note that you would leave for Harry and Linda on the pillow in the Lincoln Bedroom the night that they're in there?" And it happened to be inauguration weekend, I think, that they spent. It took a while, but in a couple weeks they came back and they said sure. So I wrote a note, and the note said, "Dear Harry and Linda: Never forget this. I was here first, and I will be back." Signed, "Your buddy, Rush."

I put it in an envelope, and then you just wonder if it ever happens. So, not long after the immaculation, the inauguration, Harry Thomason is on C-SPAN and he tells the story. "Yeah, so Linda and I get in the Lincoln Bedroom, it's a long night, we get in there, and when we pull the covers back there's an envelope on the pillow. So we open it up, and it's a note from Rush Limbaugh." I heard this, and I said, "Yes!" Then I knew they had seen the note.

You couldn't keep me out of the place. When vacation time came, yeah, I might leave, go play golf or whatever at Camp David, but Christmastime, I would be there—what a beautiful time. Thanksgiving, I would be there. Easter, I would be there. I would invite friends and family there. They would consider it an honor, too. This bunch gets outta there as fast as they can. Another reason I wouldn't travel on Christmas: the Secret Service, half of them wouldn't have to go and leave their families, but that's just me.

SPEAKING OF FUNNY STORIES: EL RUSHBO'S
EXPERIENCE WITH BALD EAGLES
The Rush Limbaugh Show, February 17, 2006

I don't know if you've heard about this. The city council of Homer, Alaska, has banned humans from feeding bald eagles. Now, for those of you that were educated in the public school system of this country, the bald eagle is our national bird. It is the national symbol, and starting next year, it will be illegal to feed them. There are hundreds of these eagles that gather every winter in Homer, Alaska, and starting next year it's going to be illegal to feed them. There is an exception. Some eighty-two-year-old woman, a famous woman named Jean Keene, whose nickname is the Eagle Lady, and she's been feeding eagles in Homer for twenty-five years. So she's going to be the only exception when the law kicks in.

Now, who's this going to hurt besides the eagles? Well, guided tour groups of photographers make this journey from all over the world with their cameras in hand and their bait fish in the other, coaxing eagles to come pose for pictures. Now, the councilman addressing the photographer safari said, "We're still going to have eagles in Homer, but you don't have to have hundreds of eagles to take a photograph." Here's why this happened: The ban resulted from complaints that bald eagles being fed was not only unnatural but it's "demeaning." It's demeaning to feed the eagles! Now, stop and think: These are the same kind of people who believe totally in unquestioned welfare. These are also the people who believe unquestionably in animal rights and so forth, but now all of a sudden, because this is the national bird, this has ties to America, it somehow is "demeaning" to see the eagles fed.

Now, it's tempting, however, on one level, not to dismiss the argument. I mean, here is our national symbol, the national bird, proud, strong—soon to be taken off the endangered species list, by the way, is the bald eagle—and the people of Alaska have made him a blue state welfare recipient. Essentially, the eagle just sits around waiting to be fed. It's embarrassing to me on one level. So, to end that picture of a welfare-recipient bald eagle national symbol of our country, ah, I can go for it. But at the same time, there's a deal taking place here that is also not good. You almost could perceive the law here as welfare

145

reform, but there's a difference. These eagles were willing to work for their food! They were willing to come take the food and then be photographed. They provided a service, essentially: posing for photographs, a fair exchange of goods and services. So, in the end, the eagle ban, the feeding-the-eagle ban is a stunning defeat for North American free trade in one regard.

I have fed eagles. Well, I didn't actually do it, but I took a fishing trip—it was a salmon fishing trip—up Vancouver Island. Two of us went out on little putt-putt boats, taking a guide where we were to fish and helping us do it all, and one day on the way back in he spotted a bunch of bald eagles (or some kind of eagles) way up in the pine trees (or whatever trees they were in). So he stopped the boat and he turned off the engine and told us to get our cameras out, and lo and behold if he wasn't able to coax those eagles to within ten feet of our boat. I've got pictures of it. I'll try to post one on the website today. You lock on when these things are racing by. I happened to get a good shot of these eagles in motion, and they're just ten feet away and he's calling them with a voice and waving bait fish just like is happening in Homer, Alaska.

I didn't realize that I was participating in making the national symbol a welfare recipient in the process here. I was doing it just to get an up-close look at the eagle, but apparently it happened regularly, because the birds were not afraid to fly down to the boat where we were, so I guess it was part of the package. It didn't happen every day because they don't see eagles every day, but this guy happened to spot a couple of them up there in the tree. It was cool. I've never been that close to an eagle, other than when I used to have fifty-cent pieces.

* * *

No media figure since Buckley has had a more lasting influence on American conservatism than Limbaugh, whose cumulative weekly audience is more than 20 million people. Since national syndication in 1988, Limbaugh has been the voice of conservatism, his three-hour program blending news, politics, and entertainment in a powerful cocktail. —Matthew Continetti, *National Review*

* * *

PART 3 — PATRIOTIC MUSIC

Rush loved music and was very knowledgeable about all genres, easily rattling off the history of songs from every era. He loved patriotic music in particular and said that we can never lose sight of the meaning behind our national anthem. The words written at Fort McHenry—"our flag was still there"—assure us that the country will go on.

One of the many attributes that made Rush unique is his incorporation of great tunes and bumper rotation music into deep political analysis. He had the time of his life writing lyrics for parodies with the very talented Paul Shanklin, putting hilarious new twists on well-known songs like "Every Cent You Make (I'll Be Taxing You)" from the Police hit "Every Breath You Take" about President Barack Obama's policies.

As many of you know, Rush lost his hearing rather suddenly, becoming 100% deaf. He could no longer hear voices or sounds in the same way he once had. This would be a devastating blow for anyone, and even more so for a career broadcaster who relied on being able to hear the sound of his voice. Instead of giving up, Rush found a way to rely on his unwavering internal optimism. While waiting for his first cochlear implant surgery to heal, Rush remarkably hosted the highest-level radio program in the country without being able to hear his own words.

He wore one cochlear implant just above his left ear and later one above the right—both were connected to magnets surgically implanted beneath the surface of the skin. In typical Rush fashion, he found humor in everything. At night he would take off both implant devices and put them into a charger on his nightstand table. As his head lay on the pillow, he would say with a huge smile, "Ah, the sound of pure silence. You can say anything you want about me. Have at it! I won't be able to hear you!"

WHITE HOUSE CEREMONY FOR POPE PRAISES GOD
AND AMERICAN EXCEPTIONALISM
The Rush Limbaugh Show, April 16, 2008

I want to play for you something that happened this morning on the White House lawn; the largest welcoming ceremony ever in the history of the White House for Pope Benedict XVI. We have audio sound bites of the president's greeting to the pope, the pope's response, and I saw something that genuinely moved me. I was sitting here staring at this and listening to this, and I was just blown away by it.

Two things happened. The event and the music itself moved me like I haven't been moved in quite a while, and the setting where it took place and the reason that it was happening. I mean, I'm sitting here thinking, "Divine intervention today at the White House."

"The Battle Hymn of the Republic" was sung by the US Army Chorus, and you have to hear this, particularly if you haven't had a chance to have your TV on today, or your radio, and you didn't hear this. You have to hear it, and you have to imagine a crystal-blue sky, a crisp day in Washington, the pope and the president on the reviewing stand with others, the camera occasionally focusing on the US Army Chorus.

You realize this is at the White House, and a song written in tribute to God is being played at the White House. In this country there has been such an effort, and it has been way too successful, to remove God from anything public. Not only was God present but the largest White House welcoming ceremony ever participated in, a ceremony thanking God and respecting God and offering up a tribute to God, and you just have to hear this. It runs about 4:47. It's infectious, so well done. The US Army Chorus, "The Battle Hymn of the Republic."

[Playing of "The Battle Hymn of the Republic"]

That is just beautiful. I'm at a loss for words to describe the impact that had on me, and I was not even paying close attention. I was looking at the computer and I had the TVs on, which are to my left when I'm sitting at the computer. I heard this start, and I told Cookie up in New York, "Get me the song. I want the song as part of the audio sound bites."

She said, "You can hear it?" I said, "I can always hear God's music." "The Battle Hymn of the Republic," that's the US Army Chorus, and that was at the welcoming ceremony for His Holiness Pope Benedict XVI at the White House today. Again, the largest welcoming ceremony in the history of the White House.

* * *

RUSH: Diane in South San Francisco, I'm glad that you called. Welcome to the EIB Network. Hello.

CALLER: Good morning, Rush.

RUSH: Hi.

CALLER: I wanted you to know that your emotions this morning at hearing "The Battle Hymn of the Republic" were shared by President Abraham Lincoln at the time of his Gettysburg Address in 1863. An army captain who had been a prisoner of war in the Civil War had gotten together a male chorus and went around singing at fundraisers, and when Abraham Lincoln heard it, his eyes welled with tears and he shouted, "Sing it again!"

RUSH: I kept singing it myself over and over here for the rest of the time. Really, I was singing the chorus over and over again. In addition to everything else that it is, it's infectious.

CALLER: Well, did you know this bit of trivia—and I will let you get on to more important calls—Julia Ward Howe wrote that in one evening in her hotel room after someone suggested she revise the original poem "John Brown's Body," the abolitionist song, she wrote all five verses of this beautiful "Battle Hymn of the Republic" and sold it to the *Atlantic Monthly* for five dollars.

RUSH: Five dollars.

CALLER: It was printed in the *Atlantic Monthly* for five dollars.

RUSH: Well, that is what it is. There's something poetic even about that.

CALLER: Yes, it is.

RUSH: Look, Diane, I appreciate the phone call.

CALLER: You're welcome.

RUSH: Thank you. You know, folks, I'm an emotional person, but I don't express it publicly on this program much. It's tough to do. Not hard, not difficult to do—I mean, I have no problem doing it. It's just coming up with the right words to reflect the way this hit me today emotionally as I was watching it, the timeliness of it, the brilliant performance, the perfection of the voices and the articulation, the musical accompaniment, the shots of the pope and the president watching in awe, listening in awe. The whole package, you watched it, you couldn't help but be profoundly moved by it, given all that is happening in the country and the world today. It was powerful, and there were lots of meanings, and some of them subtle and some of them just blaring. It had it all. This ceremony today had everything in it, and they moved from one item to the next, was not overly long, each element was bam, bam, get it, move on to the next. You were exhausted at the end of it, even though there was no frantic energy during it. Just brilliant. It was brilliantly conceived, flawlessly executed from start to finish.

* * *

I gotta play this for you again. We did this to open the program today. The welcoming ceremony for Pope Benedict XVI at the White House today, the largest welcoming ceremony in White House history, and it was just breathtaking.

A crystal-clear blue sky, crisp day in Washington, DC, just gorgeous, the pope and the president up on the podium, welcoming speeches have been made, and then it was time to turn to the US Army Chorus, one of the most moving and touching, powerful, beautiful renditions of "The Battle Hymn of the Republic" that I have ever heard. It stopped me in my tracks of show prep today to watch this. I wanted you to hear the full version of it. God in Washington today.

[Playing of "The Battle Hymn of the Republic"]

Wow. I got goose bumps listening to it again. American exceptionalism celebrated in Washington today with the arrival of Pope Benedict XVI. That's the US Army Chorus, the United States Army Chorus, with one of the most profoundly gorgeous and beautiful renditions of that song, "The Battle Hymn of the Republic," that I have ever heard, and I wanted to share that with you again.

I'm sure C-SPAN will be replaying this. No network would replay this. Fox carried it live, but I don't think the networks are going to repeat this portion of it live. I don't know if it moved them or not. It's nobody talking, there's no news being made, except to me. I think it's huge news.

In a presidential campaign which focuses on the rotten nature of the United States; the rotten nature of certain citizens; on the hopelessness that we all supposedly face; the fact that America is despised and hated around the world; that our reputation is in tatters; that our economic situation is bleak; that people are being thrown out of their homes every day; that they cannot afford food; they can barely afford gasoline; interest rates are plummeting, which is bad for seasoned citizens who live off the income of their portfolios. Everything is just rotten to the core. There's nothing about which to be happy in the United States of America.

This is the theme, day in and day out, throughout the presidential campaign. It has been the theme day in and day out of media coverage for the last six years. It has been the theme of liberal messages to this country via the media and the Democrat Party for as long as I have been alive, albeit [with] a short interruption in that when the Clintons were in the White House; then of course everything was hunky-dory and rosy. Amidst all of this pessimism, amidst all of this, the US military can't win in Iraq, that we have basically surrendered, that there is no threat to the United States other than our own hubris and arrogance.

Amidst all of this, Pope Benedict XVI arrives today, and in his remarks praised the United States of America, blessed America, spoke of its greatness, traced to our founding and our Founding Fathers and our nation's acknowledgment that we are what we are and who we are for one reason, and that is God. Amidst all of this negativism, pessimism, today American exceptionalism was the focus at the White House, long overdue and punctuated by this dramatic and goose bump–inspiring, chill-inspiring rendition of "The Battle Hymn of the Republic" by the US Army Chorus.

A LITTLE DIVERSION FOR THE STICK-TO-THE-ISSUES CROWD

RUSH EXPLAINS THE DIFFERENCE BETWEEN OPEN LINE FRIDAY AND THE REST OF THE WEEK
The Rush Limbaugh Show, June 26, 2020

RUSH: Hey, look at this. I'm here. I was not driven outta here today. I was literally driven outta here yesterday. I could not stay here. It's embarrassing, if I were to tell you why, it's embarrassing as hell. And it is part of having cancer, but it's just embarrassing as hell. Anyway, I'm here now. Everything's rocking and rolling, so let's get started.

JOHNNY DONOVAN: And now, from sunny South Florida, it's Open Line Friday!

RUSH: Open Line Friday, where we don't screen the program as tightly—you know, we got new people tuning in every day. And new people tuning in every hour. And so what's Open Line Friday? Most of you know. See, Monday through Thursday the callers have to talk about things I care about. Do you know what percentage of the audience—we have proven this statistically. This is our business. We have to know these things. Do you know what percentage of this audience ever even tries to call? You will not believe this.

And when I first learned this—and, by the way, it's true of all talk shows that have a significant audience, it's not just this one. The percentage of an audience that tries to call is less than one half of 1 percent. Our model projections are 50 million people tuning in. The official audience ratings showing us around 28 million. The percentage of people that try to call is infinitesimally small. And we know this. It's not hard to figure this out. We have a phone number, and we see how many people are dialing it. And we know how many repeats, how many redials and all this. We actually know how many people.

So, therefore, I learned early on that a talk show should never be done for the callers. They're too tiny a bunch of people. It's the listeners, it's the audience. And so, when we screen calls Monday through Thursday, they have to be desirous of talking about things I care about. 'Cause if I'm bored or if I don't care, you're gonna be able to tell. You're gonna be able to tell. And you might say, "You know what? I'm bored," and change the station or walk away. Can't afford that.

But, see, that's the great risk on Friday. On Friday we will take calls from people talking about things I don't care about, as a service to those people who are denied. I'm a benevolent dictator here. They're denied, Monday through Thursday, their chance to appear. But on Friday we open it up, but I'll take the risk, and if I have to fake being interested in something, I'll do it. So that's the difference in Open Line Friday and the rest of the week. We just don't screen calls as tightly, but we still screen 'em. So that's your guideline here—800-282-2882 is the number.

And I still am seriously thinking about a caller clinic. I haven't done one of these in twenty years, and a caller clinic is basically done per call. You explain what's good, what's bad, what's disqualifying about each call, and hopefully it provides guidance and inspiration, education for future callers to understand their role here, which I've always said is to make the host look good, 'cause the host is why people are listening.

How many times have you heard, "You know, I love listening to the X and X show. Man, those callers are the best." When's the last time anybody ever said that to you? It doesn't happen. This is not ego speaking, folks. This is the business aspect, the business side of things. And so when I say the purpose, the role of a caller is to make the host look good, the worst thing that means is praise, sycophantic sucking up.

No, making the host look good is something that inspires the host to think and be even smarter. It's not making the host look good. "Man, you're the best. Oh, I can't find anybody any better." No, no, no, no, no. You ever watched an interview of anybody—president, any president—and you know that whoever's conducting the interview is sucking up? It's not good. It looks like it's prearranged, and it doesn't work. And that's not what we're looking for here. So there's that.

• • •

"Silent Night" . . . that song, even though I've lost my hearing and cannot hear all of the frequency ranges in it—my memory supplies the melody—it still makes me tear up. —Rush Limbaugh

• • •

OPEN LINE FRIDAY QUESTION: HOW DOES YOUR HOST HEAR MUSIC WITH A COCHLEAR IMPLANT?
The Rush Limbaugh Show, December 7, 2018

RUSH: Here is Vaughan in Columbiana, Ohio. Great to have you on Open Line Friday. Hi.

CALLER: Good afternoon, Rush! How are you, sir?

RUSH: I'm doing well. Thank you much.

CALLER: Well, good. Mega dittos from a longtime listener since the early nineties. Hey, as I'm standing here lookin' at the snow and contemplating the season, a question comes up that I could only ask you probably on Open Line Friday. So here goes. Back in the early or mid-nineties, you introduced your audience to Mannheim Steamroller, and I've amassed a collection of their Christmas music and just absolutely loved it. I'm about a year older than you, Rush, and, like you, I have come to acquire a fair amount of hearing loss. Certainly nothing like you have, but I was able to mitigate it somewhat with conventional hearing aids that I'm able to control with a Bluetooth connection and that sort of thing. But it's been evident over the years listening to your bumper music and the way you brought us Mannheim Steamroller and all that that you're a fan of good music. I'm wondering, with your cochlear implants, are you able to enjoy music at all like you used to be able to?

RUSH: Well, I can if it's music that I knew before I lost my hearing.

CALLER: Okay.

RUSH: So in the case of Mannheim Steamroller, the way it works is I'm actually not hearing it. My memory is supplying memories based on the audio stimulation that I am getting. That's why I can only listen to music and recognize music that I knew before I lost my hearing. Music that I've never heard before all sounds the same note. I cannot distinguish a low piano note from a high piano note, for example. Violins, strings sound like fingernails on a chalkboard to me. I need closed-captioning even to follow [the] audio in a movie or TV show, because the music and the soundtrack will be so loud and distracting that without closed-captioning, I'll never even hear 30 percent of what's being said on any TV show. But as to music, as long as you have your natural hearing and as long as it's being amplified with hearing aids, you're not gonna suffer anywhere near the type of loss of ability to enjoy music that somebody who has totally lost their hearing will. You'll still be able to hear it exactly as it was. You just may need to turn it up—and, depending on the nature of your hearing loss, you might lose the ability to hear certain frequencies high or low. But, again, your memory will take over. If it's music you're familiar with, like Mannheim Steamroller, I predict that you'll be able to get enough of it to thoroughly enjoy it like you always have.

CALLER: Hey, after hearing you describing the amount of hearing that you lost, you won't hear me complain about mine. That's a profound amount of hearing loss.

* * *

Mega honor. Mega dittos. I am a Rush Baby. I literally grew up listening to Rush since 1988. I fought rush hour traffic, and everyone's out in their cars listening to their car radio to listen to Rush. That's why I thought that. My little toddler self called the radio in house the "Limbaugh." I mispronounced it the "Limbaugh," my parents tell me, but I thought the radio was "Limbaugh." Why else would you have the radio in your house?

—Tristan, member of the audience

* * *

OPEN LINE FRIDAY QUESTION: HOW DOES RUSH DO ALL THE SHOW PREP?

The Rush Limbaugh Show, October 5, 2007

CALLER: I appreciate you having me. I have a question for you, and I was told this is a great Open Line Friday question.

RUSH: We'll see.

CALLER: Back in the days when you started out, I remember reading your first book, and you said you read several newspapers a day. Well, nowadays we have the Internet. What are the blog sites that you prefer to read?

RUSH: I'm going to take you through a little history, because this actually turns out to be a pretty good question. When I started, the first iteration of this program was in Sacramento in 1984. And back then, it was just newspapers, and I would prep three hours in Sacramento with three papers. Maybe it was four or five. By the way, I got my first computer, Apple IIc, and that's where I first started logging on to CompuServe and the various news sources there. So the universe began to expand. And I was on the cutting edge of this—of utilizing the Internet. But it was back [in the days of] 256 baud, these slow, slow things. It was magically fast back then, but it was [a] snail's pace by today's standards. Then I moved to New York and, of course, that all changed with all the papers there, the *Washington Post,* and the Internet was expanding in terms of services available. Let's pretend tomorrow is a workday. I'll leave here, I'll get home, the printer here will go nuts and at home it will go nuts. Every morning I get in here at seven, eight o'clock and start doing the intense prep of the latest news for that particular day, coupled with what all has been found and printed for me by myself and these other three people over the course of the night, and it just keeps building, and building, and building. About eleven o'clock I stop, I take that huge stack out of the printer, and that's when I start going through and putting together what I'm going to do. On the conservative side, there's never unanimity of thought, and I disagree with them sometimes, and that helps me even further cement an argument that I want to make, but there's so much out there now, if I weren't disciplined, if our staff here [wasn't] disciplined, we could go into overload every day. As it is, I've got three stacks here today, and this is Open

Line Friday, it's a little different, but I'll get 30 percent of it done, maybe 40 percent. The stuff I don't use I'll put aside for tomorrow in case tomorrow is light. But tomorrow is never light. Every day we're overloaded.

Well, there's always going to be too much information. The key is being able to synthesize it, break it down to its essence; take the complex, make it understandable. For example, here's another trick: If I got a story from a newspaper, any website that prints out in three pages, I only print the first page, because the other two pages are a bunch of BS that comes from the Nexis database that [has] nothing to do with the story.

I don't need any more pieces of paper on my desk than I have here. I only print one page of it. But it takes a large effort. This show is huge; we have a massive responsibility to the audience, to meet and surpass audience expectations, and it's just not possible for me to do it all every day. And the blogs have become a big part of it. Show prep coming in even while the program unfolds before your very eyes and ears.

* * *

If there's something that I want to remember, I reread it ten times. And if there's something I really, really want to never forget, I write it down myself verbatim, what I've just read. I found by doing that I never forget it. —Rush Limbaugh

* * *

PART 4 — A LOOK BACK AT THE EARLY DAYS LEADING TO *THE RUSH LIMBAUGH SHOW*

FLASHBACK 1971: FAVORITE PRANKS AS "JEFF CHRISTIE"
The Rush Limbaugh Show, August 1, 2012

"JEFF CHRISTIE": I have a little joke I'm gonna play on the light company. *[Dial tone]* We'll call them up on the phone right now and give them a little grief. *[Ringing]* Phone's ringing. Let's hear.

MAN: Hello.

RUSH AS CHRISTIE: Is this Duquesne Light customer service?

MAN: Yes, this is.

RUSH AS CHRISTIE: Hi there. How are you?

MAN: Oh, just fine.

RUSH AS CHRISTIE: Well, good. Listen. I have a question for you, and I hope you can answer it.

MAN: Oh, we'll try our best.

RUSH AS CHRISTIE: Well, I just moved here from Florida.

MAN: Mmm-hmm.

RUSH AS CHRISTIE: And I have a thing for palm trees, and as you probably know, there aren't any around here.

MAN: Not outside, anyway.

RUSH AS CHRISTIE: Well, I got a big backyard, and I wanted to start a palm tree orchard, and the only way to do this is with heat lamps. And I wanted to put about fifteen thousand or twenty thousand of them out there, and I wanted to know if you could quote me a price on how much this is gonna cost me per month.

MAN: Fifteen or twenty thousand heat lamps?

RUSH AS CHRISTIE: Yeah.

MAN: You know how many watts each lamp is?

RUSH AS CHRISTIE: Be about six hundred watts per lamp.

MAN: You want fifteen thousand lamps for this palm tree orchard?

* * *

That's the Beatles, 1967, "Hello Goodbye." It's 7:03 in the morning on WIXZ Solid Rockin' Gold, the Bachelor Jeff Radio Network. For the morning rush hour, sunny and cold today, radar says near 0 percent chance of precipitation. The roads are in good shape; the salt crews did a good job, they were out early. . . . You may have some trouble on the backwoods roads out in the sticks and the boondocks, but once you hit the main thoroughfares, no problem.

—Rush Limbaugh as "Bachelor Jeff Christie," 1971

* * *

RUSH AS CHRISTIE: Around fifteen thousand.

MAN: Okay. You gonna run how many hours a day?

RUSH AS CHRISTIE: Twenty.

MAN: Twenty hours a day, six hundred watts apiece.

RUSH AS CHRISTIE: Yeah.

MAN: Wait a second?

RUSH AS CHRISTIE: Yeah.

MAN: On the average, now, this will run you 3,640-odd dollars a day.

RUSH AS CHRISTIE: Oh-ho-ho. You kidding?

MAN: Not kidding.

RUSH AS CHRISTIE: I was thinking like thirty bucks a month, maybe.

MAN: No way. *[Laughs]* You got over, what, nine million watts there.

RUSH AS CHRISTIE: Three thousand bucks a day?

MAN: Right. You got fifteen thousand lightbulbs.

RUSH AS CHRISTIE: Yeah, well, I could move to Florida cheaper than that.

MAN: Sure. Fifteen thousand lightbulbs at six hundred watts apiece comes out to about 9,120,000 watts. I mean, I don't think we even have a rate to accommodate that.

RUSH AS CHRISTIE: Three thousand dollars a day.

MAN: $3,648.

RUSH AS CHRISTIE: Well, thanks, but I'll move back to Florida if I want palm trees. But thank you for your time and trouble.

MAN: You're welcome.

RUSH AS CHRISTIE: Okay. Bye-bye . . .

* * *

RUSH (IN 2012): We played silly phone tricks, my brother and I and our friends; it was our pastime, and every time we tried one on Irene Wright, we never succeeded. Irene Wright, former drama teacher, speech teacher; we never [were] able to pull a prank on her. She was wise to us. But as I say, she never gave us up. She never warned anybody that we were on the prank path. She left the targets wide open for us to hit. She always knew it was us, but she never told anybody else in town that we were on the march. She never ratted us out. So we were able to pull off our pranks, despite her knowing.

FROZEN RACCOON MEAT TAKES ME BACK TO 1972 IN McKEESPORT WITH LILY TOMLIN
The Rush Limbaugh Show, February 11, 2015

When I saw this headline: "LA Health Officials Take Action After Local Supermarket Sells Raccoons as Food." Some of you lifers will remember this story, but for those of you who have not been here from the outset, I have to tell you this. When I was working in Pittsburgh, at a suburban station outside Pittsburgh in McKeesport, what was it? I don't even remember. Oh no, this is embarrassing. Played oldies. Fifties and sixties oldies, WIXZ, Salted Rot and Mold. That's what we called it. I was doing the morning show. And, of course, morning shows back then were not nearly as restricted in terms of how much the host could talk, the deejay could talk.

Lily Tomlin was in town appearing somewhere doing something, and her agent was calling all the radio stations and trying to get her interviews on various stations in town to promote whatever she was doing. They called and I said, "Sure." I mean, cool. I'm just starting out, my first job away from home, chance to talk to Lily Tomlin. So, we agreed the day before she was calling in to set up a bit. It was my idea, and I said, "I got an idea. Why don't I, on the radio, call a local grocery store and ask if they have any frozen raccoon TV dinners. You, as Ernestine the Operator, are monitoring phone calls and you randomly overhear mine. You are outraged that there [are] frozen raccoon TV dinners on sale at a local grocery store. You want the details, and you're gonna report me to the ASPCA."

That's what we did. We totally improvised it: frozen raccoon TV dinners. I called this grocery store—fake grocery store, of course, and there was no such thing as frozen raccoon TV dinners, the whole point. She did both voices. She did the woman answering the phone at the supermarket and she did Ernestine the Operator . . . her character from *Laugh-In.* And she was just hilarious. My mother heard the tape of that bit, and that's when my mother told me that she was convinced that after failure after failure after failure and maybe many more, that I was gonna succeed. That bit, my mother said, "I didn't know you were that funny. I didn't know you had that kind of improvisational ability." It was fun.

JEFF CHRISTIE – 14K'S "BIG HITTER" FROM 7:00PM TO 12 MIDNIGHT

Jeff Christie's not a little guy — he's a big talent, and Pittsburgh loves it. He keeps the hit music moving every night from 7:00 to 12 Midnight on 14K. Pittsburgh's youth market is turning to the All Hit Music and unique wit that Jeff offers every night.

Jeff's got a lot to say — he's an avid reader and sports fan. He's been keeping the evening hours jumpin' and the Pittsburgh listeners pleased on 14K for a year and a half. And music isn't the only kind of "big hits" he can deliver — he loves to play baseball, too.

Jeff was born in the Midwest and worked there before he moved to Pittsburgh. He was the morning man on WIXZ, McKeesport before he became 14K's night-time Big Hitter.

The Big Hits and Pittsburgh's bright night-time sound — that's Jeff Christie — he's the big man in town.

7 P.M.

So I see this headline: "LA Health Officials Take Action After Local Supermarket Sells Raccoons as Food." This is 1972 when this happened. This is eons ago. You talk about being on the cutting edge. Here I am in a bit with Lily Tomlin about frozen raccoon TV dinners in 1972, and now it actually has come true in LA. And no, I don't think there is a tape of the bit. And it would be tape if there were any in existence.

* * *

It was WIXZ, that's the station in McKeesport outside Pittsburgh that I worked at. That's the station that fired me for playing "Under My Thumb" too many times, by the Rolling Stones. Yeah, I got the call letters confused. Yeah, I played "Under My Thumb" too many times, and I got fired for not following the music playlist programming format, what have you.

∙ ∙ ∙

WIXZ 1360, where the hits roll on! "Love (Can Make You Happy)," Mercy, three chicks from New York City, and they got it together back in 1969. It's twenty before eight o'clock in the morning, and I've had a lot of requests for the Jeff Christie quickie deejay course . . . —Rush Limbaugh as "Bachelor Jeff Christie," 1971

∙ ∙ ∙

WHEN DID I FIRST KNOW THIS WAS MORE THAN JUST A SHOW?
The Rush Limbaugh Show, August 3, 2020

Rush and the EIB Network, starting our thirty-third year. You realize, our thirty-third year, and thirty of those years have been spent as the most-listened-to radio talk show in the country.

Can you stop and think as I brag here for just a second, 'cause Babe Ruth said it, it ain't bragging if you can do it. It might have been Mark Twain who said it. It might have been Winston Churchill. Hell, it might have been I . . . It was Babe Ruth? All right. It ain't bragging if you can do it. Do you know of any product or service that's been number one for thirty years?

Don't say iPhone. It's only been around since 2007. Don't say Coca-Cola, 'cause they've been up and down. Sometimes Pepsi has edged 'em out, sometimes it hasn't. Although Coca-Cola, I think maybe it has been. I don't think it's ever been eclipsed as the number one selling cola.

At any rate, it's exciting. And I thank you. We all thank you from the bottom of our hearts here. You all are the ones who have made it possible.

* * *

RUSH: Let me grab a phone call. We start quickly. John, Columbia, South Carolina, welcome to the program, sir. Great to have you with us. Hi.

CALLER: Rush, thank you so much. Thanks for taking my call. Happy anniversary, and best wishes. I have one question I've always wanted to ask. When did you realize that *The Rush Limbaugh Show* was more than just another successful endeavor—that is, this thing is really a rocket ship? 'Cause I know when it was for me, as a charter listener.

RUSH: Now, wait; I'm gonna make sure I understand the question. What do you mean by more than just an ordinary success story? I assume you mean more than just an ordinary successful radio show?

CALLER: Yes, sir.

RUSH: When it escaped the bonds of being a radio show, became that plus other things?

CALLER: Yes, sir. Just the phenomenon that it's become. When did you say, "Hey, this is maybe a phenomenon; maybe it's more than just—"

RUSH: Aw, gee, I don't know that I ever had time to think about that. I was too busy trying to do it every day. I'm not copping out. I mean, once a program was over, the only thing I thought about it was the things I thought needed improvement or the things that I wished hadn't happened that I needed to fix the next day. I never sat around and said, "Man, this thing's getting big. Man, this thing is huge. Man, I'm really important." I never sat around and did that. So I'd have to really think. I know what you're asking, nevertheless. There was a time where I actually think the honest answer to your question is in Sacramento. 'Cause this show started in Sacramento, and I had never been on a success track my whole career before moving to Sacramento in 1984. I'd always been moderately successful or the guy that might be, could be, but I never stood out 'cause I'd never been permitted to do a radio show the way I really wanted to do it. I had to conform to the programming format and all that, which everybody at any station had to do. But when I started to draw crowds . . . I would announce that I was gonna be someplace some night, and thousands of people would show up. This has never happened before. And when I would talk to these people, they were showing up not just because the program entertained them, they were showing up because they were so ecstatic there was somebody finally on the radio that sounded like they thought. So I think the realization that the radio program was gonna be more than a radio program actually began to creep in in

Sacramento. It had an effect, it had an impact on the way I did the program, 'cause back in those days I was doing so much parody, so much satire. And all I wanted back then was to be thought of as, you know, really funny, really great, really thought-provoking radio program, not just a political program but a great, great, great entertainment media program. And I found that as the program evolved and it went national, that there was less time for that, because people were taking so much of it so seriously that I had to make sure that I didn't appear to be not taking that aspect of it seriously. I still did satire and parody, but I had to make sure that it was obvious. . . . But it was pretty early on that I realized that, if I understand you right, the program meant a lot to a lot of people, and I had to take that respectfully and very seriously. And it was a great thing that it happened, by the way. I'm not complaining about it. And it's still front and center in my mind today.

CALLER: Well, I appreciate the time here, Rush. It's a thrill to talk to you.

RUSH: Thank you, sir. I appreciate it. I appreciate the question. The story that I can tell you very quickly that made me realize that I had to be really careful with satire and parody—do you all remember the Slim Whitman satanic message bit? I think I did it once. It's something I did in Sacramento, and I might have reenacted it here. But I read a story one day that some minister in Ohio had discovered that there was a satanic message in the theme song to the *Mister Ed* TV show if you played it backwards. So I said to myself, "Okay, how can I make this funny rather than just sit here and tell people what this Ohio minister claims he found?" I mean, where does an Ohio minister find a way to play the *Mister Ed* theme backwards? Why would an Ohio minister even do that? And I found a song by Slim Whitman as the updated theme, "Una Paloma Blanca," which was translated as "A White Dove." So I decided to find a satanic message in "Una Paloma Blanca." I'm sure many of you are familiar with this. So I went into the production studio and we found a way to play it backwards, and I got a guy to record a message through a harmonizer, which changes the tone of your voice. And the bit was that the devil was actually speaking to people through the Slim Whitman "Una Paloma Blanca" song, and I went through, you know, two hours of setting this up on the air and explaining it. And when it's over, I'm thinking, "Man, people will think this is the greatest thing. Johnny Carson will love it."

Anyway, Slim Whitman, we put the satanic message in "Una Paloma Blanca" played backwards. And I'm thinking when it's over that people out there listening, "This is the funniest thing I've ever heard. This is guy is really good. We are fortunate to have this guy in our town on the radio. This is the kind of stuff you have to tune to *The Tonight Show* or something like that to hear. This guy is awesome."

And I'm proud as I could be, and I can't wait for the reaction and the feedback. And during a commercial break the general manager of the radio station came in and said, "How long are you gonna go with this?"

I said, "I don't know, but I think the way this is tracking right now, I could probably get three more days out of this."

He said, "No. You have to wrap it up."

I said, "Why?"

He said, "Because people are calling their churches and reporting that there is a satanic message in what you're doing on the radio. And you admitted that you didn't know it, so people are thinking if you can be fooled, anybody can, and people are wanting to know what they should do."

I said, "Wait. You mean people are calling their ministers believing this?"

"Yes."

I said, among many other things to him, I said, "Okay. This changes a lot about the philosophy going forward."

● ● ●

I'm your host, Rush Limbaugh, with half my brain tied behind my back—just to make it fair. —Rush Limbaugh

● ● ●

FLASHBACK TO 1988

Rush's First Show on 77 WABC, July 4, 1988

RUSH: WABC Talk Radio 77. Rush Limbaugh. New York. Twenty minutes after ten. Back to the phones we go. Vinny from New York. Hello, glad you're with us.

VINNY: All right, Rush. Thank you. You know . . .

RUSH: By the way, thank you!

VINNY: Yes.

RUSH: First caller that has learned my name. And you pronounced it correctly. Thank you.

VINNY: That one of them California beach names, or what?

RUSH: No! No, I'm originally . . . *[Laughs]* California beach names. I would be, if I were, if I were in California on a beach, I'd be a whale . . .

VINNY: Oh. *[chuckles]*

RUSH: I'm from Missouri. Rush is my grandfather's aunt's maiden name. It's an old family name. . . .

RUSH: Bill. Brooklyn. You're next on WABC. Hello!

BILL: Good morning, Rush! How are you?

RUSH: Fine, thank you!

BILL: I want to take this opportunity to welcome you to New York. I'm a resident of Santa Cruz County, visiting my family, ironically.

RUSH: You are a resident of Santa Cruz?

BILL: I sure am!

RUSH: Well, it's a beautiful place. I've been here once before. I used to be with the Kansas City Royals for five years and would come in here occasionally, and it's a nice city. I like it.

BILL: Well, I hope you continue to feel that way.

RUSH: Thank you. *[Laughs]* I bet I will. . . .

RUSH: WABC Talk Radio 77. Rush Limbaugh in New York. We will be here each weekday from ten 'til twelve, from now into the indefinable future. Well, nations are nothing more than populations of people. And as a nation, I think it's been a mistake for us to be concerned about world opinion anyway, because world opinion is always going to be anti-US. Because the US is the envy of the world. So what difference does this make as far as our reputation is concerned? It doesn't hurt us a bit.

*   *   *

I caught you on your very first broadcast on radio station 770. My wife and I were on our way to the Jersey Shore. I heard you talkin', and I said to my wife, "What did he say his name was?" And she said, "I think he said 'Rush.'" And I said, "Man, I don't know who he is, but I sure like what he's saying. He's saying what I'm thinkin'," and I've been listening ever since.

—Mike, member of the audience

*   *   *

FLASHBACK TO 1993: THE DAN'S BAKE SALE PHENOMENON
The Rush Limbaugh Show, August 1, 2008

CALLER: Hello to Dan in Dallas, Oregon, who turned me on to the show.
RUSH: Yeah.
CALLER: And thanks for sending me his used *Limbaugh Letter,* since I can't afford a subscription yet.
RUSH: Wait a minute—he's sending you his used *Limbaugh Letters*?
CALLER: Well, Xeroxed copies.
RUSH: I'll tell you what we'll do. We will send you a subscription and charge it to our production budget. We'll take it out of Johnny Donovan's budget. *[Laughs]* . . . Okay. Dan, here's what we're going to do.
CALLER: Okay.
RUSH: You must organize a bake sale. Have a bake sale. Are you married?
CALLER: Yeah.
RUSH: Does your wife bake?
CALLER: Well, yeah, but she hates your show. That's another reason I can't get the letter; she won't let us put the finances to it.

Kit Carson in the New York studio on the top floor of Rockefeller Center.

RUSH: Then it is up to you to go out and earn money independently from your wife. So have her bake some stuff and don't tell her why. This is a great way to get even—bake some stuff. Also, for this to work, your friend is going to have to stop enabling you. Your friend is going to have to stop making copies of the *Limbaugh Letter* and sending them to you.

CALLER: Okay.

RUSH: And if he does not stop, you must not accept. Now, I'm serious about this. I want you to get the bake sale, the baked goods, I want you to put 'em on display wherever you work or wherever you want to do this; you're out there raising money. Have somebody take a picture of it so that we know you've done it. We'll put a picture in the newsletter of you showing how hard you worked based upon the desire you felt to have a subscription. You will appreciate it so much more than if we just acted sorry for you and gave you a subscription.

Fran, hi. Welcome to the Rush Limbaugh program. Have about a minute here, but I understand you want to donate to the guy out in Fort Collins?

CALLER: Yes.

RUSH: What do you do?

CALLER: We're offset printers.

RUSH: So you want to print the flyers advertising this guy's bake sale?

CALLER: Yes.

RUSH: You gotta ship 'em out there. . . .

Root Outdoor Advertising, owner of all outdoor billboards in Fort Collins, has offered to paint, design, and display a billboard for free advertising Dan's Bake Sale. We have heard from a printing company, Curry Printing in New Jersey. They have offered to print flyers and T-shirts and ship these to Fort Collins, Colorado, to help advertise and promote the bake sale. We have also heard from, just now, Kathy Abernathy, who is the general manager, runs Brennan's, my favorite restaurant in the world, one of my favorites. . . .

CALLER: Hello, cowboy from up here in Fort Collins.

RUSH: Yes.

CALLER: We're going to his bake sale.

RUSH: You're going to go to his bake sale? *[Laughs]*

CALLER: Yeah.

RUSH: *[Laughs]* . . . Here's the truth of the matter. These people show up, thirty-five thousand to sixty-five thousand, they drop a hundred dollars in and around Fort Collins. That, my friends, is called trickle-down economics.

KIT CARSON, MY TRUSTED AIDE-DE-CAMP
The Rush Limbaugh Show, January 26, 2015

Christopher Carson, "Kit," my trusted chief of staff, aide-de-camp, the very first staff member to join me twenty-seven years ago in New York.

When the program debuted in 1988, nobody had any idea if it was gonna work. And we had made no plans initially for it to get big. It was just a radio show with a guy doing three hours on the radio and the itinerant things that happened. But it took off. It took off faster and bigger than anybody had planned. So the phone started ringing and mail started coming in, and things needed to be dealt with.

We didn't have anybody, and Ed McLaughlin, who was the syndicator of the program at the time and the founding executive of the EIB Network, had just come from ABC and knew countless people at ABC. And in our building where we were at the time, ABC staffed its magazines, such as *Prairie Farmer* magazine and *American Homeowner, Contemporary Homeowner* or something.

And Ed said, "Look, I got this guy that's gonna come up from the magazine, and he's gonna answer the phones and deal with the mail. He's a good guy. He's here in New York. He's trying to become an actor, and he'll help us out here in a pinch."

I said, "Oh, okay, great. What's his name?"

He said, "Some guy, Kit Carson."

I said, "Kit Carson? Kit Carson, like the cowboy?"

"Yeah, that's what he says: Kit Carson."

Okay. So, the next day, in walks this guy, cargo shorts, white ankle socks, black Keds, and red hair that looks like it's got yeast in it piled so high on top of his head. I was immediately jealous. I said, "What did you do, put yeast in your hair?" He didn't know what I meant. But I spotted it immediately. He wanted to be an actor, he had a performer's ego, and he thought I was crazy. After one radio show, he thought I was crazy.

Affectionately referred to as part of "The Overrated Staff," James, Dawn, and Brian at the Southern Command.

He's listening to "homeless updates" and all this stuff, and he just thinks that I'm a lunatic. But he's gonna stick with it, 'cause it looks like it could be fun for a while. And he said, "What do you want me to do?"

I said, "Well, when it comes to the phones . . ." And I did my best to explain who I was, what I did, and what we're all trying to accomplish, and he just said, "Yeah, yeah, yeah, the latest to get to New York, gonna hit it big, right, right, okay, got it, got it. What can I do?"

I said, "Well, when you're answering the phones, I want you to really learn how to do something, and I really want you to learn how to do it, and it's [to] say 'No.' You're gonna have people calling wanting me to do this, do that, requests for all kinds of things, and I don't care what and I don't care who, your first answer is no, and then you come tell me and we'll review who called and then we'll decide what to do." It's harder than you think, folks. It's easy to say yes to people and make friends, have a good relationship.

Saying no to people does not promote good friendships right off the bat. He said no. He loved saying no. He said, "Really? I have the power to say no to anybody?" I said, "Yes, you do." He started answering mail. Anyway, it just evolved to where he became the resident expert on me and the program. He became its number one champion, defender, evangelist, and, of course, he ended up doing much more than—well, he never stopped saying no.

That job remained as important twenty-seven years later as it was that first day. He enjoyed it as much as ever, except the people calling later on were like from the White House and *Good Morning America* and the *Today* show, and he still said no and then came and told me about it.

He loved everybody here, and everybody loved him. He did not allow me to be pessimistic or negative. He didn't allow me to get down in the dumps about anything. And if he sensed that I was, he would do anything that he could that enabled me to get the best out of myself, even if it was just a social soiree that we were at, or some business trip. I was thinking about it last night. I can't remember a time when he complained about things.

MARK STEYN: Kit Carson was Rush Limbaugh's chief of staff, so Rush dubbed him "H. R."—as in H. R. Haldeman, who fulfilled the same role for Richard Nixon. The dramatis personae of the Nixon White House aren't quite as reflexively familiar to an unassimilated foreign guest host such as myself, and it took me awhile to get on top of it: On one early show, I referred to him as "R. F.," which bemused him. "Where did that come from?" he asked. After thinking about it, I figured I must have confused H. R. with R. F., the studio boss of Monumental Pictures in *Singin' in the Rain*.

Kit liked that. He had been an actor, dreaming of Broadway, not talk radio. But twenty-seven years ago he accepted a job with a guy whose radio show was growing a little faster than he could handle. So Kit came on board to deal with Rush's mail, and one day he handed Rush a couple of news stories with a very slender connection between them, and Rush riffed off it for a few minutes on air. And after the show he asked Kit, "Do you have any more stuff like that?" Kit's "stack of stuff" was a big part of the show for the next quarter-century.

RUSH EXPLAINS EARLY "RUSH TO EXCELLENCE" TOURS

After I left KFBK to do this program nationally, there was a natural pull to go back there and to express gratitude for all of the people there who had made it possible. So we started the Rush to Excellence Tour—which, if you've seen a Trump rally, it's what the Rush to Excellence Tour was. When this program started, nobody knew who I was, and nobody thought syndicated radio in the daytime had a prayer. A bunch of people had tried it with moderate success, and I was just the next one—and if it didn't work, nobody would think anything of it other than "Nice try."

I figured it would set me up for a better job later if it didn't work, 'cause it never had. People thought you had to be local, local, local in the daytime doing radio. I didn't believe that and wanted a chance to show it. So I started the Rush to Excellence Tour. Every time we'd get a new affiliate, I would go there. I would go for a weekend. I'd arrive on Friday night, have dinner with the radio station people, and do a personal appearance on Saturday.

I'd fly back to New York on Sunday. I did that forty-eight weekends a year for the first two years to cement a relationship with the stations that took the show and to cement a bond with the audience. I was stunned at how many people showed up. It'd be five thousand. If the place held ten thousand, that's how many showed up. I would do an hour and a half, sometimes two hours, with just some notes to remind me [of] things I wanted to say. That's why, when Trump started his rallies, I knew exactly what was going on.

. . .

GOLDEN "BO SNERDLEY": I've been on radio since I was fourteen years old in one form or another. This is the number one broadcast in the world, and I'm damn proud to be working with him.

RUSH (ON TOUR STAGE): I want to introduce some people I have brought with me from New York. Kit Carson. Kit, would you stand up? Executive assistant. These are the people behind the scenes who do work that you don't even know to enable me to do what I do.

. . .

THANK YOU, HIGHLY OVERRATED STAFF: A RARE REFLECTION ON TWENTY-FIVE YEARS
The Rush Limbaugh Show, August 1, 2013

Welcome, ladies and gentlemen, to the first day of the twenty-sixth year of the Excellence In Broadcasting Network, a network named after the talent and ability of the host. That comment dedicated to all twenty-four- and twenty-five-year-old women. The door just opened *[staff enters]*. I thought we'd already done everything. It's the twenty-fifth anniversary of the Excellence In Broadcasting [Network]. August first of 1988 is when this program began on a national scale.

[Staff sings "Happy Anniversary" to Rush.]

Thank you all very much. Ah, that is a gorgeous-looking macaroni cake. That is gorgeous. The whole staff is here. Well, the Florida contingent is here.

I don't often look back. I don't often spend time thinking about the past, because I'm so focused on the next day. And I'm obsessed with meeting everybody's expectations every day, and there are many days where I think I haven't been nearly as good as I could have been, so I look to the next day to fix that, get better. So I don't sit back and reflect.

When I was younger and climbing my own ladder, one of the great perks of my success has been to meet other successful people, people who are the best at what they do. I haven't met everybody I would like to meet, but I've met a number of them, and a number of them became very good friends and I was able to get very close and learn from them.

I asked the question to each and every one of them, because when I was younger and imagining what it was like, when I was younger and imagining the kind of success I envisioned for myself, the kind of success that I wanted—and it was specific—I was aiming to be number one. I didn't want to be top five.

I wanted it to be real. I wanted to be number one because my audience was the largest, not because a bunch of PR or buzz, people *saying* that it was big but not really *being* big. I wanted it to be substantively the biggest. And I moved to New York in 1988 with that objective. In those days, I imagined what it would be like if I ever did succeed and get there.

So it was August first, 1988, but before I got there—I was in New York—before I got there, I had to get, you know, a lot of breaks. And it's dangerous, risky, when you start mentioning people that have helped you along the way, because success has many fathers. Failure is an orphan. But whenever there is success, there are all kinds of people who want to touch it.

In my case, there were a lot of people, and I can't mention them all, and I don't mean to slight anybody by leaving them out. But the first name that I would mention [is] Little Willie Brian, who gave me my first-ever radio job at age sixteen, having not ever done it, in Cape Girardeau, Missouri. He's a well-known raconteur in our little town. Little Willie, we called him. He was a radio personality himself, and he owned this little radio station.

Norman Woodruff was a broadcast consultant from San Francisco who I met when I was about to get fired for the fourth time in Kansas City in 1983. He was consulting a station there. And, sure enough, I got fired because of a commentary I did about Jesse Jackson and Gary Hart in the '84 Democrat presidential primaries. And by today's standard, it was nothing. I mean, all I did was express an opinion. Back then you did not do that. You did not. They called me on the carpet. I said, "Well, Peter Jennings does." "No, he doesn't." "Yes, he does, every night. Why can't I?" "You can't. You're gone."

Two weeks out of work and I get a call from Woodruff asking me, "How would you like to be a star in California?"

The Southern Command Studio in Palm Beach, Florida.

"California. Wow. Ooh, I've never been there."

Now, in radio when you hear "California," you think San Francisco, Los Angeles, San Diego. So I waited. Which of those three was it gonna be? And he would not tell me what city until I had said yes, which told me immediately it wasn't one of those three. It turned out to be Sacramento, California, and he consulted that station, KFBK. Sacramento became, as you all know by now, my adopted hometown. But that was 1984, and I started in radio [in] 1967. In 1984, that was the first time, after all those years, the first time anybody ever really let me do a radio show the way I wanted or thought it should be done; first time. From 1967 to '84—what is that, seventeen years?

And that led to meeting another consultant named Bruce Marr, who was instrumental at that stage because the radio show succeeded there, and there were pressures to change the show. "You gotta do guests. You can't do a show without guests. Every talk show's gotta have guests." I said, "I don't want guests, precisely because every other show has guests."

But I said the main reason I don't want guests is because they're not interested in whether or not my show succeeds. So why should I turn over hours and hours and hours of my show to people that don't care about it, other than how it might help them sell their book? They're gonna be on every other radio station and radio show. I don't need it. And it was Bruce Marr who ran interference for me and made sure that the local management did not force me to change the way I was doing it.

That led—you talk about a confluence of events—to Edward McLaughlin, who was the president of the ABC Radio networks. Short version of this: When Capital Cities merged with ABC, a lot of the ABC executives were given retirement packages as the Cap Cities people were installed in management positions. And one of Mr. McLaughlin's exit package items was they gave him two hours of satellite time from noon to two.

They said, "This is yours, and you can do with it whatever you want. You can put whoever you want in there, and you can sell it, monetize it, however."

So, Ed knew these people in California. They had told him about me. Unbeknownst to me, he's in town listening, and it led to my going to New York. This is no longer applicable in radio, but in syndication you have to be in the number one market. Your sponsor's commercials have to run in New York or you don't have a prayer.

It's all academic if that's not the case. And that's still true today. But there was nobody in New York that was gonna take a national show, because back then, as I said, everything had to be local—local numbers, local guests, local hosts, local issues; nobody was interested, particularly people in New York who had never heard of me.

So McLaughlin had to pull strings and get me a local-only show in New York on WABC, and when that show was over I went to a different studio and did the two-hour national show. This was for the first two or three years. In order to, quote, go national, I had to do an exclusively local New York show for two hours, and WABC agreed to run our national commercials in my show, and that's how we were able to tell our advertisers that their spots were gonna be heard in New York. That's how hard it was. I mean, there was no other way.

Then on August first the national show started, and the Sacramento station picked it up. New York didn't, so I'm still doing two shows, and that went on for two or three years. But it worked.

I never believed that radio listeners actively said to themselves, "I'm not listening to something that doesn't come from my town," because they did at night, and they didn't care where it came from. So I had to shoot that formulaic belief to smithereens, and did, and the rest is history. So that's just a brief recap of how it happened: Key people who took great risks, and it was a risk. I mean, Mr. McLaughlin's given two hours of satellite time, and he puts a no-name on? And it was. It was fun. You know, all kinds of excrement started hitting the fan. *[Chuckles]* Ed never planned on any of that. Ed had two hundred radio stations, and they were producing a little income and fine, but my ambition was not two hundred radio stations, it was six hundred, it was twelve hundred, whatever. But everybody involved hung in there. Everybody. My family's always hung in there. Everybody has always hung in with me.

My gratitude goes so deep for so many, I couldn't possibly mention them all to you.

· · ·

For you young whippersnappers out there, it is hard to understand what life was like before Rush. There was no one, and I mean no one, like him. There was no Fox News, no Sean Hannity, not really even a talk radio format, not on a national level. Rush started it all. And the bond he built with his audience was based not on politics alone as much as it was humor. No one was funnier than Rush.

—Nick Searcy, American actor, February 17, 2021

· · ·

Starting from the early days in radio, Rush had an incredible sense of self-deprecating humor. He never took himself too seriously and made us all laugh with famous lines like, "I know the left like I know every square inch of my gloriously naked body!" Seth MacFarlane, the creator of *Family Guy*, asked Rush if he would be willing to appear in an episode of the popular cartoon show. Rush knew full well he was taking a great career risk by being turned into a cartoon figure, but said, "Why not? What could possibly be said about me in a cartoon that isn't said in real life on a daily basis by the Drive-by Media?"

FAMILY GUY: A CAREER CHALLENGE
The Rush Limbaugh Show, October 4, 2010

RUSH: I guess the most frequent criticism I'm getting is that I allowed conservatism to be "cartooned." Ha! But everything in the show is cartooned. It is a cartoon, but that ending, folks? I'm running down the street, I morph into an eagle flying into the sky, into a big American flag? I mean, it doesn't get any better than that. Conservatism looked pretty good to me. *[Laughs]*

BRIAN (DOG CHARACTER ON *FAMILY GUY*): Listen, Limbaugh, my name is Brian Griffin, and I have got something to say to you. Our republic has been bastardized and royally screwed up thanks to you jackasses. You suck! And you're terrible.

RUSH CHARACTER: Yes, uh, valid points you're raising, my friend, and I respect you for raising them. But may I ask you a question? Okay. Have you ever read anything I've written?

BRIAN: Well, no, I haven't. But I've read things other people have written about the things you've written, and I do not approve of the things I've read from others about the things they've read from you. Not one bit, sir.

RUSH CHARACTER: For crying out loud, Brian, read my book. Judge for yourself.

LOIS: Brian, are you reading the new Rush Limbaugh book?

BRIAN: Yeah, I picked it up at the mall yesterday. I . . . I can't believe I'm saying this, but this might be the best book I've ever read.

LOIS: Brian, you've got to be joking.

BRIAN: No, I mean it, Lois. You know, I've never actually read any of Limbaugh's stuff, but this book makes an excellent case for personal accountability, fiscal responsibility, and steak-eatership.

● ● ●

Okay, so I officially today announced that I identify as skinny. From this day going forward, I am skinny. Now, in the old days, people's reaction to that would be to call me delusional and maybe think I needed some help. Today, I'm brave. It's a courageous act to identify as skinny when one is not. I'm sure I will get accolades all across Twitter and accolades all across Facebook, and accolades all across the Drive-by Media for positive thinking, now that I identify as skinny. And I'm fully expecting that Weight Watchers and others will identify with me and welcome me to the fold as a skinny, since I now identify that way. The way I see myself is the way I am, not how you see me, and if you don't see me that way, you're the bigot. I'm brave! —Rush Limbaugh

● ● ●

RUSH EXPLAINS THE RUSH BABES PHENOMENON
The Rush Limbaugh Show, May 9, 2012

"Rush Babe" is not demeaning or insulting of women in any way. It is an acknowledgment, ladies and gentlemen, that a proud conservative woman is innately attractive for her independence or intellect or commitment to real values and doesn't mind being called a babe. It's a compliment to a well-adjusted woman. Hey, babe, how are you? It's not an insult. Rush Babes for America is a compliment. Only in the land of the left would calling a woman a babe to her face be insulting, such as stigmatizing or ignoring the existence of her brain.

Do you remember—I never forgot this, just to show you the generation—a great director was married to Julie Andrews, Blake Edwards. He got a lifetime achievement award at the Oscars one year, and he gave all of his thanks to the best "broad" in the world. The best broad he'd ever met—his wife, Julie Andrews—and you could hear a gasp in the room amongst the young actors and actresses who thought he was insulting her.

He was engaging in shock value, but back in his day, World War II generation, women were broads. It did not mean they were cows like it meant when I was in high school. The dames, they were broads. Go read a Mickey Spillane novel. Anyway, he just called her a great broad. It was the best compliment he could give her, and she took it that way, of course. And that's what Rush Babes is. It's not at all insulting.

• • •

In 1994, my wife, Cindy, and I and another couple of friends, Bill and JoAnn, went into NYC to see the show. We had a great time. During intermission we were able to speak with Rush and have him autograph his new book. I told Rush that we were going to Patsy's restaurant after the show, since he always spoke highly about it. Rush called ahead and reserved us a table without our knowledge. It was such a nice surprise when we arrived, and a thoughtful gesture on Rush's part! The sweet sausages were delicious, and we had a great time. We still talk about it to this day with the same friends. God bless you. —Joseph, member of the audience

• • •

IT'S THE SON OF ONE OF THE EIB NETWORK'S MOST FAMOUS CALLERS
The Rush Limbaugh Show, October 18, 2019

RUSH: We're gonna go back to the phones to Phoenix, Arizona, and we have somebody here, folks . . . For those of you who have been lifers, we used to have a semi-regular caller [come] in over the transom way, way back. One was Mick from the high mountains of New Mexico. The guy was a classic, he was an American classic, and he instantly became an audience favorite here. We have Matthew from Phoenix. You are Mick's son, is that right? Or grandson?
CALLER: *[Garbled cell connection]* No, I'm his son.
RUSH: You're his son.
CALLER: Yes, I am.

RUSH: Well, this is amazing. You know, I met your dad at Dan's Bake Sale. He showed up. That was the only time I ever met him—and I tell you, Matthew, he looked exactly the way he sounded.

CALLER: Yep, he did. Just one quick question to you. Do you still have the elk skin that hung on your back wall with your TV set? The one he sent you.

RUSH: Oh, yeah, we still have that. It's just like the Legacybox *[digital preservation advertiser]*. I do not throw that stuff away.

CALLER: Great. I'm one of four generations that have been listening to you. My millennial son listens to you. He's an avid follower, solid conservative, his wife also. And then my three grandsons, every time that they're in the kitchen, you know, with the radio on, they've got you on. And I just wanted to thank you, you know, for educating America and also, you know, every time you have an anniversary show, I hear my dad's clips on there and it just brings a smile to my face. And, you know, thank you for educating America. But my old man would have backed Trump a hundred percent. There's no doubt in the world.

RUSH: Matthew, how old would you have been back in the early nineties when he was calling here on a regular basis?

CALLER: I was about twenty-six, twenty-five, twenty-six. I'm fifty-five, fifty-six now.

RUSH: Okay. So you were an adult when he was making those calls.

CALLER: Yeah.

RUSH: I mean, you had to be laughing yourself silly every time he got through, 'cause the guy was a genuine American classic.

CALLER: Rush, I actually got on the show with him and with you, and we talked about his stories, you know, talking about, you know, some of the things he talked about, you know, things like that. And, you know, he was—he was genuinely a great character, and just a great man.

RUSH: Oh, he was. Folks, I'll just give you one example. He would call here and describe how to prepare roadkill and make it edible, or the latest animal he had killed for food. Just irritating the animal-rights crowd. The animal-rights crowd was huge back then, and he tweaked them out the wazoo and he made it sound like it was the most natural thing in the world to go out and slaughter wildlife to convert it to food and so forth. He was just an original.

CALLER: You know, I'm getting up early and I'm carting myself up to northern Arizona, picking up my son, and we're gonna go squirrel huntin'.

RUSH: *[Laughs]*

CALLER: So, you know, I'm passing on my legacy. This is what we do.

RUSH: Squirrel hunting? Who goes squirrel hunting?

CALLER: I promise you! I'm not lying to you.

RUSH: I know you're not. I'm not trying to express disbelief. I'm just . . . *[Laughs]* Squirrels, everybody has 'em in the yard. Who has to go squirrel hunting? But there you are, out hunting the things. Anyway, Matthew, I'm glad you called. I'm glad you waited. We all loved your dad here. Like I say, he was a classic. A little *Rush Limbaugh Show* history here to remind you of the early days of the program.

RUSH REFLECTS ON HIS BROTHER, DAVID, AND FAMILY
Fall 2020

I am so thankful for my brother, David. He is just such a good person . . . hilarious, smart, a great lawyer and writer. He's been there for me from the beginning. I have so many memories of us over the years . . . I could talk about them for hours. We used to do these pranks as kids in our hometown of Cape Girardeau. Who knew we could grow up to be such law-abiding citizens? He may be embarrassed that I'm saying all this, but I just love him very much and am grateful. He has a very patient and special wife, Lisa. They have five really great kids. Can you imagine having that many kids in diapers at the same time? I love them all.

. . .

I don't talk about my nieces and nephews too much on the radio . . . to protect their privacy. But I love them all very much. I want them to go after their dreams and be whatever they want to be . . . whatever that is . . . find their passion. I know they will have challenges along the way, we all do, but most important, I want them to be who they are! —Rush Limbaugh

. . .

Chapter 4

THE AMERICAN DREAM

TRIBUTE
by Dr. Ben Carson, Renowned Neurosurgeon

One thing that really impressed me about Rush was perspective. He had perspective. He was able to look at the big picture. We see so many of our political leaders get bogged down in small stuff. And Rush recognized that in order for America to remain a place of opportunity and freedom, it was a persistent fight. It wasn't a fight that occurred during World War II or during the Vietnam War. It's a fight that we have to fight every single day....

And Rush recognized that—he also talked so often about opportunity, and taking advantage of that frequently. You know, I'd be operating and somebody would say, "Did you hear what Rush said about you today?" because he was always talking about people who perhaps didn't start out on the right side of the tracks but took advantage of opportunities. And we're able to take those to a place where not only their lives were improved but they're able to improve the lives of other people around them.

And then, also, he recognized that freedom of speech is not a problem that only the government can solve. You know, freedom, our loss of freedom of speech can come from anyplace. And you have to be wary of big tech and media, and people who impose the concept of shutting up, closing people down, because that is such an important part of who we are.

America is not so much a place as it is an idea, an idea of freedom, freedom of speech, freedom of expression, freedom of religion, the ability to lead your life to where you want to, as long as it's not negatively impacting other people. That's where the government comes in. But the government

was never intended by our Founders to be involved in every aspect of our lives. And I think that's what Rush realized so much, and did a yeoman's job in terms of creating the pathway for others to begin to think that way and to express themselves; he opened up the whole pathway for talk radio and conservative thinking.

And he was a tremendous person. He was also a very nice person. Some people probably don't really realize that he was.

PART 1 — IN AMERICA, ALL IS POSSIBLE

Rush wanted every American to believe that the American Dream is alive and well. He encouraged us to find our passion and strive to become the best version of ourselves. Rush was inspired by extraordinary people like Dr. Ben Carson, who overcame tremendous obstacles from a young age to become one of the most renowned surgeons in the world, and one of the leaders of our nation. Rush wanted all of us in the United States of America to know that anything is possible in this miraculous country.

DR. BEN CARSON SHARES HIS INCREDIBLE STORY

Music Hall Center for the Performing Arts, Detroit, Michigan, May 4, 2015

My mother came from a very large rural family in Tennessee and was shuffled from home to home. She always had a desire for education, but she was never able to get beyond the third grade. And she married at age thirteen with the hope of escaping a desperate situation. She and my father moved here to Detroit, and he worked in a factory. . . .

But, some years later, my mother discovered that he was a bigamist and had another family. And, of course, that occasioned the divorce, and you know she only had a third-grade education. And, consequently, we were thrown into a situation of dire poverty. And she still maintained that dream of education, but now it was for us more so than for herself. We moved in with her older sister and brother-in-law in Boston. Typical tenement. Large, multifamily dwelling. Boarded-up windows and doors, sirens, gangs, murders. Both of our older cousins, who we adored, were killed. . . .

But my mother was out working extraordinarily hard. Two, sometimes three jobs at a time, as a domestic. Trying to stay off of welfare. . . . She didn't want to be dependent. She wanted us also to be independent, and she decided she would work as long and as hard as necessary, leaving at five o'clock in the morning, getting back after midnight, day after day after day. . . .

You know, my mother's dream was for us to move back to Detroit, and we eventually were able to do that, but I was a terrible student and my brother was a terrible student, and she didn't know what to do. So she prayed. She asked God for wisdom. . . .

My brother and I didn't think it was that wise. Turning off the TV and making us read books and submit to her written book reports, which she couldn't read. But, you know, it didn't matter, because, because it worked. That was the key. As I started reading those books, which I really didn't want to do, and I started reading about people of accomplishment, I began to recognize that the person who has the most to do with what happens in your life is you. It's not somebody else.

And you don't have to be dependent on the good graces of somebody else. You can do it on your own.

IMMIGRANT SCULPTOR THANKS RUSH
The Rush Limbaugh Show, August 21, 2008

RUSH: Here's Raj in Houston. You're next on the EIB Network. Hello, sir.

CALLER: Dittos, Rush, from a twenty-year listener and a first-time caller.

RUSH: Thank you very much, sir.

CALLER: Rush, I just wanted to give you a perspective, my perspective on this horrible country.

RUSH: Yeah? Yeah?

CALLER: I got here with twelve dollars in my pocket—

RUSH: That's about how much Obama's half-brother has in a year!

CALLER: *[Laughs]* Well, I had it all at one time. I was a high school dropout from India. I cleaned latrines. I dug ditches, planted trees. At the age of fifty, after my second successful business, I retired and started to do what I really wanted to do, and that's become a sculptor and an artist.

RUSH: And it took you 'til you were fifty to get to start to realizing that? That was like a hobby for you?

CALLER: Yes, sir, and being what many would consider as a man of color in this country, I can tell you: having listened to you, there's never been a day I can say anyone discriminated against me for that. I would not tolerate becoming a victim. I would not allow anybody to treat me differently or as if I was not as good as anybody else. And finally, Rush, I found out why I'm a Republican. I have three air-conditioning units in my house.

RUSH: *[Laughs]*

CALLER: I drive a Yukon XL and I have two homes, I hate to admit.

RUSH: You drive a Yukon XL?

CALLER: Yes, sir.

RUSH: That's big!

CALLER: Well, I'm an artist. I gotta go all over the country to different shows, haul my bronzes around.

RUSH: I don't know why you'd be afraid to admit that. You don't need to be afraid to admit that you drive a Yukon XL.

CALLER: *[Laughs]* Oh, I love the gas-guzzling monstrosity that I have. . . . Thank you, Rush. And God bless you for what you do.

RUSH: Thank you, Raj. I appreciate it. Nice to have you here.

THE AMERICAN DREAM IS NOT DEAD
The Rush Limbaugh Show, August 29, 2013

RUSH: Martin Luther King Jr. was interesting. If you read a lot of what he said or wrote, Martin Luther King did not blame the Constitution. Martin Luther King acknowledged that the Constitution did indeed spell out the right thing for all people. He said that it was just not properly applied at first, but eventually it was and has been. He did not rip the Constitution. He did not think the founding of the country [was] immoral or unjust.

He thought the implementation, in the early days, was flawed. It's real simple. The thirteen original colonies, in order to rebel, in order to form a union, had to accommodate the southern colonies. In some of them, slavery was the thing for them, and they weren't gonna give it up. A number of the Founders knew it. Jefferson, Adams, they all wrote, "This is gonna lead to trouble down the road," but they had to talk about compromise.

• • •

Rush Limbaugh, the most powerful and successful conservative radio talk show host in the country. —Barbara Walters

• • •

They had to make compromise, accommodation, in order to found the country. Martin Luther King knew all of this, and he said that the founding was proper and actually a blessing, just improperly applied. He was about integration, not separatism, and not segregation. But that's what was on stage yesterday. Everything about the civil rights movement today is back to segregation. We've gone back to pre–Martin Luther King days, essentially. It's about a never-ending race battle.

It's about segregation. . . .

The sad thing is that so many people, particularly young people, are losing faith in America, the American Dream. There is no America if there's no American Dream, and a lot of young people don't think the American Dream is possible. They're losing faith in it. . . .

CALLER THANKS RUSH FOR INSPIRATION
The Rush Limbaugh Show, May 29, 2009

RUSH: Travis in western Kansas. Great to have you on the program, sir. Hello.

CALLER: Hey, Rush. How are you today?

RUSH: Good, sir. Thank you very much.

CALLER: Rush, I know you've heard it a million times, but it really is a thrill to speak with you, and I don't think that you realize how much of an inspiration you are to millions of us across this country. There's a very short list of people that have had a profoundly positive effect on my life, and you, sir, are right there at the top of that list.

RUSH: Well, I appreciate that. Thank you. Thank you very, very much. I very much appreciate you saying that.

CALLER: If we contrast the message that you're giving us every day—self-sufficient, self-reliance, get out there, do what you love, be aggressive, be bold—if we live our lives by the principles that you are espousing, we'll all be successful. If we listen to those, the liberals out there that are beating us down, tell us we can't do it, everything is against us, you know, this country is going to be headed in the wrong direction. I don't think you realize what an inspiration you are to so many of us, you know. You've always been there,

• • •

Rush was the man that brought conservatism from the brink of extinction and made it great again. He was the familiar voice on the radio that led so many young Americans like myself into the ideals of what we truly believe. The greatness of America, the freedoms that we hold so near and dear . . . He was that voice. With all of us taking that great legacy and continuing it, there's no doubt that the future of conservatism is bright, because of Rush Limbaugh. —Donald Trump Jr., Tribute to Rush, 2021

• • •

and I don't think that I would be where I'm at today without some of the things I've heard you say through the years.

RUSH: Well, I do appreciate that.

CALLER: Yes, I certainly do, I really do from the bottom of my heart. I was in an industry. I was a loan officer in a bank, was not terribly happy with it. I was good at it but not really happy, and part of the encouragement that I've taken from listening to you all these years gave me the encouragement to step out and do something that I truly love, and, Rush, I've never been happier. I've never looked back. I've never worked harder, and you're a big reason for part of that success.

RUSH: Well, I appreciate that. What are you doing?

CALLER: I am a professional gun dog trainer. I train those dogs that run around in the fields and find birds and then us, you know, terrible hunters go out and shoot 'em. *[Laughs]*

RUSH: Now, that, to me, is just fabulous, quintessentially American. Here is a guy, folks—undoubtedly working in the bank, loan officer, this is part of some formula, but what he really, really liked was working with dogs. But to tell people that, I mean, they might laugh at you. "A dog trainer? They make jokes about dog trainers in movies." The guy finally did it. Now he trains dogs that run around in the field and find birds when people are out there

202

hunting. He's doing what he loves, working with dogs he loves. That's absolutely fabulous. I'm glad you called, I really am, Travis; thank you so much, and continued good luck to you. Remember, luck is where preparation meets opportunity, and you obviously prepared yourself for this. You created the opportunity out of necessity. Bam! You struck gold.

FIFTEEN-YEAR-OLD WANTS TO KNOW: IS THE AMERICAN DREAM AN ILLUSION OR REALITY?

The Rush Limbaugh Show, January 5, 2018

RUSH: Here is Adam. He's fifteen years old. He is in Champlin, Minnesota. Great to have you. I'm glad you waited, Adam. Welcome to the Rush Limbaugh program. Hi.

CALLER: Thank you. It's an honor to be talking to you. . . . So, recently, the United Nations did this investigation into poverty in the United States, and they concluded that the American Dream has become the American illusion. My question is, is the American Dream an illusion or is it still a reality?

RUSH: Let me ask you a question. It's not a diversion. I need to know. You're fifteen. Do you have a definition of the American Dream yourself?

CALLER: Yes. I think it means social mobility, that you have the potential ability to change your economic status for the better or the worse.

RUSH: Okay. The American Dream is alive and well. . . . This country still is the best place to realize your dreams. There is no place anywhere on this earth better for being able to live your dream, or to have an opportunity to do so. It is in no way over. Now, I'm gonna be honest with you here, Adam, and I run the risk of you thinking that I'm just a partisan hack, but I'm telling you, if the Democrat Party were still running this country and were in charge of the US economy, I would tell you that the American Dream's still there, but it's tougher because you now have more obstacles to overcome in the form of the United States government.

CALLER: Right.

RUSH: People have been overcoming obstacles in this country from the beginning. Ordinary people have accomplished extraordinary things, and it

happens every day. And you can, too. It depends on your degree of ambition, how much you want it, how hard you're willing to work at it, and how much luck might come your way—luck being defined as when preparation meets opportunity. Adam, you're gonna have no trouble finding people all over your life who tell you something can't be done or that you can't do something. But as long as you're an American, as long as you live here, you will be able to seek opportunity, you'll have opportunity to be and do whatever you want. That opportunity has not been destroyed. It has not been eliminated. There are people who have tried to whittle away at it, but nobody is gonna succeed totally as long as we have our constitutional liberties and freedoms.

CALLER: I believe that. Yeah.

RUSH: Do, because it's the truth. You know, you could always find people who failed at something. Don't listen to 'em. You can always find people that haven't succeeded. They're legion. And you can always find people that tell you how to fail, 'cause everybody knows how.

• • •

Rush Limbaugh was a fierce defender of the First Amendment and a leader of the conservative movement.

—US Senator Joni Ernst of Iowa

• • •

THE AMERICAN DREAM AS DESCRIBED BY MARCO RUBIO IS REAL
The Rush Limbaugh Show, August 31, 2012

RUSH: [The Republican National Convention] was real. And the stories that they told about America were real. Here, grab sound bite eleven. Every one of these speakers had a story like this, a quintessential American story. This is what this country has always been, and this is what's under assault. This is what the Democrats don't want people to believe is possible anymore.

RUBIO: My dad used to tell us, *"En este pais ustedes van a poder lograr todas las cosas que nosotros no pudimos"*: "In this country, you're gonna be able to accomplish all the things we never could." A few years ago, during a speech,

I noticed the bartender behind a portable bar in the back of the ballroom. I remembered my father, who worked for many years as a banquet bartender. He was grateful for the work he had. But that's not the life he wanted for us. You see, he stood behind a bar in the back of the room all those years so one day I could stand behind a podium in the front of a room.

RUSH: That's it, in a nutshell. Parents want a better life for their kids than they had themselves. That's the point of parenthood, and America is what made that possible.

⊛ ⊛ ⊛

This wasn't a radio show host broadcasting; it almost was like a friend talking to you. It was rip-roaringly hilarious and entertaining to begin, and once you were connected, there was a great deal to learn. Rush didn't spoon-feed you—he taught you how to think. Rush managed to convey what conservatism is about to a mass audience much better than any teacher ever could.

—Rajan Laad, *American Thinker*, "Remembering Rush Limbaugh," 2022

⊛ ⊛ ⊛

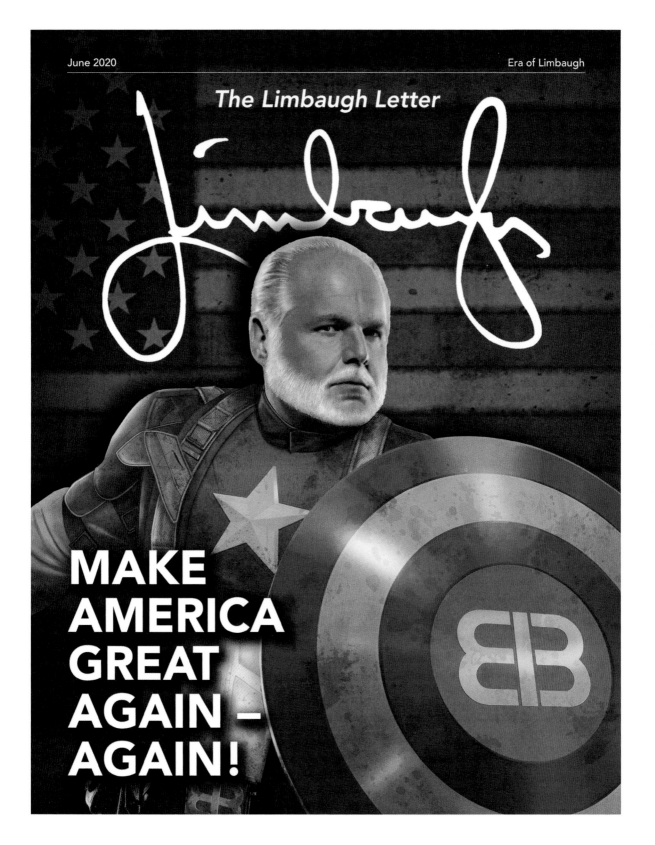

The Limbaugh Letter

**MAKE
AMERICA
GREAT
AGAIN –
AGAIN!**

PART 2 — ALL AMERICANS CAN SUCCEED WITH HIGH EXPECTATIONS

Rush always believed the best way to truly care for someone is to encourage them to have high expectations for their lives and to strive to have individual purpose. He felt that if people believe in America, anything truly is possible, regardless of where they began and the hardships they faced. Rush could not stand groupthink or any kind of stereotypes. He often said the easiest way for a liberal to get out of a debate is to call you a racist, sexist, bigot, which takes no actual thought and is intended to distract from the actual issues.

He routinely pushed back on the idea that Democrats are the so-called caring party, saying that sticking people in groups or treating them like perpetual victims is not caring at all. Following a golf tournament in Connecticut, Rush challenged a group of liberals to come up with an answer to a question he'd been asking for years: "If the Democrat Party is the party of caring individuals, what have they actually done in fifty years to show it?" He laughed, recalling the group's response: "It was complete radio silence."

AMAZING! CALLER SAYS LISTENING TO RUSH IN PRISON TURNED HIS LIFE AROUND

The Rush Limbaugh Show, May 18, 2018

RUSH: Jerome in Traverse City, Michigan. You're next on Open Line Friday. Hi.

CALLER: How's it going, Rush?

RUSH: Hey! We're doing great today. Thank you.

CALLER: Well, I'm just calling in to say that, you know, you saved my life, man. You changed my life completely around. You saved me from a bad place. I made a mistake when was eighteen years old and got sentenced to eight years in [jail] in Texas, right? I'm from Traverse City, though, up here in Michigan. And four years into my eight-year sentence I got segged up [put in Administrative Segregation, a form of solitary confinement] because I had got into a fight with a guard. Well, whenever I got segged up, they took away all my TV privileges. All I had was my radio, and they play the same songs over and over. So I was like, "You know what? AM talk shows! That right there could be like TV or whatever," and I switched over to AM, and I discovered 1470 KYYW in Abilene, Texas. And listening over . . . I started listening about four and a half years ago, give or take, and it just completely changed my whole shape of view in life. And now I'm out. I've got me a good phone, I've got me a good job, I've got . . . I'm out of my parents' house and stuff. I immediately just hit the streets, and I'm a twenty-six-year-old millennial. So this is coming from a millennial and stuff. I just am constantly getting in debates in the streets with people who don't really know what they're talking about and also trying to teach people what conservatism really is and trying to teach people how our government's really supposed to run.

RUSH: This is incredible. This . . . I've got goose bumps listening to you.

CALLER: *[Chuckles]*

RUSH: I really do. The way you described it, you are a hell of a storyteller.

CALLER: I mean, like, four years into my sentence, I was still talking about jumping it up from burglaries of houses to armed robbery, and then I discovered your show.

RUSH: And you discovered it because they took your TV privileges away.

CALLER: Because I was screwing up that bad.

RUSH: Can I ask you a question about when you got sent to prison?

CALLER: Yes, sir.

RUSH: I'm not gonna ask you why, what for, but when you look back on it . . . Where you are in your life now, you think that a lot of people told you things that weren't true?

CALLER: Yes.

RUSH: They had you set up for different things. Do you think that any of that contributed to the life you were living that got you thrown in jail, or was that nothing to do with it—you were just doing stuff you shouldn't have been doing?

CALLER: Well, I wouldn't say . . . I mean, well, actually, there was a lot of stuff, though, as far as like how I would see all in the media about, like, how bad the police are and stuff like that. And that gave me no respect for authority and stuff, because I felt like everybody . . . They were all out to get me and stuff like that, because I was brainwashed into thinking, "Okay, well, you're in the streets. You don't have, like, a lot of . . . You know, you don't come from, like, a lot of money and stuff like that." You know, my mom worked as a waitress and stuff—

RUSH: So they talked you into or they influenced you—

CALLER: —and that talked me into believing that I didn't get a chance.

RUSH: —into an adversarial relationship with law enforcement?

CALLER: Exactly. They taught me that I had no chance really, and [I] try to preach to people every single day that you do have a chance. You do have a chance to become an elitist. I was talking to my stepdad one day and, you know, I told him that I wanted to open up rehab and I also wanted to open up a string of businesses. And he told me, "Well, you know, you should just focus on your factory job." I've already signed up for college. I know what I'm gonna do, and he'd say, "Because all those dreams just might not come true. They might just not come like that. There's a lot more . . ." And I told him, I said, "You know the difference between me and you. You're an average citizen. Me, I'm an elitist. I know I can make it to the top. Nobody can tell me I can't. You know—and that's the thing, though. There's so many success stories. Look at Dr. Ben Carson."

RUSH: Let me tell you, what you just said there is so important, and I have often thought that many people end up in life where they end up because family members or parents or other people who were influential with them basically said, "Don't start dreaming. You're just gonna get disappointed. Just stick with the way the family's operating now. Just stick with it. Take the safe route. Be this. Don't take any risks. Don't take any chances. You're not gonna succeed, 'cause they're not gonna let you," that kind of stuff. And you finally decided to stop listening to them.

CALLER: Exactly. And the thing is, too, like, I'm considered the black sheep of the family, probably. Me and my sister. I mean, my grandparents are conservative. My mom doesn't really get into politics. But anytime she does, though, it's always leaning conservative. My aunt, my uncle? Die-hard conservatives. They're actually listening right now, because I texted everybody because I was so excited because I've had this dream since I was in prison of talking to you on the radio.

RUSH: Wow. This is boggling my mind. What—

CALLER: I can remember pacing in my cell back and forth listening to your show on Open Line Friday, just thinking, like, "You know what? One day I'm gonna be out of here and one day I'm gonna call and tell him how [he] saved my life."

RUSH: And here you are.

CALLER: And like—

RUSH: Here you are. And you're back home, you're in Traverse City.

CALLER: Yes, I'm back home in Traverse City. . . .

✶ ✶ ✶

RUSH: That was nothing short of amazing. I'm still kind of speechless about it. I'm asking myself, how does—he's in prison, and he's a malcontent, and he gets privileges removed, including not being able to watch television because he's misbehaving, in his early twenties. Gets tired of listening to music, and all of a sudden discovers this program and goes through a transformation.

• • •

The left doesn't want to be judged on the results of anything they do. They only want to be judged on their good intentions.

—Rush Limbaugh

• • •

WHAT CONSERVATIVES WISH FOR ALL PEOPLE
The Rush Limbaugh Show, December 12, 2014

My fervent hope, and as a conservative—and I know I speak for every conservative when I say we love everybody, and we want everybody to succeed. And that desire is really the foundation of every conservative economic and social belief.

We don't want people to have to be dependent on people that really don't care about them. We don't want people to have to be dependent on people that are really not interested in them. We don't want people to have to be dependent on people who are using them. We want people to experience the great things about achievement and accomplishment and success, because that's how we have a great country. That is how we have a wonderful society.

Now, it's obvious not everybody's gonna be able to do it. Some people are never going to find what it is they're good at. Some people simply are not gonna find what it is they want to do. And that's always been somewhat disappointing, because I was lucky. I found out really early in life. I was eight years old when I knew what I wanted to do, some form of it. I knew what I wanted to do when I was eight years old, and I have been nothing but dedicated to those desires.

And it's true, the old saw that if you're doing what you love, you'll never work a day in your life. It sounds kind of clichéd, but it really is true. And if more people had the good fortune of actually discovering their passion, their true passion, and if they can figure out a way to get paid for it, then they would know life and success and all kinds of happiness in ways that eludes them otherwise, and that's what I wish for people.

ANYONE—REGARDLESS OF RACE OR GENDER— CAN SUCCEED IN AMERICA
The Rush Limbaugh Show, October 21, 2020

My friends, there are a lot of things that I know, and there's plenty that I don't know. But one thing that I know in 2020: We have to reject this narrative, this idea that a certain race or a certain gender cannot succeed in our country. It's just bogus. This is the message of the left. The message of the left is that America hasn't changed from the days of our founding. We are still a racist slave state. If you're African American, you're locked.

You're stuck! You don't have a prayer of moving up. You don't have a chance at succeeding. If you are gay, you don't have a chance of moving up. This stuff has to be dispelled; it has to be nuked; it has to be swept away. The whole notion that America's best days are behind us is silly. America's best days are always ahead of us. But that's what's on the ballot.

What will America's best days be? How tough is it going to be to continue riding this massive rocket that is the United States of America? We have to reject the idea that you have to vote Democrat if you are of a certain race or background, and the way to reject this idea is to simply point to the people who have been voting Democrat for the last fifty years, and then tell people: You notice they're still complaining about the same things? They're still unhappy about the same things. They've been investing in the Democrat Party with their votes for fifty years! The Democrat Party has been promising to end discrimination, to bring about social justice, police justice, whatever justice.

They've been promising to fix economic inequalities and all that—and yet every group of people that votes for the Democrat Party is still complaining about the very things they continue to vote for the Democrat Party to fix. It is fundamentally racist and not true to say that the only chance you have if you are of a certain race or background is to vote Democrat.

In fact, voting Democrat may be the worst thing you can do in terms of achieving the American Dream, because they don't believe in the American Dream anymore, folks! The whole point of the Democrat Party is to convince you it doesn't exist, that it was only ever for a very few select number of people. It was never for everybody. It was a gigantic trick—and they're trying to get you and as many people to believe that the American Dream itself is phony and nonexistent.

Well, it's not. The American Dream is still attracting millions and millions of people from all over the world every year. Take a few moments and educate yourself. Make it a little project: Educate yourself and others on what Donald Trump's policies have actually done for minority communities and what his plans for the future are. Before the pandemic hit, African American unemployment reached an all-time low since records started being kept in the early 1970s.

African American and Hispanic and women unemployment records, all-time lows. The fact of the matter is that all Americans have an opportunity for a remarkable future, a great future no matter where you begin. It's all there waitin' for you to come grab it and take it. It's all there waiting for you to give it your best shot to grab it. Don't let people tell you "You can't." You can!

*　*　*

It doesn't matter if you come from the inner city. People who fail in life are people who find lots of excuses. It's never too late for a person to recognize that they have potential in themselves.
—Dr. Ben Carson, 17th Secretary of Department of H. U. D. and Founder of American Cornerstone Institute

*　*　*

EXPLAINING THE LEFT'S SOFT BIGOTRY OF LOW EXPECTATIONS WITH THE HELP OF SHELBY STEELE
The Rush Limbaugh Show, January 16, 2017

I mentioned Shelby Steele. I've quoted him often. He is a scholar at the Hoover Institute on the campus at Stanford. He is African American, a very brilliant man, and, very much to our benefit, a conservative. One of the most recent pieces of his that I've come across is headlined "The Perils of Political Correctness." And here's how he begins this piece: "Societies have many of the qualities individuals have. America is a particularly great society. There's been no country like this ever before in all of human history."

He's exactly right about that. But, see, that is actually one of the roots of the problem. The Democrat Party today . . .

"One of the points that I feel very strongly about," writes Mr. Steele, "coming as a Black [man], is that the deference that America has shown us since the sixties with the War on Poverty and the Great Society and welfare, these deferential policies that defer to our history of victimization now victimize us more than racism did."

Let that sink in. Let me read that again: All of the great things that American has done for African Americans "since the sixties with the War on Poverty and the Great Society and welfare, these deferential policies that defer to our history of victimization now victimize us more than racism did," and it does. It doesn't just victimize, it stigmatizes.

It's the "soft bigotry of low expectations." It's the presumption that because there is this thing that happened to African Americans two hundred years ago, it makes it today impossible for them to ever be full-fledged, because they've got so many strikes against them.

So it's the low expectations, the constant victimization, the stigmatization that they can't do anything without the help of liberals—and so we need these programs. And Mr. Steele is saying this is not helping us. This is not helping African Americans or any other minority.

It's continuing to perpetuate the idea that we're prisoners of American society in general. Not plantation owners anymore but just the country itself. And we can't escape this penalty box we're in without the help of liberals, government programs, or what have you.

RUSH ENCOURAGES AUDIENCE TO OVERCOME SELF-LIMITATIONS
The Rush Limbaugh Show, July 19, 2011

One of the reasons I'm fascinated by computers, folks, is one of the reasons I'm fascinated by high tech. It's one of the things that keeps my mind as active as I want it to be, and current and hip and what have you. It's just something I want to happen and something I want to be the case.

And in the process, if you're open to what you're learning, doors open that you sometimes didn't even know existed, and then you have to have the

• • •

Think about every problem, every challenge we face.
The solution to each starts with education.
—President George H. W. Bush, 1991

• • •

courage to walk through the door, if it indeed opens up. . . . Most of the limitations are not placed on you by others but rather by yourself. Good and bad. . . .

Once people can overcome this notion of self-limitation, then the world opens up to you and your perspective on life changes. Anything within your dreaming and imagination becomes possible. And we want people dreaming. We want little kids dreaming. We don't want school kids being corrupted with the notion that their very existence is destroying polar bears. We don't want little kids to be raised with the idea that their existence is destroying the planet, but this is what liberals do to people. . . .

Young people need to have the vistas of their dreams as wide open as possible. There's nothing wrong with anybody thinking they can do anything. How many times have you heard a highly successful person say that throughout their life everybody told 'em they couldn't do it? Common. Because it happens.

There are millions of people who tell you you can't do it. They do it for a number of reasons. Some are trying to be helpful, trying to keep you grounded in reality. Some are bitter because they have failed. I've always said if you want to succeed in radio, for example, don't go talk to failures. Don't go talk to people who are bitter about it. You know, find people who love it, find people who have succeeded at it; try to get hold of them, learn from them. Whatever it is you want to do, find the people who have succeeded; find the people who have passion for it; find the people who love it and see if you can absorb something from them.

But negativism is easy. Bitterness is easy. Comes naturally. Nobody has ever had to write a book on how to think negatively. But guys who write books on how to think positively have become multimillionaires. It takes effort, it takes discipline, particularly when you haven't had any experience yet that generates positivity. But if you stick with it, you will.

It's the great promise and the great offer of this country, why so many people are working so hard to preserve what this country's always been, because this is a country where dreams come true. People all over the world dream about coming here because this is where dreams do come true. And most dreams—not talking about fantasies here—most dreams are grounded in reality. They can happen. They don't happen overnight, and when they happen, they may not last.

DR. MARTIN LUTHER KING JR.: "BE THE BEST OF WHATEVER YOU ARE"
The Rush Limbaugh Show, August 28, 2013

RUSH: Dr. King, October 26, 1967, in Philadelphia at Barrett Junior High School.

KING: What I'm saying to you this morning, my friends: Even if it falls to your lot to be a street sweeper, go out and sweep streets like Michelangelo painted pictures! Sweep streets like Handel and Beethoven composed music. Sweep streets like Shakespeare wrote poetry. Sweep streets so well that all the host of heaven and earth will have to pause and say, "Here lived a great street sweeper who swept his job well!"

RUSH: You don't hear that, sadly, from anybody in politics anymore. You certainly don't hear that on the Democrat side, and, sadly, you don't hear this on the Republican side from very many people. . . . This is years after the "I Have a Dream" speech, which was 1963. This was five years later in Philadelphia, to some junior high school students. The school was Barrett Junior High. . . . If I may translate this, this was a man speaking to the weak. He wasn't coddling them. He's saying be as strong as you can be. Be the best you can be. He was not coddling the weak. He was not excusing them. By "weak" I mean meek, whatever. I'm not talking about weak in character. It's clear what he's talking about. There's value in every job. Work is its own reward. Do it the best you can and be known for it, because ultimately your judgment is with God.

* * *

Be a bush if you can't be a tree. If you can't be a highway, just be a trail. If you can't be a sun, be a star. For it isn't by size that you win or fail. Be the best of whatever you are. —Dr. Martin Luther King, Jr.

* * *

FORMER DEMOCRAT MAYOR FINDS RUSH, REJECTS VICTIMHOOD

The Rush Limbaugh Show, June 24, 2019

RUSH: Jim in Middletown, Pennsylvania. You're next. It's great to have you with us, sir. Hi.

CALLER: Rush, it is an absolute pleasure to talk to you. I have been a converted . . . I was a Democrat. Now I've been listening to you for the last couple years. I was elected as a Democratic mayor of Middletown, Pennsylvania. I ended up voting for Donald Trump, left the Democratic Party as quickly as possible. I am a millennial, thirty-five years old. And the reason I don't support it is it was my personal choice to further my education and become an attorney. That's what my daily job is, and I think if I made the personal choice to further my education . . .

RUSH: You mentioned that you found the program two years ago. I'm sure you had heard about the program before you found it. What caused you to show up and come over here?

CALLER: Well, you know, I just was tired of the rhetoric on the Democratic side. It's victimhood. It's all about self-preservation in government. I thought, "You know what? I really need to open my eyes here."

RUSH: I tell you, I am . . . It's so refreshing to hear that you arrived at all this on your own, especially that you figured out what victimology is.

CALLER: Yes.

RUSH: I mean, victimology is a license to fail. Victimology is an excuse to not amount to anything. Victimology is one of the most convenient cop-outs, and we have a political party [that] is pushing it on as many people as they can. And when I say that you have the built-in excuse to fail, that's exactly what being a victim is. You aren't amounting to anything. You're not getting a job. You're not getting a career. You're not getting anything done because somebody is mistreating you. You're a victim of this person or a victim of that circumstance. Once you succumb to that, once you adopt the fact that you are a victim, your life is over. You're never . . . You don't have to accomplish anything because you've just told yourself that you can't. You have just told yourself the deck is so stacked against you, you don't have a prayer, that everything's lined up against you, that all these powerful forces are aimed at you, making sure you don't succeed, so you're gonna sign up as a victim of something and let other people take care of you and get even with whoever it is that's keeping you down. It's one of the greatest concessions a human being can make in life. Now, look, there are legitimate people, legitimate victims of . . . In fact, you could make the case that we're all victimized by something, and in many cases [by] many things over the course of our lives. It's when you succumb to the idea that you are a permanent victim, you have just given up. It's exactly what that means. You have just cashed out. You have just admitted to yourself that there's nothing you can do. You can't succeed, however you define it. You probably cannot find happiness, however you define that. You have to be in pretty much a constant state of misery once you acknowledge that you are a victim. And the Democrat Party is pushing this on people because that's what they want—a nation of as many victims as possible with the Democrat Party promising to get even with all the oppressors, to get even with the people who did it to you and to take care of you at the same time. They love people becoming victims because it means people have given up on being self-reliant. It's one of the greatest mistakes a human being can make. Even people who are legitimate victims of something. A lot of people are legitimate victims of crime. A lot of people are legitimate victims of harassment, personal and otherwise. A lot of people are legitimate victims of many things. But it doesn't define you. It shouldn't. It shouldn't define the rest of your life. It also permits constant rage. It also allows you to be permanently angry. It's much easier to be angry than happy. Much easier to be negative than positive. And assuming and adopting victim status? That's your free ticket. That's your red carpet to constant misery, constant unhappiness, and a constant excuse for the sorry state that you find yourself in. So when you said you got tired of it, that made my day. That's good.

FREEDOM AND OPTIMISM, NOT COLLECTIVISM, MADE AMERICA GREAT
The Rush Limbaugh Show, May 31, 2007

Some people in this country are not so far removed from 9/11, and they know what actions need to be taken to keep us safe. Some of them have forgotten what built this country, what allowed this country to lead the world. Some of them know and resent that we lead the world. They resent how the country was built, because it's led to their misery. They don't think that they're factors. They don't think they're that important. They think that life's an excrement sandwich, and some days all they get's mayonnaise on it. So they're out there, and they want everybody else to be miserable. "We're all in this together."

My parents would not any more understand my life . . . You know what my dad was . . . ? When I got out of radio when I was twenty-nine, I figured that was about the fifth time I'd been fired. "Well, if I haven't made it playing top-forty records when I'm twenty-eight or twenty-nine, I'd better get out of it, because, you know, it's a teenage market."

So I went to work for the Royals. When I lost my last radio job, I was making something like $22,000 or $23,000 a year. I was out of work for three months. I decided what I want to do, and I was in Kansas City, and I liked living there, so a friend of mine at the Kansas City Royals said, "Why don't you come work for us? We need a group sales director." Okay, I got $12,000 a year to start at age twenty-nine. I called my dad. My dad could not have been happier. God bless him. He thought radio was a waste of time. He never forced me out of it because I quit everything else prior to that. I quit everything—except baseball, Little League baseball. But that was just vocational stuff. So he never pulled me out of radio, but they were constantly worried. "Where is playing Donnie Osmond records going to lead our son? Nowhere! What's the social relevance?"

So when I called and told him that I was joining the Kansas City Royals, ah, he was ecstatic. Twelve thousand dollars a year, and this is 1979. He said,

"Son, if you play your cards right, and you be there thirty years, you may make $50,000 and get a car, company car." His formative experience was the Great Depression and World War II, and if you didn't get a college degree (which I don't have), you didn't have a chance. That was just his world. He was trying to be a good father. He was ecstatic.

After five years I left the Royals, making $17,000 a year. I got a thousand-dollar-a-year raise every year and went back into radio, and he started getting worried all over again. But I was just pursuing my passion. The point is, my father would no more relate to my life today—he'd be thrilled by it, don't misunderstand—and I think, you know, we've always had arguments in this society about, "Well, is this the generation that's not going to do as well its parents?"

We are nowhere near that yet, but the misery index crowd would love for you to believe that that's the case. You know, over the course of my career, people have come up to me and sought advice on getting into radio, and I said, "Well, the worst thing you could do is go talk to people who have failed at it, because they'll tell you that you shouldn't do it, that the business will eat you up and spit you out. Make sure you talk to people who have succeeded at it."

It's easy to run into people who'll tell you won't be able to do something. You can find people to tell you you can't do something because many of them don't want you to if they've failed at it. It'll make 'em feel bad. You can always find negativism. You can always find pessimism. You can always find these things. But the opportunities in this country today are profoundly better, and yet people do not grasp it.

I'll tell you what made the country great. It's the "I" who make this country work.

I don't care if they're rich, middle class, third or fourth quintile. It's the people that make this country great, not government, and not government policies, and not government regulations. It is the freedom that we all acknowledge we have that allows us to pursue whatever our dreams and ambitions are, as unfettered as any people in the history of civilization have ever been.

That's what sets us apart from all other countries in the history of human civilization, and it's the liberals who are trying to look this prosperity right in the eye—which is right out in front of our faces every day—and tell us we

· · ·

You are my best friend that I have never met, as others have said. You have entertained, educated, and inspired me all these years. I pray to our Lord for you and Kathryn when I hear your voice. I pray for America, and hope you can help guide us through these troubled times ahead. —Orlando, member of the audience

· · ·

should be miserable, that it's unfair, that it's not right, that it's not going to last, and this all needs to be torn down.

LIBERALS DON'T WANT TO HAVE A REAL CONVERSATION ABOUT RACE, THEY JUST WANT TO CALL US RACISTS
The Rush Limbaugh Show, May 12, 2015

When you get down to it, the left does not want to have a conversation on race. . . . The bottom line for me is that it depresses me. You know, I'm an American. I love this country. I know what is possible in this country for everybody.

I see immigrants from various parts of the world coming into this country and just doing gangbusters. I see people natively born in this country doing gangbusters. I know it's still possible. I know that it's likely if certain steps are taken. I know that the American Dream is alive and well. It's sad that so many people have given up on it, but it's because of the way they've been conditioned. It's the way they're influenced. It's the way they're taught.

And it breaks my heart, folks, because it's so unnecessary. It's not cliché to refer to the US as a land of opportunity. Always has been, still is. There are steps one needs to take in order to access it. It just doesn't come knocking. Well, maybe once in your life it will.

You have to know to open the door when that happens, but for the most part the recipe is pretty much the same: hard work, dedication, desire, preparation, study, passion. Those things are still required, and if they're present, you can write your ticket.

AFTER TWENTY-YEAR INVESTIGATION, BLACK CONSERVATIVE CLEARS YOUR HOST OF RACISM ALLEGATIONS
The Rush Limbaugh Show, March 15, 2019

RUSH: Paul in San Antonio. Great to have you, sir. Thank you for waiting. Hello.

CALLER: Good afternoon, Rush. I am a conservative who just happens to be Black. And I wanted to personally thank you for your commentary, but more so than your commentary, I wanted to thank you for the information you provide with it, because that's what ties everything together.

RUSH: Thank you. I appreciate that, sir, very much.

CALLER: I wanted to give you a brief explanation of how I came upon this journey of being conservative, especially coming from the Black community. As you would say, at seventeen I was a young skull full of mush. I was beaten over the head and terrified that if I didn't vote for Jimmy Carter in my first election, we were basically gonna go back to slavery. Well, I did notice that after he was elected it got worse, not necessarily for Black America but just for America in general. So I chalked that one up. Then Reagan came along, and I really heard we were about to get lynched, we were about to basically go back to slavery. And that didn't happen. And I noticed that America actually got a little bit better overall. I'm like, okay, what's going on? I'm the kind of person that needs to know why. So your show came along. And at the time I heard somebody talking about how you were racist. So, much like the Mueller investigation, I embarked upon a journey to find out, to see what was going on. After twenty years, just like the Mueller investigation, I finally had to close the investigation down after finding out that you have not colluded with or have ever been a racist. You've been cleared, and I just wanted to personally let you know that.

RUSH: I love this! I love this analogy! You conducted a twenty-year investigation [that] required frequent, constant listening—

CALLER: Yes.

RUSH: Okay. So you are sitting out there, and you're fully expecting the country to go spiraling down. You've been told that Reagan is gonna bring back slavery and racism, and the exact opposite happened. So while that's happening, while America's getting better all around you, what are you thinking?

CALLER: Well, Rush, I'm the type of person, I gotta know why. So I'm always in search of facts or something to prove or disprove. And one of the theories that I have is, in this situation, minus the absence of information, it makes it easier to control people with emotion. So, since I was in search of facts, I was starting to get out of the emotional tie that I had to what I was being taught. Because every time I would listen to you, and I started looking for other sources and I'm like, okay, I'm hearing this mostly in my community and in this segment of the media, but in reality, as they used to say, here's the rest of the story. And the rest of the story is usually where all the important information was.

RUSH: Now, wait a minute. Hold on. Now, that's key. Because it wasn't just me telling people what I thought. What you heard me also offer was backup information or facts that were what they were regardless [of] what I thought?

CALLER: That's it. That is what got it.

RUSH: So you were able to rely on not just my opinion. You were able to tell, no, I'm not just telling you what he thinks, and you were able to relay information that you heard backing all that up?

CALLER: Rush, you're kind of like a treasure map. You're not actually digging up the treasure, but you gave me clues as to where to find the treasure. And the treasure would be the truth.

RUSH: You are filled with great analogies. So you had a twenty-year investigation to try to find the racism on the program, you couldn't, and then you discovered this program is a treasure map to the truth!

● ● ●

Rush Limbaugh—opening the American mind one listener at a time. We're up now to about 40 million minds opened, which still means there's a lot of room for growth. —Rush Limbaugh

● ● ●

Happy Birthday Rush. Hope your
big day is a special one.
Ronald Reagan

PART 3 — BIG GOVERNMENT IS NOT THE SOLUTION

Like you, Rush adamantly opposed the idea of big government encroaching on our individual lives. The Founding Fathers and early patriots fearlessly fought to establish a nation run for and by the people, with laws in place to limit the overreach of government. Rush would often say that history repeats itself, and every few years those who believe government is the solution come up with a new program aimed at growing the government under the guise of fixing a problem. More often than not, these types of programs, paid for by our taxes, just create dependency. Rush knew government in a limited form is necessary for a society to function; however, he was entirely against inefficiency and false rhetoric in any form. As always, he would make us laugh while tackling serious issues. "Have any of you ever been to the DMV? Well, then you know government is not exactly known for speed, efficiency, or actually getting anything done."

RUSH'S MORNING UPDATE: FAILURE OF BIG GOVERNMENT
The Rush Limbaugh Show, June 30, 2010

The Democrats tell us that Big Government is the answer. So they took over Big Auto, they took over housing and health care. Now they're in the midst of taking over banking and Big Energy. They've inserted their tentacles deeper into the private sector, despite a dismal track record. Medicaid and Medicare are bankrupt, Government Motors is billions in debt, Fannie Mae and Freddie Mac own trillions in worthless subprime home notes, and Obama can't even plug the hole in the Gulf.

On the other hand, they tell us Big Government's not the answer: Vice President Joe Bite Me says that many of the eight million jobs lost will never come back . . . though Reagan created over 20 million. Russia is ferrying our astronauts to outer space because Obama says NASA can't cut it. Last week, Obama said America cannot be counted on to be the engine of world economic growth because we can't cut it.

And this week, Big Sis Janet Napolitano said the border is "big"; sealing it before taking on immigration reform is "not an answer to the problem." So the very things the government is tasked with doing, Obama's Big Government can't do: We can't protect ourselves, we can't grow the economy. But everything the government should not be doing—screwing around in the private sector—Obama's Democrats are doing, and doing poorly. It's a total failure from a bunch of Ivy League theoreticians who talk out of both sides of their liberal mouths . . . and a couple other orifices as well.

* * *

I mean, look at the Department of Motor Vehicles. Do they care a whit about making you happy or satisfying you there? Now, imagine that when you go to the doctor under nationalized health care. —Rush Limbaugh

* * *

LIMBAUGH: I HOPE OBAMA FAILS
The Rush Limbaugh Show, January 16, 2009

I got a request here from a major American print publication. "Dear Rush: For the Obama Inauguration we are asking a handful of very prominent politicians, statesmen, scholars, businessmen, commentators, and economists to write four hundred words on their hope for the Obama presidency. We would love to include you. If you could send us four hundred words on your hope for the Obama presidency, we need it by Monday night, that would be ideal. . . ."

Look, what he's talking about is the absorption of as much of the private sector by the US government as possible, from the banking business to the mortgage industry, the automobile business to health care. I do not want the government in charge of all of these things. I don't want this to work.

So I'm thinking of replying to the guy, "Okay, I'll send you a response, but I don't need four hundred words, I need four: I hope he fails." What are you laughing at? See, here's the point: Everybody thinks it's outrageous to say. Look, even my staff, "Oh, you can't do that." Why not? Why is it any different? What's new, what is unfair about my saying I hope liberalism fails? Liberalism is our problem. Liberalism is what's gotten us dangerously close to the precipice here. Why do I want more of it? I don't care what the Drive-by story is. I would be honored if the Drive-by Media headlined me all day long: "Limbaugh: I Hope Obama Fails." Somebody's gotta say it. . . .

He is the president of the United States, he's my president, he's a human being, and his ideas and policies are what count for me, not his skin color, not his past, not whatever ties he doesn't have to being down with the struggle, all of that's irrelevant to me. We're talking about my country, the United States of America, my nieces, my nephews, your kids, your grandkids. Why in the world do we want to saddle them with more liberalism and socialism? Why would I want to do that? So I can answer it, four words: "I hope he fails." And that would be the most outrageous thing anybody in this climate could say. Shows you just how far gone we are. Well, I know, I know. I am the last man standing.

I'm happy to be the last man standing. I'm honored to be the last man standing. Yeah, I'm the true maverick.

MORE PEOPLE ON UNEMPLOYMENT BENEFITS GROWS THE DEMOCRAT PARTY
The Rush Limbaugh Show, December 6, 2010

Boy, the libs are out in full force in my email. "How dare you say that Pelosi, Reid, and Obama want people unskilled and dependent?" For crying out loud, about the only thing that's gonna grow the Democrat Party is unemployment. The only thing unemployment stimulates is the Democrat Party, pure and simple. I can't say it any plainer. I hit you right between the eyes with it. Unemployment stimulates the Democrat Party. Unemployment grows Democrat voters.

Look, everything since 1965, every Democrat welfare initiative, folks, has been to grow a bigger and bigger crop of Democrat voters who are dependent on the government. Europe has had a permanent underclass for a long time. That's why the Communist, socialist base is so tremendously strong in Europe,

● ● ●

If you put the federal government in charge of the Sahara Desert,
in five years there'd be a shortage of sand.
—Milton Friedman, recipient of the Nobel Prize for Economics

● ● ●

and has been since World War I. The whole point of these social welfare programs is to create more Democrats, because that's who these people end up depending on for what meager existence they end up with. Now, the Democrats in the United States have wanted to accomplish that here, a permanent growing underclass, and they've been working on it since 1965. And they're well on their way to accomplishing it. This is why the numbers are what they are. There's five to six, maybe ten years to stop this and turn this around.

Look at every initiative: Welfare in general, money for not working; food stamps, making it even more painless not to work, and more money for each child; aid to women with dependent children, more money for every child, a substantial amount of money per child, and a disincentive to get married. The Democrats in this country have wanted to accomplish all of that here.

They've been working on it steadily and steadily and steadily, and now they're trying to create more government dependency from the middle class with endless unemployment benefits. Nobody in their right mind, nobody daring to be honest with you would tell you that extending unemployment benefits is going to grow employment. Nobody in their right mind would tell you that unemployment benefits and their extension is stimulative to the economy, yet they do. The only way they can say this is under their breath; behind closed doors they say stimulus for our economy, meaning for our party.

Why don't we ever hear about how many jobs are going to be *lost* if the rich have to pay higher taxes? We always hear about how many jobs are created if the government does this or government does that.

You know, people who own businesses (you've heard 'em; they call here all the time) will sell their yacht and they will cut payroll. But whatever else they have to do, they will cut payroll. Now, keeping the current tax rates in place as opposed to raising taxes will do a hell of a lot more to keep this economy from slipping into a depression than the Democrats' phony stimulus bill, because it will provide some certainty and some confidence. People will be able to know, whatever the temporary nature of these tax rates is, whatever it is, they'll be able to start making some plans.

Why don't we see any polling of the business community? Ask how many employees they have had to lay off to pay their taxes. I would love to see that poll: "How many employees have you had to lay off in order to pay your state and federal taxes—workers' comp, whatever it was—every other payroll?" We get polls about everything under the sun, but why not that? "How many jobs have you eliminated at your business in order to pay taxes?" Ho-ho-ho-ho! What a poll that would be.

* * *

The best way to convince anybody of anything is to believe in it yourself, and to be able to explain it and be passionate about it.

—Rush Limbaugh

* * *

AN ADDRESS TO THE UNEMPLOYED
The Rush Limbaugh Show, January 12, 2009

I want to talk for a moment to those of you who are out of work. Can I have your attention, please? Those of you who have been fired, those of you who have been laid off—not just recently, either, but maybe in the past six months or so, but particularly to those of you laid off in the past couple or three months. I want to speak brazenly honestly with you, extremely openly with you. As you know, I'm an optimist, and I have a philosophy that guides me most of the time. Even I, strong and committed, a rock, a spine of steel, even sometimes I slip, and the negative outweighs the positive. I catch myself. One of my operating philosophies and theories is that no matter how bad something is, there's always good to be found in it. . . . The first thing that I think those of you who are out of work . . .

233

You now have, out of necessity . . . an opportunity to choose what you want to do. . . . But there are plenty of opportunities out there, and those opportunities are only going to increase over time, because, again, statistically, the odds are that this down cycle will come back, despite what government does.

So, my point here is, a job's a job. A career is a different thing. And a career has goals, objectives, short- and long-term. A career, somebody has a career vision, more than likely has a passion for what they love to do and knows what it is. So that's, to me, wherein the opportunity lies. . . . You may not like it, may wish it never happened to you, but while you're out of work anyway, and those of you remember to whom I'm addressing, you want to go back to work, figure out what it is you really love.

Figure out what it is you really want to do, and then look into how to do it and get it done. Now, it may seem like, "Oh, Rush, it's so hard." I know it is. But everything starts with the first step. I don't care who somebody was before they were somebody or something; it started with the first step. And if it is something you love, it won't really be like a job. It won't really be like a career. And you may not know what it is yet. That, again, is part of the opportunity. You have the chance to choose.

SET AMERICANS FREE, DEMOCRATS! FOLLOW THE WAL-MART EXAMPLE
The Rush Limbaugh Show, November 21, 2008

If millions of Americans are set free . . . then millions of Americans will create jobs through innovation, risk taking, and just the natural order of things. It might not be a new way forward, but we should remember one of Reagan's timeless truths: Government's not the solution; government is the problem.

See, this economic crisis was not caused by you or me or anybody else in the private sector. We're sitting here minding our own business, and these people throughout the bureaucracy—Fannie Mae, Freddie Mac, and the pressure brought to bear on banks and lending institutions on Wall Street and so forth—the public sector created this problem, and it's so damn frustrating to have people think that the very people [who] created the problem are the only ones that can "solve" it. This problem can only be solved by people in the private sector. That's known as the market. The problem we face is that the people that cause the problem don't want to get out of the way. It's the source of their power. They, as Rahm Emanuel said . . . Grab sound bite number five. We can't play this enough. This crisis is just too great to go to "waste."

EMANUEL: You never want a serious crisis to go to waste. And what I mean by that, it's an opportunity to do things that you think you could not do before.

RUSH: Stop. "[A]n opportunity to do things that you think you could not do . . ." He's not talking about you. This crisis doesn't afford you any opportunity. He's talking about agenda items of the Democrat Party. This crisis gives the Democrat Party an opportunity to do things they've always wanted to do but haven't been able to do because it was too big a leap. But now with the crisis it's easier to get health care nationalized; it's easier to raise taxes on whoever they want to raise taxes on; it's easier to get all these regulations. He's talking about himself, his party, the Democrat Party and their agenda. He's not talking about you.

MAYOR DOOMBERG'S NEXT TARGET: STYROFOAM
The Rush Limbaugh Show, February 14, 2013

RUSH: You know, in Staten Island, New York, there are still citizens of New York City living in tents—part of the aftermath of Hurricane Sandy. In light of this, the mayor of New York City, Mayor Doomberg, in Brooklyn just this afternoon at the Barclays Center delivered his final State of the City Address. And as part of his final, and I say supposedly his final, State of the City Address, he made this suggestion.

BLOOMBERG: One product that is virtually impossible to recycle and never biodegrades is something Marty [Markowitz] made fun about, but it's not just terrible for the environment, it's another thing that's terrible for the taxpayers. Styrofoam increases the cost of recycling by as much as twenty dollars per ton because it has to be removed. Something we know is environmentally destructive that is costing taxpayers money, and that is easily replaceable, I think is something we can do without.

AUDIENCE: *[Applause]*

RUSH: That was applauded? Styrofoam? So let's think how many ways that you could get how many years in jail in New York City or how much money you could be fined. You get caught with a Big Gulp full of sugar, soft drink. That's a fine. If you are caught eating salt and trans fats in your food, a problem. If you sell food with too much salt and trans fats, the Board of Health can come in and shut you down. And if you put your sugary soft drink larger than sixteen ounces and whatever food item with salt and trans fats in a Styrofoam container, you might go to jail in New York City.

Now, Reuters has the print version of the story, and they say at the bottom of their article, they mention in passing, "The plan is likely to meet opposition from small businesses, since alternatives to Styrofoam tend to cost between two and five times as much." So? Isn't big business and small business getting away with murder already? It ought to cost 'em two to five times as much. Styrofoam is a problem in New York City!

● ● ●

I hate to break it to you, folks, but it's very tough out there to compete with Santa Claus. There are a lot of people who will gladly accept free stuff. Little do they know it's not exactly free!

—Rush Limbaugh

● ● ●

IN A NATION OF CHILDREN, SANTA CLAUS WINS
The Rush Limbaugh Show, November 7, 2012

Hey, any of you guys in there want to come sit in my chair today? Anybody? Nobody wants to come sit in my chair here? None of you? I mean, I'm giving you a golden opportunity to speak to, what, 50 million people.

I can handle it. Okay, all right. So nobody wants to come sit in my chair today. Greetings, my friends.

But first, let me tell you, small things beat big things yesterday. Conservatism, in my humble opinion, did not lose last night. It's just very difficult to beat Santa Claus. It is practically impossible to beat Santa Claus. People are not going to vote against Santa Claus, especially if the alternative is being your own Santa Claus. The old standby: American route to success, hard work. That gets sneered at. I'm sorry. In a country of children where the option is Santa Claus or work, what wins?

We're outnumbered. One of the greatest misunderstandings in this country, if you boil all this down, is what creates prosperity. The traditional American view and history—vision, as well—of what creates prosperity. The old capitalism, the old arguments of hard work, stick-to-itiveness, self-reliance, charity, helping out in the community.

All of these things that define the traditional institutions that made this country great were rejected. That way, or that route to prosperity was sneered at. That route to prosperity was rejected. The people who voted for Obama don't believe in it. They don't think it's possible. They think the game's rigged. They think the deck is stacked against them.

They think that the only way they're gonna have a chance for anything is if somebody comes along and takes from somebody else and gives it to them. Santa Claus! And it's hard to beat Santa Claus. Especially it's hard to beat Santa Claus when the alternative is "You be your own Santa Claus." "Oh, no! I'm not doing that. What do you mean, I have to be my own Santa Claus? No, no. No, no, no. I want to get up every day and go to the tree. You're the elves," meaning us.

＊ ＊ ＊

I am the Doctor of Democracy, America's
Real Anchorman. —Rush Limbaugh

＊ ＊ ＊

237

Rush had the time of his life tweaking the media while making us all laugh. When asked about his favorite parodies of all time, he replied, "Well, there were many great ones. Barack O'Claus was pretty good, you gotta admit."

FROM THE GREATEST PARODIES HITS ROSTER . . .

BARACK O'CLAUS IS COMIN' TO TOWN

Barack O'Claus is comin' to town
You better not work, you better not try
Get your hand out, I'm telling you why
Barack O'Claus is comin' to town
If you're a success, I'm taxing you twice
Gonna reverse who's naughty and nice
Barack O'Claus is comin' to town
I'll pay you just for sleepin'
Don't work, stay home and play
You will care if you're bad or good,
'cause if you're bad you get more cake.

First broadcast in 2012
Paul Shanklin for *The Rush Limbaugh Show*

HOW RUSH LEARNED SELF-RELIANCE
The Rush Limbaugh Show, July 8, 2008

During the break here I'm thinking about the call from Rafael in Charlotte, North Carolina. I want to make sure I heard this right, you guys. He said that he learned self-reliance from this program, that his father did not teach him self-reliance, is that right?

That's what I thought, and I was thinking about that during the break, and I have to admit, I was kind of blown away by that. I think our most recent show on slackers in America was like five years ago, the theory that 5 percent of the population is pulling the cart and 95 percent of the population's in the cart demanding to be pulled, and never thanking the 5 percent who are pulling it.

We've done shows on this. To me, the whole concept of self-reliance—I guess I learned it from my parents, the way I was raised and so forth. It seems as natural as breathing. And I am always stunned when I hear people say that it is a new concept that they had to learn and that only when exposed to its explanation did it make sense to them. And I asked myself, "How can this be?" In this country, how can this be? One of the things that we often then realize, self-reliance is impugned.

Liberals, the Drive-by Media, attack people who are self-reliant as though it's not fair that they are and therefore they need to share and be punished for their achievements. So the whole concept of not being self-reliant is pushed by the American left with aid and abetment from the Drive-by Media. Of course, the less self-reliant you are, the more what you are? Dependent. And upon whom?

Well, many people have been trained to be dependent on government. A lot of people view the concept of being American as being entitled. So still, though, self-reliance seems something natural to me: do it yourself, take care of yourself. The idea that my wants, my needs are the responsibility of others is foreign to me, but yet that's another great thing about Rafael's call: It was a wake-up that there's still a lot of people to be taught or reached or what have you.

* * *

Conservatism vests in and depends on the widespread, informed understanding of human nature, self-governance, and the First Principle of Progress: free people interacting in free markets produce the greatest good for the greatest number always, but only, when tethered to virtue and morality. —Mary Matalin, Former Senior White House Official and Political Advisor

* * *

DEMOCRATS CELEBRATE FIFTY YEARS OF DEFEAT IN THE WAR ON POVERTY

The Rush Limbaugh Show, January 8, 2014

Today it's the fiftieth anniversary of the War on Poverty. Did you know that? So today we're celebrating fifty years of defeat in the War on Poverty. But it's a valiant effort that we continue to make, fifty years of defeat in the War on Poverty.

Robert Rector, Heritage Foundation, the expert on the War on Poverty. Here's the number. We have spent $20.7 trillion on means-tested aid since 1964. In other words, we have redistributed $20.7 trillion trying to wipe out poverty, and the poverty rate is pretty much exactly where it was in the mid-sixties, 14 percent.

We haven't changed anything. As a percentage, there are as many people in poverty today as when this whole War on Poverty started. It's an abject failure. It's been an absolute disaster.

But we're not supposed to look at that. We're supposed look at the intentions of those who started the War on Poverty. We are to be moved by "At least they tried. At least they tried. You didn't even want to do anything for 'em," is how the refrain goes. In every Big Government attempt to cure a social or economic problem that is structurally societal, a dismal failure.

In that vein, these people are victims of an unfair, immoral, unjust country that is controlled by the rich, who will not share any that they are stealing from everybody else. You can take all you want, but entrepreneurs, producers, hard workers are gonna go do what it takes to get it back. Everybody's differ-ent. There are different ambitions, levels of ambition, desire, education, overall intelligence, ability.

Yet the Democrats want to make everybody the same, particularly when it comes to outcomes. It's not possible. So everything's done under the rubric of fixing the inequality that exists—and that's what sucks in a bunch of young people, by the way. That, to them, is the essence of compassion: Every-body being equal. Nobody should be denied. There should be "equality"; [it's] a magic word when they're young, idealistic, and so forth.

The Democrat Party claims to want to help people. What they actually do is grow government. What they're really interested in is expanding government, not helping people. Conservatives literally, factually want to help people.

❋ ❋ ❋

Rush, congratulations on twenty years of the most informative and entertaining broadcasting in the history of radio. You are like a brother to me, a mentor, role model, a true patriot. I don't know what the country would do without you. I do know that conservatives would be lonely and leaderless without you. You educate us, you inspire us, and you make us laugh. You're an extremely generous man in ways that others don't know, but I know I speak for millions in saying, "Thanks for everything, and don't leave us." And, by the way, if you play your cards right, maybe I'll nominate you for the Nobel Peace Prize again next year. God bless. —Mark Levin, phone call into show on the twentieth anniversary

❋ ❋ ❋

PART 4 — A LOOK BACK ON RUSH'S INFLUENCE: "MAJORITY MAKER"

Rush will forever be a national treasure and an unwavering American patriot. He was undeniably a hero in our country's history, making a significant positive impact on the political landscape and in the lives of so many.

RUSH LIMBAUGH SALUTED AS A "MAJORITY MAKER"
Kevin Merida, *The Washington Post*, December 11, 1994

House Republican newcomers made Rush Limbaugh an honorary class member tonight, a symbol of their gratitude. . . . Limbaugh was presented a "Majority Makers" pin, the emblem of the newcomers who have given their party majority status in the House for the first time in forty years. For some of the GOP freshmen-elect, Limbaugh is a symbol of their birth into politics and a reminder of their victories.

RUSH LIMBAUGH'S ADDRESS TO INCOMING HOUSE GOP FRESHMEN
December 10, 1994, Baltimore, Maryland

Thank you all very much. Thank you. Thank you. Thank you very much. They asked me to keep it short because there's a lot going on, so: Don't screw up. Thank you very much for having me. It's been a pleasure.

Now, I'm overwhelmed. I really am. And you've taken me off my game here with these platitudes and introductions. I was just sitting here in my seat and some reporters from newspapers who have early deadlines came up and started asking me some questions. And among those questions was, "So you really think you're responsible for all this, don't ya?"

I said, "No, no, I really don't."

"Well, what do you want? What role do you think talk radio played?"

I said, "No, look, you people in the press have got to understand something. This country is conservative. It has been for a long time. Get used to it. You tried to change it and you failed, and tonight proves it."

I don't mean to be confrontational here. I really don't. But, my friends, I've gotta speak openly and honestly about this. To all of you in this room, the freshmen class of 1994—for me to sit here and actually think I had some serious, profound role in it—you are the ones who took the risks. You are the ones who ran for office. You are the ones who raised the money. You're the ones who took the flak. You're the ones who took the heat.

I'm just a media guy who happens—and this is a key, and I think all of you should never forget this, because these reporters who were asking me questions about talk radio were all trying to say in a roundabout way that I took a bunch of brainless people and converted them to mind-numbed robots, and every day would send out code in my show that would force them to march to the polls on November the eighth and pull the lever I wanted them to pull. And the fact of the matter is that's not what's happened.

There may be some talk show hosts who do that—and there may be some talk shows; I don't think they're the majority. I think that the reason you're sitting here tonight and liberals aren't is that you understand that the American people are intelligent; they are aware; they care; and they know what's going on, and they are not a bunch of mind-numbed robots. They may have been at one time and have awakened from it now.

And what happens on talk radio is real simple: We validate what's in people's hearts and minds already. These people are living their lives conservatively. They care about what happens to their kids. They care about their own futures. To think that I came along and got people concerned about those things for the first time in their lives is ludicrous; and I mean this from the bottom of my heart. You guys are the ones—and I mean that generically—I'm in awe of you. You people, you took the risks. You are the ones who engaged the opposition—for whatever reasons you were motivated to do so. (Those are individual, and maybe some people had roles in it.) But you actually went out and did the work.

Rush with newly elected US Republican senator Fred Thompson celebrating the big win, 1994.

● ● ●

*Rush may be the most consequential person in political life at
the moment. He is changing the terms of debate. He is doing to
the culture what Ronald Reagan did to the political movement.*

—William Bennett, former Secretary of Education, 1993

● ● ●

THE REAL LESSONS OF 1994
The Rush Limbaugh Show, October 19, 2010

The lesson of 1994 is not the government shutdown. For crying out loud,
these analogies amuse me. Here's the lesson of 1994, and I'll tell you exactly
what it was, and I said this over and over again. The biggest mistake that was
made after 1994 was that Newt and the boys believed that the country had
gone conservative, and they stopped teaching. They removed all ideology
from what they did. When it came time to balance the budget or implement
any new legislation, they didn't say, "And this is because of X, Y, and Z, conservatism, what we believe." They just did it, assuming that people knew.
That assumption should never be made. The reasons for doing things must
always be explained. It's in the Constitution. It's in the best interests of the
people. We care about people. We care about the country. We need to fix
what's wrong. That's the biggest lesson of 1994.

We quit. We quit educating. And we quit fighting, essentially. There was
something else that happened in 1994, and this is key, too. I was made an
honorary member of the freshman class of 1994, and I went to their freshman orientation at Camden Yards. I went there 'cause they asked me to stand
up there and speak to them. And I said, "Do not think the media is happy
you're here. Do not expect Cokie Roberts to come bat her big eyelashes at
you and say, 'Let's go to lunch.' Cokie Roberts and the rest of the media are
agitated that you are here. They're not gonna treat you like the ruling-class
Democrats. They're gonna treat you as though you're not the majority. You're
interlopers. They have no interest in dealing with you [with] a form of
respect." I remember making that statement as plain as day, and I warned

*   *   *

*Without Rush, I doubt if we would have won control of the House
in 1994, because he clarified the issues. He gave our candidates
arguments to run on. He created a huge number of people—his
impact was more than the 20 million listeners a week, it was all of
the people they would go talk to. My guess is that the ripple effect of
Rush was 80–90 million people every single week, because people
would go out and say, "Did you hear what Rush said today?"*

—Newt Gingrich, fiftieth Speaker of the US House of Representatives

*   *   *

September 6, 1993   49145 $2.95

Child
Abuse: The
New Witchhunts?

Wm. F. Buckley Jr. on the Clinton Falsifications

NATIONAL REVIEW

THE

LEADER

OF THE

OPPOSITION

James Bowman on Rush Limbaugh

them that the idea that they were going to be the majority and have automatic respect as a result of that—not going to happen.

There's a third lesson. For forty years Republicans had been losers. For forty years Republicans had been in the minority, and then one day they weren't. There was nobody on the Republican side who knew what it was like to be in the majority. I've drawn the analogy—those of you who have had weight problems over the course of your life know exactly what I'm talking about: You lose a lot of weight but you still stop at every mirror to make sure it's still gone. Every storefront, every piece of glass, you still look, you turn sideways. "Am I gaining it back?" You still are thinking fat. You still think you gotta turn a different way to get through a turnstile when you don't anymore. You become accustomed to being what you are, and all of a sudden, when you're now the majority and leading and you have no experience at it, what do you do?

AN EIB HISTORY LESSON ON 1994
The Rush Limbaugh Show, March 11, 2009

RUSH: Here is Tom in Manhattan, Kansas. Thank you for waiting, sir, and hello.

CALLER: Hello, Rush. It's an honor to talk to you, sir.

RUSH: Yeah.

CALLER: Rush, I grew up in the nineties and my parents were singing your praises all—because of your effect on the '94 elections, and I was, you know, kind of praying that I hope we see something similar in 2010. I was only seven when Clinton, you know, his administration began. So I was just wondering if you could maybe talk about some of the similarities and differences you've been seeing between the beginning of the Clinton administration and now.

RUSH: Oh, hell, yes. Damn right. It's an excellent question. That is a hell of a good question! I applaud you. You're twenty-three years old, right?

CALLER: Yes.

RUSH: Oh, this is a great question. I can tell you right now what the big difference is. Starting in 1988, when I started this program, through 1989, there were two huge scandals in the House of Representatives. The big one was the

House Bank Scandal. Do you remember that, by any chance, or did your parents tell you about it?

CALLER: I heard about it, but I don't really know the story.

RUSH: Here's basically what it was. The House of Representatives at the time had its own bank for members, and their paychecks were automatically deposited there. But it really didn't matter what they were paid. They were allowed to write checks for money they didn't have. Some of these people were overdrawn hundreds and hundreds of thousands of dollars, with no attempt ever to recoup it. If they needed to spend $50,000 on something, they just wrote a check. The House Bank covered it. This blew up, because everybody could understand this. Nobody else can go to their bank and write a check for money that they don't have. The second scandal that was discovered shortly thereafter was the House Post Office Scandal. That is where members would take a check from a constituent, a campaign contribution check or whatever, and go into the post office and buy a dollar's worth of stamps and get $50,000 in change. I mean, that's a bit of an exaggeration, but the House Post Office and the House Bank were personal piggy banks. That blew up. Then while all this was going on, there was an agitator in the House of Representatives who was trying everything he could to take out the leadership—Jim Wright, Thomas Foley, you name it. His name was "Newt" Gingrich. Newt Gingrich was leading the Reagan Revolution in the House of Representatives. He was contrasting, starkly so, the views of Reagan conservatism with the liberalism of then, which is identical to the liberalism of today. The liberalism of today is no different than the liberalism Newt was fighting then. It's identical: abuse of power; wanton spending; doing everything they could to tax the rich and limit individual liberty and opportunity. And Newt was having none of it. Because of the scandals and because of the emergence of this show that provided a national media platform to focus attention on the Democrats and their scandals and their corruption—combined with what Newt was doing, after years and years of doing this—finally the American people were fed up with forty years of one-party rule in the House and decided that they [wanted] change. They wanted some change, and Newt and the boys (with the help of a couple consultants) came up with a Contract with America that had ten understandable items in it.

"Here's what we're going to do when we get into power"—such things as term limits, balance the budget, and so forth—and the third thing they did, they went to all of these House of Representatives districts that Democrats had all over the country and they nationalized those elections. Rather than [make] the elections about who brought home the most pork or who built the newest old folks' home, they instead talked about the danger this Democrat had been to American foreign policy, with the Soviet menace racing and so forth in Central America—and that combination of things won. But it was primarily that there was an army of conservative Republicans in the House hell-bent on throwing the Democrats out. That's what does not exist today, and the leader of that revolution somehow doesn't see liberalism today as he saw it then.

MR. BIG OF THE "VAST RIGHT-WING CONSPIRACY"

Rush kept a white coffee cup on his desk in the library for years that said "Right-Wing Conspiracy!" with his signature printed in gold. Shortly after the Drudge Report broke the news of Bill Clinton's affair with White House intern Monica Lewinsky on January 17, 1998, Hillary Clinton was interviewed by Matt Lauer on the *Today* show. She implied that the reports of infidelity were being manufactured by the political right to discredit her husband. "I do believe that this is a battle," she said. "The great story here for anybody willing to find it and write about it and explain it is this vast right-wing conspiracy that has been conspiring against my husband since the day he announced for president."

On January 26, 1998, President Bill Clinton stated forcefully that he did not "have sexual relations with that woman . . . these allegations are false." In August 1998, Bill Clinton admitted to having an "inappropriate relationship" with Lewinsky. Based on the accusation that he was behind the efforts by conservatives to discredit the president, Rush proudly called himself "Mr. Big of the Vast Right-Wing Conspiracy."

• • •

Mary Matalin, I hate to correct you, but Hillary is not the "Energizer Bunny"; it's Bill Clinton who took the licking and kept on ticking. —Rush Limbaugh

• • •

RUSH LIMBAUGH, AN EXCEPTIONAL CAREER

The list of incredible accomplishments achieved in Rush's life is extensive. Below are just a few.

- Presidential Medal of Freedom recipient, 2020

- Inaugural recipient of the Titan of Conservatism Award, The Heritage Foundation, 2020

- Marconi Award for Syndicated Radio Personality of the Year, National Association of Broadcasters, 1992, 1995, 2000, 2005, 2014

- Children's Choice Author of the Year Award for *Rush Revere and the Brave Pilgrims*, 2014

- #1 *New York Times* bestselling Adventures of Rush Revere series, including *Rush Revere and the Brave Pilgrims*, *The First Patriots*, *The American Revolution*, *The Star-Spangled Banner*, and *The Presidency*, 2013–2016

- Hall of Famous Missourians inductee, 2012

- Named to *Forbes* magazine's list of 50 Most Powerful Celebrities in the United States, 2010+

- Named to *Time* magazine's list of 100 Most Influential People in the World, 2009

- CPAC Defender of the Constitution Award, 2009

- Named one of Barbara Walters's 10 Most Fascinating People, 2009

- Named one of the Giving Back Fund's 10 Most Generous Celebrities, 2008

- Named Human Events Man of the Year, 2007

■ William F. Buckley Jr. Award for Media Excellence, Media Research
Center, 2007

■ Claremont Institute Statesmanship Award, 2004

■ National Association of Broadcasters Hall of Fame inductee, 1998

■ Named an honorary member of the Republican freshman class in
the House of Representatives, 1994

■ Radio Hall of Fame inductee, 1993

- #1 *New York Times* bestselling author of *The Way Things Ought to Be* (1992) and *See, I Told You So* (1994), which have collectively sold more than 10 million copies

- Author of the *Limbaugh Letter*, the most widely read political newsletter in the country, first published in 1989

- Featured on numerous national and international broadcasts, including *60 Minutes*, *20/20*, *Nightline with Ted Koppel*, *Crossfire*, *Good Morning America*, *CBS This Morning*, the *Today* show, *The Phil Donahue Show*, *The Late Show with David Letterman*, *The Tonight Show*, *This Week* with David Brinkley, *Meet the Press* with Tim Russert, *The Drew Carey Show*, *Family Guy*, *Hearts Afire*, and various programs on Fox News

- Featured in numerous national and international publications, including *U.S. News & World Report*, *Newsweek*, *National Review*, *Time*, *The New York Times Magazine*, *USA Weekend*, *The Washington Times*, and *The Washington Post*

* * *

Rush loved life. And he was, as everybody has said, the most generous man I ever met. When I was the Regent at Mount Vernon in 2007, he was sitting on my right on the Piazza, talking. We were all talking about the great George Washington. And he leaned across with his left hand, and he said, "Gayse, look!" And I said, "What's that?" He said, "It's an iPhone. It's the first Apple iPhone." And then, all of a sudden, while people were talking, he said to me, "Look!" And he zoomed in on our house on North Ocean Boulevard, and his house, just two houses over. I had never seen anything like it. Soon he gave me one. And from that day on, every new iPhone that came out, Rush gave me one. And I know he did that to thousands.

—Gay Gaines, eighteenth Regent, Mount Vernon Ladies' Association

* * *

OPEN LINE FRIDAY: WHY I'M AN APPLE GUY
The Rush Limbaugh Show, February 1, 2019

RUSH: Here is Brian in Minneapolis as we head back to the phones on Open Line Friday. Glad you called. Hi.

CALLER: Hi, Rush. I was wondering if we could switch a little gears here and talk about tech.

RUSH: Sure!

CALLER: Why don't you ever talk about Android? Why are you an Apple guy?

RUSH: Well, I learned on Mac. I learned computers on Mac, and then I just gravitated to everything else Apple because of the ecosystem, and I've never been curious other than to . . . There's never been . . . Apple has yet to disappoint me. It's something else, too. You're gonna find this strange, maybe. The fact that you go buy an Android phone and you're not gonna have that operating system upgraded for years. Android just doesn't upgrade. I am so addicted to operating system upgrades featuring additions, new capabilities on the phone that Android just doesn't offer, unless you go out and buy a new phone by a different vendor. It's such a fractured operating system that I don't think I could ever get comfortable with it.

CALLER: I would love to hear a review from you after doing a week on a Pixel, which does get updates instantly. A good tech review by Rush on Android operating system using a Pixel phone for a week. If we can make this happen, I would be more than willing to purchase it for you and send it to you.

RUSH: Well, that's awfully nice. You're talking about the Pixel 3?

CALLER: Yeah.

RUSH: This is the one with the great new camera tech that basically you take a picture in the dark and it looks like it's broad daylight?

CALLER: Yeah. I mean, one of your big concerns with Android was that you just said that it doesn't get operating system updates instantly. Now, that would be true for, like, Samsung or LG or Motorola. However, Pixel is Google's operating system, and—

RUSH: Yeah, it is.

CALLER: —Google—

RUSH: And Google is getting ready to abandon . . . Well, they're not gonna abandon Android, but they're coming out with something. What is it, Google Q or some such thing?

CALLER: Yeah, it's still a ways away.

RUSH: Anyway, here's a problem. I look at the . . . I'd be happy to do a review, but I look at the sales of the Pixel 3, and I don't mean to be insulting here. I'm just looking at the market. I'm not trying to talk you out of what you love, but nobody's buying them, compared to other phones. Now, that may have more to do with marketing and other things. But I've never been disappointed enough with what I've got to want to try something else, is the basic answer to your question.

* * *

There are a couple of other things that I want to add in answering the previous caller's question, "Why not Android over Apple?" The vast number of reasons are totally due to Apple and not much to do with Android. I actively love my Apple devices. I am immersed fully in the Apple ecosystem. I have no desire to leave it. There is . . . For example, I don't use the phone much because of my hearing. My primary communication tool in life is iMessage. It's not on Android. Apple has not ported it to Android, and they probably will not. . . . The Apple ecosystem, in terms of marketing and construction, it's brilliant the way it's been put together and the way it does ensnare people like me. I know what they've done, and I don't care. I know exactly how they've snared me. I know they don't like me politically. But I don't care. Using their stuff is fun and productive at the same time. So that's the full-fledged answer.

● ● ●

I gotta hurry out of here, folks. It's Apple beta day!

—Rush Limbaugh

● ● ●

257

RUSH GIVES APPLE IOS 14 TUTORIAL
The Rush Limbaugh Show, September 17, 2020

Oh, Snerdley, did you install iOS 14? Have you gotten around to it yet? You have? You wanted to ask me . . . *[Laughs]* If there are, or are there? No, no. There aren't any, no, there are no problems with the install. It's clean. There's no bugs in it. It's actually one of the cleanest releases that they've had in a long time. I knew what was gonna happen. The changes that have been made, say in the widget area, you can't just tell people verbally how to do it.

I have been recording instructional videos on my phone to show people what all can be done with the widgets now and how to do it, 'cause you can't, if you wanted to text them or send them an email, you'd be writing thousands of words, and you'd still need to take screenshots and pictures. Once you've taught them how to do it, it's rather simple, but it is that first step of the learning curve. So that's why I turned on the "do not disturb" yesterday.

I didn't want to get hassled by anybody, 'cause I'm the go-to guy in my *familia* and in my group of friends. Whenever anybody has a tech question, I'm the one they call, so I turned on "do not disturb" last night so I wouldn't be bugged by it.

So I just wanted . . . I thought about putting some of the videos on the website, but they're on my phone. I mean, bye-bye, privacy. See, that's the thing. You people would not believe how my life has been so severely limited because I'm too famous.

And so, yeah, I would love these videos, they would be great instructional videos to put on the website to show people how to do this. But it's my phone that I use. It's my homepage. I didn't stop to think to do this on a dummy phone. I don't have a dummy phone anyway. Every phone I use has got a purpose.

* * *

The Stick-to-the-Issues Crowd is very, very oriented toward sticking to the issues. Like, if I had spent some time today talking about the US Open, which starts today, started today, it's under way at Winged Foot, I'm sure I would have been ripped a new one.

Chapter 5

THE AMERICAN PEOPLE

TRIBUTE
by Vice President Mike Pence

Rush inspired generations of American patriots. He opened the minds of men and women, young and old, of every race and color and creed, with his wit and his wisdom and his boundless energy.

Rush made us think. Rush made us laugh. And he made us proud of our heritage of freedom. But most of all, he made us believe in our country, in our values, and in each other, and in the boundless potential of every American to live the American dream, just like he did. As long as Rush Limbaugh was on the air, every day was morning in America....

You know, I hardly believe that I would have had the opportunities I've had—to serve in Congress, to serve the people of Indiana as governor, or to be your vice president—without the life, the example, the encouragement, and the friendship of Rush Limbaugh, and I'll always be grateful.

Rush Limbaugh was a force of nature, but he was also a genuinely good man who had a heart for our country, and for the American people. He was never afraid to stand up for our most cherished values, and he gave millions of Americans the same courage to stand firm for life and liberty, and our timeless American ideals.

PART 1 — CAPITALISM, NOT SOCIALISM

During the holidays, Rush loved to burn pine-scented candles throughout the house, with the smell wafting into every room. As we put gifts together, we often played his favorite Christmas songs on the sound system overhead, including Mannheim Steamroller's "Silent Night." Every year, Rush was extraordinarily generous with bonuses for his radio staff and everyone who worked with us. He genuinely appreciated sharing with the people in his life, and with many whom he'd never met. This past November, we surprised Rush by lighting as many of the large palm trees around the estate as we could.

When Rush got home from the studio, he saw the red and white lights illuminating the yard for the first time. He was overcome with emotion and said, "This is a winter wonderland." Rush considered himself to be truly blessed in every way and thanked God for everything in his life, including you.

One of Rush's favorite annual traditions was telling the "True Story of Thanksgiving." In addition to marking this special time of year when we gather to give thanks, Rush thought the leader of the Pilgrims, Governor William Bradford, illustrated the difference between capitalism and socialism with a brilliant experiment.

THE TRUE STORY OF THANKSGIVING
The Rush Limbaugh Show, November 24, 2020

RUSH: Here's the version you were probably taught: The Pilgrims arrived here after an arduous trip across the Atlantic Ocean. They didn't know where they were, had no idea what to do. They had nothing. The Indians took pity on them. The Indians saw them, and the Indians saved them. The Indians taught 'em how to do things they didn't know how to do, like grow food, catch beavers, stuff like that. . . . That's where it ends. And that's the feel-good story. But that doesn't even get close to the true story. . . .

Now, here's the part that has been omitted. The original contract the Pilgrims entered into in Holland—they had sponsors. They didn't have the money to do this trip on their own. They had sponsors. There were merchant sponsors in London and in Holland. And these merchant sponsors demanded that everything that the Pilgrims produced in the New World would go into a common store, a single bank, if you will. And that each member of the Pilgrim community was entitled to one share.

So everybody had an equal share of whatever was in that bank. All of the land they cleared, all of the houses they built belonged to that bank, to the community as well. And they were going to distribute it equally, because they were gonna be fair. So all of the land that they cleared and all the houses they built belonged to everybody. Belonged to the community. Belonged to the bank, belonged to the common store. Nobody owned anything. They just had an equal share in it. It was a commune.

The Pilgrims established a commune, essentially. Forerunner of the communes we saw in the sixties and seventies out in California. They even had their own organic vegetables, by the way. Yep. The Pilgrims, forerunners of organic vegetables. Of course, what else could there be? No such thing as processed anything back then.

Now, William Bradford, who had become the governor of the colony 'cause he was the leader, recognized that this wasn't gonna work. This was costly and destructive, and it just wasn't working. It was collectivism. It was socialism. It wasn't working. That first winter had taken a lot of lives. The manpower was greatly reduced. So William Bradford decided to take bold action, which I will describe when we get back.

★　★　★

William Bradford, the governor of the Pilgrim community, saw that none of this was working. The Mayflower Compact was not working. Giving everybody a single share of stock in the common store, in the common bank, was not working. Collectivism. It was as costly and destructive to the Pilgrims as it is and has been to anybody who has ever tried it.

266

So Bradford decided to scrub it. He threw it out and took bold action. He assigned a plot of land to each family. Every family was given a plot of land. They could work it, manage it however they wanted to. If they just wanted to sit on it, get fat, dumb, happy, and lazy, they could. If they wanted to develop it, if they wanted to grow corn, whatever, on it, they could. If they wanted to build on it, they could do that. If they wanted to turn it into a quasi-business, they could do whatever they wanted to do with it.

He turned loose the power of the capitalist marketplace. Long before Karl Marx was even born. Long before Karl Marx was a sperm cell in his father's dreams, the Pilgrims had discovered and experimented with what could only be described as socialism, and they found that it didn't work. Now, it wasn't called that then. But that's exactly what it was. Everybody was given an equal share. You know what happened? Nobody did anything. There was no incentive. Nothing worked. Nothing happened.

What Bradford and his community found was that the most creative and industrious people had no incentive to work any harder than anyone else, unless they could utilize the power of personal motivation! But while most of the rest of the world has been experimenting with socialism for well over a hundred years—trying to refine it, perfect it, and reinvent it—the Pilgrims decided early on to scrap it permanently. What Bradford wrote about this social experiment should be in every schoolchild's history lesson. If it were, we might prevent much needless suffering, if the true story of Thanksgiving had been taught for years and years and years.

* * *

So, William Bradford, after putting everybody in a common store, the Mayflower Compact . . . They wanted to be fair. They wanted everybody to have one common share of stock in everything that happened that the Pilgrims produced—and it bombed. It didn't work.

There was no prosperity; there was no creativity, because there was no incentive. Here's what Bradford wrote about the failure: "For this community [so far as it was] was found to breed much confusion and discontent . . ." They were not happy, in other words. "[T]his community was found to breed much confusion and discontent and retard much employment that would have been to their benefit and comfort."

In other words, nobody worked.

The way they set it up killed and discouraged work.

There was no need.

"For young men that were most able and fit for labor and service" sat around and did nothing. "[T]hey should spend their time and strength to work for other men's wives and children without" being paid for it? Why should they do that? So they didn't. "[T]hat was thought injustice." Why should you work for other people when you can't work for yourself? What's the point? Do you hear what he was saying, ladies and gentlemen?

"The Pilgrims found that people could not be expected to do their best work without incentive. So, what did Bradford's community try next? They unharnessed the power of good old free enterprise by invoking" capitalism, "the principle of private property," all the way back in the 1600s. It was incredible. "Every family was assigned its own plot of land," and they could do with it whatever they wanted to do.

"This had very good success," wrote Bradford, "for it made all hands industrious, so as much more corn was planted than otherwise would have been." So when profit was introduced, when the opportunity to prosper was introduced, it went gangbusters. That, my friends, is the essence of the True Story of Thanksgiving. Now, this is where it gets really good, folks, if you're laboring under the misconception that I was, as I was taught in school.

"So they set up trading posts and exchanged goods with the Indians" after they had enjoyed this prosperity. It was not the Indians that brought them to prosperity. It's not said to insult anybody. The Indians assisted in their arrival, undeniably. But what led to prosperity for these original settlers was [when] the common store failed. Socialism didn't work.

It's when they introduced what turns out to be capitalism. They didn't have the name for it, but when they turned loose individual incentive—keep what you produce, sell what you don't need—it went crazy. This is not something they were taught by anybody by self-experience. It was not the Indians. None of this is said to put anybody down. Don't misunderstand.

The Indians did a lot of things that helped them, which I'll get to in just a second, but it was their own industriousness. "[T]hey set up trading posts and exchanged goods with the Indians." They sold stuff to them, and those

I used to think I was a pretty famous person. I'm not a famous person compared to Rush. I'm that guy, I'm the nerd that works in the upstairs office right now; he's the superstar on the field. Nicest, most generous man you could ever meet. —George Brett, Hall of Fame baseball player, Kansas City Royals, 2021

"profits allowed them to pay off their debts to the merchants," their sponsors in London and in Holland, and you know what? The success of that colony after they had abandoned socialism and tried what was essentially capitalism, the word spread throughout the Old World of this massive amount of prosperity that was there for the taking in the New World. And guess what happened? The New World was flooded with new arrivals. "[T]he success and prosperity of the Plymouth settlement attracted more Europeans and began what came to be known as the 'Great Puritan Migration.'"

And all it took was prosperity and the word spreading across the Atlantic Ocean of how there was prosperity and it was there for the taking. All you had to do was get there and give it a shot. The lesson is—the True Story of Thanksgiving is—that William Bradford and his Pilgrim community were thanking God for the blessings on their community after the first miserable winter of a documented failure brought on by their attempt at fairness and equality, which was socialism.

It didn't work.

"One of the most important legacies of early settlers is that they experimented with socialism in the 1620s, and it didn't work. Private property rights and personal responsibility, two pillars of a free-market economy, saved the Plymouth Colony from extinction and laid the economic foundation for [the] free and prosperous nation that we all enjoy today."

MY DEFINITION OF CAPITALISM
The Rush Limbaugh Show, November 3, 2020

So, I got an email: "Rush, could you say something besides 'capitalism'? You have to understand, people have been trained to hate the word. People have been trained to oppose the word. They don't even know what it means."

That's a fair point. Here's what it is: We want an economic arrangement. We want a country. We want a society. We want a place where people provide what other people need and want as efficiently as possible and are rewarded for how well they do it—meaning innovators invent products, they create new services, what have you, that people end up wanting or needing and are willing to pay for, if they're priced fairly.

And that "priced fairly" results in the innovator being rewarded with a profit so that he can continue, or she can continue to make and provide and earn a profit and then hire other people as the business grows. So, it's all good. The Democrats don't like that because in the midst of all that is self-reliance. The Democrats prefer to take from the people who work hard. They want to take from the innovator. They want to punish success on the basis that it isn't fair that some people succeed and others don't.

So, they want to take from the successful and give it to people who don't want to bother with having to work for it, who don't want to bother with having to earn it. And the Democrats cultivate that culture. They cultivate the culture of transfer of wealth. And if you destroy the wealth creators, if you disincentivize them, if you raise their taxes, if you take away their profit, then why should they continue to do what they do? And they are demonized. The Democrat Party, the American left, demonizes the successful, then sets about punishing them, and they want to be applauded for it.

Success feeds off of itself. And it is a great motivating factor. It's what we're all oriented toward. We all want to succeed, until the Democrat Party gets hold of enough of us and convinces us that we can't. You can't succeed because of your race, your gender, your sexual orientation; the deck is stacked against you because America's unfair, America's racist, sexist, bigoted, homophob[ic]; you don't have a chance. That's what the Democrat Party tells people. Turns 'em into victims.

MILTON FRIEDMAN SCHOOLS PHIL DONAHUE ON CAPITALISM AND GREED

The Rush Limbaugh Show, July 31, 2012

Milton Friedman—some of you in this audience may not know—Milton Friedman, University of Chicago, a brilliant economist. He and his wife were a dynamo. They were a dynamic team. In economics, free-market capitalism, Milton Friedman's a rock star. Milton Friedman should be the Bible for young people, or anybody, trying to understand capitalism and free markets. Back in—I think the year was 1995—back in 1995, I interviewed Milton Friedman for an issue of the *Limbaugh Letter.*

Milton Friedman, while being interviewed by me—Snerdley will remember, 'cause this is back in the days when Snerdley hung around to listen to the interviews taking place. I wish I could remember the exact words, but Milton Friedman paid me a high compliment. I think he suggested that it would be very helpful if more people listened to me. I think that's what it was, wasn't it? And that, believe me, made my month, day, even year, because Milton Friedman, if he wasn't in a class all by himself, it certainly didn't take long to call the roll. He ended up at the Hoover Institution, the conservative think tank out at Stanford.

He would be a hundred years old today. I have a sound bite I want to play for you. Actually, two sound bites. One sound bite is two minutes of Milton Friedman schooling Phil Donahue and his audience in greed and capitalism and virtue. Phil Donahue interviewing Milton Friedman, and they had this exchange. And Donahue starts off wanting to know about greed and capitalism. Here it is. And listen to this.

DONAHUE: When you see around the globe the maldistribution of wealth, the desperate plight of millions of people in underdeveloped countries, when you see so few haves and so many have-nots, when you see the greed and the concentration of power, did you ever have a moment of doubt about capitalism and whether greed's a good idea to run on?

FRIEDMAN: Well, first of all, tell me, is there some society you know that doesn't run on greed? You think Russia doesn't run on greed? You think China doesn't run on greed? What is greed? Of course, none of us are greedy. It's only the other fellow who's greedy. The world runs on individuals pursuing their separate interests. The great achievements of civilization have not come from government bureaus. Einstein didn't construct his theory under order from a bureaucrat. Henry Ford didn't revolutionize the automobile industry that way. In the only cases in which the masses have escaped from the kind of grinding poverty you're talking about, the only cases in recorded history are where they have had capitalism and largely free trade. If you want to know where the masses are worst off, it's exactly in the kinds of societies that depart from that. So that the record of history is absolutely crystal clear that there is no alternative way, so far discovered, of improving the lot of the ordinary people that can hold a candle to the productive activities that are unleashed by a free-enterprise system.

DONAHUE: But it seems to reward not virtue as much as ability to manipulate the system.

FRIEDMAN: And what *does* reward virtue? Do you think the Communist commissar rewards virtue? Do you think Hitler rewards virtue? Do you think American presidents reward virtue? Do they choose their appointees on the basis of the virtue of the people appointed or on the basis of their political clout? Is it really true that political self-interest is nobler somehow than economic self-interest? You know, I think you're taking a lot of things for granted. Just tell me where in the world you find these angels who are going to organize society for us.

DONAHUE: Well—

FRIEDMAN: I don't even trust you to do that.

RUSH: Milton Friedman back in 1979 schooling Phil Donahue, and everybody else who heard that on the notions of virtue and greed and just basically upsetting Phil's applecart. Phil wasn't smart enough to know it was happening. He's still running around lamenting the accident of birth. If he'd been thirty miles south, he would have grown up in poverty. Anyway, we wanted to play that for you and recognize Milton Friedman, one hundred years old today, and now, in a testament to Milton Friedman of free-market economics, here is our first obscene-profit time-out of the day. I'll tell you, the guy was great. He was a genius.

THE BEAUTY OF CAPITALISM: ANYONE CAN BECOME "SUPER RICH" IN USA

The Rush Limbaugh Show, July 20, 2011

RUSH: Fred in Orlando, Florida, Open Line Friday as we keep on. Hello, sir. Welcome.

CALLER: Good time, down low, Black conservative dittos, Rush.

RUSH: Thank you, sir.

CALLER: I teach business and calculus. I tell my students that we need as many millionaires as possible, because only millionaires can pay you thousands of dollars for your degree—and the more millionaires we have, the more opportunity you have to actually get hired for thousands of dollars. I tell them it's a factor of about a thousand. Millionaires can pay [a] thousand dollars. I'm a "thousandaire." I can only pay people in the hundreds. The NFL pays players in millions. That's because they make billions.

RUSH: Right.

CALLER: You need as many billionaires as possible to have as many millionaires, and you need as many millionaires to have thousandaires.

RUSH: You say you are a college professor?

CALLER: Yes.

RUSH: What's so hard about . . . ? What you said is just common sense. What's so hard for people to learn that?

CALLER: Because the students have learned it all backwards. When they hear me say this, their opinion is that we have too many millionaires and they're sucking the money out of the economy.

RUSH: I know. They think it's a zero-sum game.

CALLER: Yeah.

RUSH: They think if you get a dollar, somebody has to have lost one.

CALLER: Yes, and I had to kinda un-teach all that.

STEVE JOBS: AMERICAN SUCCESS STORY
The Rush Limbaugh Show, October 6, 2011

Over all of the years that I've been hosting this program—twenty-three—I have been an evangelist for Apple Inc. products. I love them, and one of the things that I have always done on this program is talk about my passions and share my passions with all of you. I think a large part of life is passion. When you find it, when you have it, it's fabulous.

It's a magnet for other people, and it's self-invigorating, and sharing those passions is something that I thoroughly enjoy. Over these twenty-three years, each time I would discuss Apple products—a new one that I couldn't wait to get or one that I was having problems with or frustrated with—I'd always get emails from people, "Would you stop talking about Apple? They're nothing but a bunch of liberals! I don't want to hear about Apple. Why do you talk about Jobs? It's nothing but a bunch of liberals."

Rush worked tirelessly to achieve profound success and live the American Dream. Our home in Palm Beach, Florida.

I talk about Apple and Jobs because I love greatness. I just love greatness. I am fascinated by it. I am intrigued by how it happens. I'm intrigued about every aspect of greatness and excellence, because it's so genuinely rare. It is genuinely rare and exciting, and I am mesmerized by it. I'm inspired by it. I've many times told people (and you, too) that one of the greatest perks of the good fortune that I've had has been to meet people. I have had the opportunity to meet people who are the best at what they do, and that is exhilarating and fun and inspiring to me. So I attach myself to these things that create childlike wonderment in me. It's difficult as an adult to have childlike wonderment. How soon do we all outgrow the excitement that as children we all felt on Christmas Eve, and how many of us wish by magic that we could recapture it?

To find out, to rediscover that total, unbounded passion of childlike exuberance, excitement, innocence, uncluttered by the rigors of life lived as an adult. . . . And for me, speaking honestly, the introduction of every new Apple product ignited that in me. That's just me. I am fascinated by what Apple products do; how they do it, the invention process, the whole way . . .

Steve Jobs epitomized American exceptionalism. His life epitomized it. His philosophies epitomized American exceptionalism. . . . There hasn't been, in the last ten years, an Apple product that has not created wonderment in me, that has not exceeded my expectations.

Using Apple products is genuine fun for me; and at the same time, they have increased my productivity. I know I'm making this sound like it's a lot about me, but it's the best way to explain all this to you. What Jobs did literally changed the way human beings receive, transmit, enjoy all media. One guy did this. He had a lot of great people around him, but one guy did it. One guy's vision. To me, it's mind-boggling.

. . .

The problem with socialism is you eventually run out of other people's money. —Prime Minister Margaret Thatcher

. . .

HOW'S SOCIALISM LURING THE YOUNG?
The Rush Limbaugh Show, April 17, 2019

RUSH: Here's Robert in Julian, California. Hi. Great to have you here.

CALLER: Hello, Rush. Glad to be on your show.

RUSH: Thank you, sir.

CALLER: I'm living in it. You said it 100 percent correct. This is the new example for failed socialism. California is definitely it.

RUSH: Well, not yet.

CALLER: The people out here are crazy. Oh, it's bad. I'm already there. It's not good.

RUSH: Oh, I know.

CALLER: Everything is given to everybody, and they bill the people that are actually working for everything that's given away.

RUSH: I know. And the taxes are going up and the things being taxed are going up and the state's been overrun. You can't afford to live where you work, all that. But it's not there yet. It's trending. It's a one-party state with a declining Republican Party. But it's not yet—to you who live there it is, but to a millennial in Illinois, California, "Hollywood, Hollywood, Silicon Valley." It's not yet. It's going to be. My whole point was—this guy I was talking to on the golf course Sunday—the lure of socialism. What is it? When we were growing up, there was the Soviet Union for all of our lives as a testament to what Communism is. It kills people. Communism kills people. There is no prosperity. There is no plenty. There's no abundance. There's nothing but fear every day of your life. We had that. There was no magic allure to socialism. We did have the sixties and the leftist radicals who hated America and actually were enthralled with the idea of a Castro, Che Guevara, Soviet Union, because they were jealous of the power. But young people today, there is no equivalent of the Soviet Union. Venezuela doesn't work, the ChiComs don't work for it, because the face of China is not what the face of the Soviet Union was. My only point was that California is trending in a direction that will someday be an example of the failures of socialism and liberalism for one and all to see. Look. It's beginning now. People are leaving the state. Not in droves, but it's been a trickle, and it's continuing. But it isn't there yet. For those of you who live there and

 Rush Limbaugh

understand, yeah, it is, but for people outside of California looking at it as the land of fruit and opportunity and hope, it still is that. It's gonna be a while. That was my only point, is that young people today don't have a living example of the horror. So it's left to their imaginations to dream of this utopia that they are going to build and create, even though it hasn't ever been done. It hasn't been done because they haven't been alive when it has been tried, but now they are alive, and people like Alexandria Ocasio-Cortez and Ilhan Omar are going to lead the way over the carcasses of brontosauruses like Schumer and Pelosi and take your pick of the rest of them.

*　*　*

Through our company, Premiere Networks, we were privileged to be able to help feature Rush on radio stations across the country for well over twenty years. From the time we first met, Rush was far more than a colleague, and far more than the most talented, loved, respected, and appreciated person in talk radio history.
—Rich Bressler, President, COO, and CFO of iHeartMedia

*　*　*

RUSH EXPLAINS THE BUSINESS SIDE OF THE PROGRAM
Personal Recording at Home with Kathryn, Palm Beach, Spring 2020

Started in New York, the national show, August first, 1988, with fifty-six radio stations. The total audience was not even one hundred thousand people—that's how small the stations were. The objective is to get on radio stations in markets that are big. If you can get on the top twenty stations, or the best twenty stations in the market, you are covering 85 percent of the country.

And that's what's necessary, because you can't sell advertising at exorbitant rates without a large audience. That all worked out, and by 1992—four years—we're up to five hundred radio stations, and we've covered 80 percent of the country with the top twenty markets that were in—probably in the first three years of the show's existence.

There's a misconception put out there by our friends in the Drive-by Media that it was the arrival of Bill Clinton that built my show. I just want to reiterate, we were at five hundred stations at about 15 to 16 million cume [the estimated number, of different people who listened to a station for a minimum of five minutes in a quarter-hour] by the time Clinton was elected in 1992, takes office in '93, and by 1995–96, when the Republicans clinched the House for the first time in forty years—that's when we were at 615 radio stations and a [cume] of 20 million. So, we built during the Clinton years, but it wasn't because of Clinton. Our growth happened before he was even elected.

* * *

I remember every market that carried or carries this program. It's my business to. They're all special. Every darn one of them is special. —Rush Limbaugh

* * *

CURIOSITY: THE EIB BUSINESS MODEL
The Rush Limbaugh Show, May 20, 2011

RUSH: David in Warminster, Pennsylvania, Open Line Friday. You're next, sir. Great to have you on the program.

CALLER: Great, Rush. Hope you're having a great day.

RUSH: Thank you, sir. I am.

CALLER: I wanted to just express my gratitude. You are a driver of this economy. I didn't realize that you make more wealth for people in one segment than Congress does in, well, decades. I started an advertising agency with some people, and we specialize in radio, direct-response radio.

RUSH: Right.

CALLER: And, you know, we're starting customers and putting them on your show locally, and I'm actually gonna have a couple customers launching on national, Rush, in September. So it's amazing, you know, what the right advertising can do.

RUSH: Well, there are secrets to why this works. The business model of this program has never really been fully explored, which is fine with us. Of all the curiosity there has been about this radio program, the business aspect of it has really never been looked at. People are quite understandably fascinated by the content side, and they assume that the content side explains the revenue side. And while it does, in a way, that doesn't quite cover it all. There is a precise business model. There are different kinds of advertising strategies. When we started on this program, the most common network radio advertising strategy was called CPM, which is translated "cost per thousand," which meant that Campbell's Soup would go out and buy as many syndicated radio programs as possible, just trying to make sure as many people as possible heard the commercial, just get the brand name out there. And so the advertising rate was based on how large the audience being assembled was by combining a whole bunch of programs. Campbell's Soup and General Motors, whoever, they wouldn't touch us because of the so-called controversial nature of the program, and they didn't want complaint letters, which are always fake anyway, from activist listeners trying to have a negative impact on the business side of our program. It didn't matter. Every letter they assumed was real, and they didn't want to deal with it. So, of course, we had to sit here and devise a different strategy if we were to make it, because while the content, of course, is crucial, without business-side success, any content's academic. Without business-side success, nobody's gonna hear the content; not gonna be there. So we had to devise a strategy. We had to find a way to get sponsors and advertisers who had never used radio before, national radio. We went out and we found people who were in the same situation we were, start-ups, who were willing to take risks and go outside the conventional wisdom and the bounds of how it was always done, 'cause this radio show blew those boundaries away anyway, why not do it on the advertising side, and it did. And he gave it away here. He used the phrase here that has made the difference. If you missed it, I'm not going to tell you, because it's still a trade secret. But basically he's an agency, he's [an] advertising agency, he's calling here to essentially thank me, the host, for the profound success that advertisers on the program have, and I appreciate that, because if that doesn't happen, folks, all the rest of this really is academic. So thanks for the call.

● ● ●

I think if we go back to the beginning, thirty-plus years ago, and we think about what was going on in radio, there weren't the large radio audio companies that there are today. There were thousands of small radio owners, and FM had just come into play; all of the music and the audio from the AM was moving over to the FM, and these small owners were saying what are we going to do for programming. And then appeared Rush. He was a pioneer. He came through and talked about, in an entertaining way, his beliefs on conservative politics and life, and he captivated audiences, and he started one market at a time. There wasn't anything like social media in those days, so it really was viral in the sense that brothers called sisters, cousins called cousins, neighbors told neighbors. And Rush was magnetic when he came on air. It always seems like three hours a day is pretty easy to do; it's a very difficult task, and Rush did it spectacularly. When he rolled out from one market to fifty-six, we grew to over 650 stations, and we reached over 20 million listeners. And in that day part of his—he was across all those stations—he remained number one throughout his career. And we look at each other and say, "How could anyone have really done that?" And it was his adaptability, his flexibility; he loved technology. He is a legend.

—Julie Talbott, President, Premiere Networks

● ● ●

ADVICE FOR YOUNG PEOPLE ON HOW TO ACHIEVE SUCCESS
The Rush Limbaugh Show, December 23, 2019

RUSH: Independence, Missouri, up next. This is Mark. It's great to be with you, sir. Hello.

CALLER:... Do you have any advice for ... all of us on success? ... I'd proudly ask you for advice for success, not necessarily in the radio business but in life and taking advantage of our great country as this year approaches, and I'm sure many young people would like to hear your advice as well.

RUSH: Okay, I'll give this a shot. I have said over the years that there haven't been, by comparison . . . I remember when I was a young teenager—I wanted to do radio since I was eight. So when I would run into anybody who was in it, I'd just ask them question after question after question. I asked so many questions, one guy said, "You know, it sounds to me like you're more interested in how to do it than [in] actually doing it." I said, "What do you mean?" "Well, at some point you gotta stop asking questions and start doing things." And I said, "Well, I'm not old enough to start doing things. I'm not old enough to get hired yet." "Well, yes, you are, if you really want to, but at some point you gotta stop asking and you gotta start doing. You can't learn everything about doing something just by asking about it." Which I knew. It was still some relevant advice, probably from somebody who was tired of all my questions. . . . Now, then there are basics. I don't care what it is that you want to do, you have to have a well-rounded knowledge, and, more importantly, the ability to demonstrate that you have it. This is not just broadcasting and radio. You have to be able to communicate what you know. You have to do things that are going to inspire confidence in yourself. You have to really like yourself to be confident. And it is confidence that will open up opportunity to you. It's confidence that will allow you to transmit what you know in ways that are persuasive and impressive. Now, there's some other things that are common, too. . . .

* * *

When I started, the wizards of smart and the powers that be in radio tried to talk me out of doing what I do. They said, "You can't do a show without guests, and you have to take calls, and it has to be about local things." I didn't want other people to be the reason my show had an audience. . . .

Don't think there's only one way to do anything, because there isn't. There are countless ways, and even now, depending on what it is you want to do, there are countless ways to do what you want to do that may not have been done before or may not have been done very often or frequently.

And remember that the pressure on everybody is to conform. Conformity creates the least amount of problems for bosses and managers. Nonconformity, that's a problem. I am a nonconformist. It's why I would never

287

* * *

Today's a day on which to honor Rush Limbaugh's impact and presence in the lives of so many Americans who have made it their habit to listen to their friend on the radio each and every day. Rush epitomized excellence in all he did, on and off the air. —Kraig Kitchin, Chairman of the Radio Hall of Fame, *Inside Radio* interview, 2021

* * *

succeed in any corporate structure. Some people are made for it, though. This is the thing: There's no right or wrong about whatever it is you want to do. Just find it. That's half of it, if not more.

And how you find it is being honest with yourself about what you love and what your passions are, and what you want to be. Some people, "What do I want people to think of me?" Other people, "What do I want to do?" Whatever it is that motivates you.

I've often found that one of the worst things you can do, though, is to get even with people you think wronged you in the past. "I'm gonna succeed at this just so those people will see they were wrong." Fine. Let it motivate you awhile, but don't let that be why you're doing what you're doing, 'cause they'll never acknowledge it anyway. You'll never get the satisfaction you seek.

YOU DEFINE WHO YOU ARE
The Rush Limbaugh Show, January 14, 2004

Life is what you make it; life is what you do. Too many people have the attitude that life is what happens to you. You grow up, you go out there, and here comes this glob of mess thrown at you, and . . . you have no choice but to take it. You do have a choice! You don't have to take it. . . .

Anyone is free to grab hold of the reins of life and make life what they want it to be. It's hard sometimes, because . . . for most people, grabbing hold of the reins of life and making your life what you want it to be is change, and change or anything new is very, very hard. Routines are easy, habits are easy, and sitting there and being a victim and blaming somebody else for your lot in life, that's easy.

Victimhood is the easiest thing in the world to do, and it's a trap. . . . Some people think life is not meant to be enjoyed. You're having too much fun, then you're not doing enough serious stuff. You're not doing enough serious stuff, then you're not working hard, whatever. We have all of these conventional wisdom ideas we're raised with that imprison us. . . .

Life could be made whatever you want it to be, but if too many people sit around and think they've got no control over it . . . It's not, unless you allow it. Who's to say you shouldn't be happy? Who's to say you shouldn't have peace in your life? Who's to say that you have to go through suffering twenty-four hours a day, seven days a week? Why do you have to do that? Who said that? . . .

You've got to take control of your life, and you've got to realize that you're the one that defines it, not anybody else. Not your mom, not your dad, not your sisters, not your grandparents. You define who you are, and you define your life, and you are the one that gets to set the rules as to how life is going to be enjoyed and how it's going to be pursued. And if you give up those rules to somebody else, then you are to blame for where you are if you don't like it. I know this is hard. I'm here to tell you this is hard, because none of us are raised this way, and none of us are told this. We're all told the other. We're all told that people who are rich and doing things great are lucky, that it just was handed to them or that they're different, or that—forget rich—people that just appear to be happy to us, and if we're not? It's just the luck of the draw. . . . Life is to be lived. Life is to be grabbed onto. Life is to be defined by you, nobody else—including your parents. It's to be defined by you. If you let somebody else define it, and you sit around and be worried what other people think of you, then you're imprisoned by it.

* * *

You know when I was growing up—this is the big difference. And I think it has to do with how values are inculcated. When I was growing up, I've been fired seven times, I've been broke a bunch of times. And from the time I left home, I left home when I was twenty. So from the time I left home at age twenty until 1987 . . . so almost twenty years, I never made more than $22,000 or $23,000 a year. And for many years I never made more than $15,000 or $10,000. And I did what a lot of people do. I drove around town where the rich people lived and I would try to imagine how they got there. And wherever I lived I would do that. But at no time did I hate 'em. And at no time did I resent them. I wanted to enjoy the kind of success that I saw all around me! —Rush Limbaugh

* * *

290

SHINING SHOES? BEEN THERE, DONE THAT
The Rush Limbaugh Show, June 19, 2020

My first job, the first job I ever had outside of the house, you know, chores and that kind of thing, the first paying job I had was to shine shoes in a barbershop, thirteen years old. I was fascinated with making shoes shine. I wanted to be the best at it. I wanted to figure out how to do it. . . .

But one of the things, when I first got the gig, the shoeshine stand was as far back in the barbershop as you could go, and I'd sit back there and I'd wait for customers to show up, and nobody would show up. . . . And after the first four or five days, one of the barbers—the owners—said, "What are you gonna do to change this? You think they're just gonna come to you back there?" I said, "Well, if I wanted a shoeshine . . ." He said, "Exactly. They don't want a shoeshine. You gotta understand: Everybody's shoes you're gonna shine in here does not want one, so what you're gonna have to do . . ." He gave me an idea.

He said, "Whenever we have somebody . . ." We had four barber chairs. "Whenever somebody's in the chair, just go up and start buffin' the shoes, and they're gonna say to you, 'Wait, wait, wait, wait! I don't want you to do that. I'm not paying for this,' and you say, 'I'm not charging you, sir. This is a service offered by me and the barbershop at no charge.'"

The barber said to me, "You watch how many of them will then ask you to go ahead and do it for real, ask you what you charge for it," and that's exactly what happened. So I gave 'em a free buff, and it led to—I'd say—over half of the customers wanting a shoeshine. Then when they saw how good I was at it and how I could pop that shoeshine buff rag, I learned something else.

You go to the barber supply store, and you have access to pieces of equipment and various types of shoeshine and other things that were never sold retail. It's the same thing in the restaurant business. Restaurant supply stores have things that you'll never find at even the biggest grocery store or Costco or what have you. So I would always use that. "I've got stuff you can't get at home. I've got stuff that will make your shoes shine like

I think one of the reasons why I listen to you and never get tired of listening to you is 'cause I think your voice just makes people want to listen, like myself. I think you have the type of voice that just makes people want to listen. —Ace, member of the audience

you can't make your own shoes shine." I said, "I have studied the spit-shine technique of the US military. I've perfected it. You want to see how it works?" "Oh, yeah!" So, fifty bucks in three months at fifty cents a pop. I loved it—absolutely loved it.

FROM THE GREATEST PARODIES HITS ROSTER . . .

THANK THE LORD RUSH LIMBAUGH'S ON

Talent, on loan, from God

Oooh, let's give it up for Rush

Thank the Lord (thank the Lord) Rush Limbaugh's on (Rush Limbaugh's on)

Thank the Lord, Rush Limbaugh's on the EIB

You hear him every day on the EIB (talent from God)

He likes to tease Bill and Hillary (talent from God)

You love every word that he says, the liberal leftists feeling sad

C'mon, join me, Dittohead (talent from God)

Thank the Lord (thank the Lord) Rush Limbaugh's on (Rush Limbaugh's on)

Thank the Lord Rush Limbaugh's on the EIB

Talent on loan from God

First broadcast in 2005
The Rush Hawkins Singers

PRAISING RUSH'S INSPIRATIONAL SHOW
The Rush Limbaugh Show, July 3, 2009

RUSH: Gulfport, Mississippi, this is Paul. Welcome to the EIB Network, sir.

CALLER: Thank you, Rush, for taking my call.

RUSH: Yes, sir.

CALLER: I just wanted to say that I'm twenty-one years old and I'm currently in school, and you have inspired me to—instead of let the recession beat me down—create my own job. So I did just that, and I work all across the United States through the Internet, and it's working.

RUSH: Congratulations, sir. So you're another that's not all that greatly affected by the recession.

CALLER: That's correct. As a matter of fact, I'm going to Washington, DC, next week just for fun. So thank you for being an inspiration to me and to many others.

RUSH: Oh, now, see? If I were a liberal, what I would say to you is, "Go ahead and take your trip, but don't brag about it. That's going to hurt people's feelings. Do you realize how many people are hurting, and here you are, calling here bragging about going to Washington to have fun? You ought to be ashamed."

CALLER: *[Laughs]* Well, at least I'm not on TV every day.

RUSH: *[Laughs]* Thank goodness.

CALLER: So thank you, sir, for all that you do, and the heart that you've given to other people.

RUSH: I appreciate that. I really do. Thank you very much, Paul.

● ● ●

How did Limbaugh do it? No one really knows, because few have been able to duplicate his success, despite a number of gifted hosts who have tried. For all the criticism that Limbaugh was crass, over some twenty-five thousand hours of the syndicated Limbaugh show, there were few embarrassments. And in cases where Limbaugh said something he regretted, he later apologized. He certainly could grow animated but seldom shouted and yelled. He talked about having talent "on loan from God," but could turn self-deprecatory and compliment callers for insights that he found original and noteworthy, saying, "I hadn't thought of that." He mocked identity politics, but at work and in life often surrounded himself with talented people who were not white, and he seemed oblivious to any significance of that fact other than that he'd found friends and employees who were competent and whom he liked. He was a self-made multimillionaire many times over and proud of it, and yet felt and acted more comfortable with those of the Midwestern middle classes with whom he'd grown up.

—Victor Davis Hanson, Senior Fellow, Hoover Institution

◦ ◦ ◦

DOCTOR INSPIRED BY RUSH TO SUCCEED
The Rush Limbaugh Show, March 2, 2020

RUSH: This is Larry in Fall River, Massachusetts. Hey, Larry, great to have you. I'm glad you waited, sir. Hi.

CALLER: Thank you, and dittos. I wanted to say that I thank you and I'm glad I got the chance to do this, but I became a doctor thanks to you. I've been a doctor a long time now, but it's thanks to you. And my second point is, I remember—

RUSH: Wait. What kind of doctor are you?

CALLER: I'm a spine specialist.

RUSH: A spine specialist. And how did this program make you want to become a doctor?

CALLER: I was a schoolteacher, and you talked about following your passion and how you've never worked a day in your life because you love what you did. And I was convincing myself that, you know what, I should do that, too. And of course I had the grades and the academic ability, and of course I went to school in New York, NYU, so they're probably gonna lose credit now, but that's okay.

RUSH: I love hearing stories like that. I really do. Because, see, it was in you all the time.

CALLER: Yes.

RUSH: This passion was in you all the time. You just needed a little kick that told you you could do it.

CALLER: Absolutely. And the money and everything just appeared. It was a miracle, if you want to use that term. But it just occurred. And I've been practicing a lot now, and still passionate about it, I'm getting a little older in my years and long in the tooth, but I have as much passion today [as] the day I walked into the school and walked into the anatomy lab. So it's there.

RUSH: Well, thank you very much. I love hearing stories like that, when anybody is able to get out of a rut, find out what they really love doing, and go do it. That's fabulous. Thank you very much. Now, I know you had something you wanted to add to that. That's when I interrupted you.

CALLER: I remember when you got scammed also on a virus back when they had the HTLV-3, now called HIV, on that talk show. You were on a panel show as a guest host, and they tried to do the same thing they're doing now. It's the same thing. It's the same stuff. You were right then. You're right now. And that's something that they can't grasp.

RUSH: You know what he's talking about? He goes back to [the] very beginning. He's talking about when I got set up and scammed guest hosting *The Pat Sajak Show*.

CALLER: Correct.

RUSH: That's what he's talking about. Yeah, you're right. You're right. I took those producers at their word, and honestly, I thought it was gonna be an opportunity to reach out to some people that misunderstood me, and instead it was a gigantic setup. You're absolutely right about that.

CALLER: And you learned from that, and you became—so you're right now, let me tell you, you are so right now about these viruses, and you're right then, and you're right about it. So you know your stuff. You do your research.

RUSH: Well, I do. Thank you. I do. You're exactly right.

OPEN LINE FRIDAY QUESTION: HOW DO I ORGANIZE MY STACK OF STUFF?

The Rush Limbaugh Show, October 30, 2020

RUSH: Suzette in The Woodlands, Texas. I'm glad you called. You're up first today. Hello.

CALLER: Are there any tips that you can pass along to us about organizing your Stack of Stuff and how you do that?

RUSH: Ah. Let me give you the process by which I do this each and every day. I'll do this as briefly as I can. Starting the night before—that's when show prep begins, and that's when I start reading things and looking at things. And things I find interesting I print to the printer here that's right behind me. And then I promptly forget about it. And I do that for two to three hours a night, get up, get here at the time I arrive, and start doing the same thing over and over. I start looking at everything that I rely on as a source. Things that interest me, I print them. And then about eleven o'clock I stop what I'm doing and I go grab everything out of the printer and I start organizing it into probably four different stacks based on the kind of news it is. And then I put those stacks together, and at about 11:45 I stop, and that's the show, or it used to be. But now the news is breaking and made throughout the three-hour program, and so prepping it is an entirely different process. I still do it the way I've always done it. What I'm really blessed with, Suzette, is a good memory. I happen to know everything I've put in these Stacks. The one thing I can't keep track of sometimes is which Stack something is in. But I know I've got it somewhere here, and I think the key to good organization is passion. You know, I love being informed. I love having things at my fingertips. I love being able to tell people off the top of my head things that I know. And that's just passion. That's having a desire to do it. I've developed a system here over thirty-some-odd years that works for me. And, interestingly, it's all individual pieces of paper. I don't use a computer once the program starts. I use a computer exclusively to prep. But once the program starts, it's all individual pieces of paper. I have to remember where things are. But my memory comes in handy, and I have to know pretty much everything in the stacks. I just have to go get it to get the exact wording now and then. But I'm blessed.

Bestselling author Vince Flynn and Rush shared great laughs together over the years.

I'm blessed with that kind of skill set, and it works perfectly, this kind of application, doing a radio program like this.

CALLER: How are you able to recall stuff from long ago? You seem to always be able to bring it up right at your fingertips.

RUSH: You know, that's a good—I think that's another thing that—every one of us has different skills that we are blessed with or good at. I have been blessed that the skill set I have is 100 percent applicable and useful to my job. And because of that I have spent so much time perfecting it and learning how to make it work for me that I've got years and years and years of experience here. And, you know, how do you account for a good memory? This is where my profound belief in God comes in. When I say that I've got talent on loan from God, that's part of the recipe. It's one of the things that I mean. I've got specific talents here that are exclusively applicable to this program. And who knows why I'm able to remember something from thirty years ago? I mean, I wish I knew what the synapses occurring in my brain were. All I know is that instantly I have the recall. And it's just a blessing.

. . .

Folks, I've told you this before. I flunked speech. Speech 101—I flunked it. I went to every class and I gave every speech. The reason that I flunked . . . Well, actually I didn't. I came close to flunking. I was given an opportunity to pass the course if I redid one of the four speeches or five speeches I had to do during the semester. . . . I'd already developed a way that I felt comfortable doing public speaking, and it did not involve using notes. It certainly didn't involve outlining. So I show up, I give every speech, and I get an F "pending" because I didn't outline any of the speeches. —Rush Limbaugh

. . .

From 1988 on, *The Rush Limbaugh Show*'s audience and ratings continued to climb. It is extremely difficult to remain number one in any industry, let alone consistently, year after year, for more than thirty-two years. Tina Turner's hit "The Best" often made its way to the bumper rotation, and the lyrics are perfect in reference to Rush: "Simply the best / better than all the rest." Rush dominated markets from coast to coast, including major cities like New York and Los Angeles.

EIB AUDIENCE NUMBERS SHOOT THROUGH THE ROOF: TWENTY-SIX MILLION AND GROWING!

The Rush Limbaugh Show, April 27, 2017

Before we get into the meat and potatoes of the program, I got a fascinating email today from a friend thanking me for doing something. You know, it's good. Sometimes I do need an assist in staying in touch. Now, don't misunderstand here—the letter, the email thanked me for announcing what the latest audience figures, ratings are on the program, and I did this yesterday. I've actually mentioned it twice. But let me do it again just to set up the email.

As you know, for the last thirty, twenty-five years, whatever, we've been floating between 20, 22 million people, depending on when you take audience ratings. It's a weekly [cumulative] number. Radio does ratings different than TV. We talk about average quarter hour, and that's how many are listening in any fifteen-minute sweep during an hour. Then there's the weekly cume and the monthly cume. That's the grand total of everybody listening, the cume is. And there is the daily cume. The daily cume number here is up. It's always been around 10 to 12 million, and that's up, too.

The upshot is that after the election, the audience of this program continued to grow. Subscribers at Rush 24/7 continue to grow. Subscribers at the *Limbaugh Letter* continue to grow. This is not usual. Now, hang on, I'm not bragging here. I'm setting this up to get to the email I got. And the numbers are just pouring in now for March, but prior to those numbers the weekly cume had been up now to 26 million and climbing.

Usually on a program like this when you have an intense election that features a campaign of a minimum one year or longer, once the election's over, the results are in, the intensity usually lightens and fades away and audience levels go back to what their historic norms were. Not the case this year on this program. The audience has continued to build. So I mentioned this, and the email I got thanked me for doing so.

"It's good to know that it's growing. It's good to know that we can tune in here at noon Eastern time every day and know that like-minded people are still here and in greater number." Now, I just assume everybody knows this. And maybe I assume too much, but I assume that everybody knows where the program ranks and that nothing has changed. 'Cause believe me, if it had, that would be the only thing in the news. And so, since that's not in the news, I figured everybody was just up to speed. But that's a mistake. I shouldn't assume people know these things. So the emailer wanted to thank me for mentioning this because it was a reinforcement, like a validation.

Ratings are taken now constantly. It used to be they were taken four times a year. Now they're taken constantly. They fluctuate depending on a lot of factors, which is why I don't spend an inordinate amount of time talking about them. But I did, because what's happened here is phenomenal, actually, if I don't mind saying so myself. And I just happened to mention it in passing and got this [gratifying] thank-you email note, so I wanted to repeat that.

* * *

RUSH: Scarlett in Scottsdale. Great to have you on the EIB Network. How are you doing?

CALLER: I'm doing great! Thank God for you and answering my call.

RUSH: *[Laughs]*

CALLER: I've listened to you since 1990, and I used to live in California, and I took my little friends to Long Beach one time to see you, and I've listened to you ever since. And now I'm in Scottsdale, and I listen to a California station 'cause I like to listen early.

RUSH: Well, thank you very much. I remember there was a Long Beach, California, Rush to Excellence Tour stop. I remember it well.
CALLER: Yes.
RUSH: Good to know you were in the audience there. It was a massive crowd.
CALLER: Yeah.
RUSH: Thousands and thousands of people out there.

. . .

Rush, it's Rich Lowry at National Review. *I just want to give you the hardiest congratulations. You've been an affliction to liberalism for twenty years, and to the rest of us you've been an inspiration, a joy, a comfort, an education, and a friend. You long ago joined the annals of conservative greats, the defenders of ordered liberty, our civilization's highest accomplishment. I know how proud Bill Buckley was of you. Rush, it's been an inspired twenty years. Now we expect twenty more. Take care, and God bless.* —Rich Lowry, Editor, *National Review*, phone call on Twentieth Anniversary Show

. . .

PART 2 — YOU MAKE AMERICA WORK

Rush had a brilliant way of describing scenes in a way that made us all stop what we were doing and laugh. He joked about highbrow professors sheltered in Ivy League faculty lounges waxing poetic about policy, and Washington swamp bigwigs with no idea what was going on in the real world. None of them, he said, would set foot in "flyover" country, Middle America, if they could possibly help it.

Rush believed with all of his heart that you are the people who make this country work, and not the government. You are the backbone of America, out there working hard to provide for your families and contribute to the economy. Rush maintained if the government would just get out of the way, the American people, who are the most ingenious in the world, would know exactly what to do.

There were many times when Rush demonstrated how deeply he cared about fellow Americans. When a large tornado hit the small town of Joplin, Missouri, causing widespread damage, Rush flew in to personally deliver a financial contribution to aid in their recovery and donated a full semi-truck of his iced-tea beverage to the town's Fourth of July celebration. He was not seeking any kind of publicity or recognition; he simply wanted to show the people of Missouri how much they meant to him.

Rush was one of the most generous people you could ever meet, and he deeply cared about fellow Americans. He delivered a few rallying words to inspire the people of Joplin.

A proud son of Missouri, Rush Limbaugh was a voice for the voiceless. He changed talk radio, but more importantly, Rush changed the conversation to speak up for the forgotten and challenge the establishment. He lived the First Amendment and told hard truths that made the elite uncomfortable, but made sure working men and women had a seat at the table.

—US Senator Josh Hawley of Missouri, Tribute to Rush

RUSH VISITS JOPLIN, MISSOURI, AFTER TORNADO
The Rush Limbaugh Show, July 5, 2011

HOST: Welcome to the stage, Rush Limbaugh!

AUDIENCE: *[Cheers and applause]*

HOST: Maha Rushie!

RUSH: Thank you all very much.

AUDIENCE: *[Cheers]*

RUSH: Thank you so much, but I can't hear you. I'm a little hard of hearing.

AUDIENCE: *[Wild cheers and applause]*

RUSH: I gotta tell you, folks: Thank you so much for allowing me to be part of this tonight. It was a thrill. It was an honor to be here tonight among all of you. It's the Fourth of July, and do you know what we're celebrating today?

AUDIENCE: *[Cheers and applause]*

RUSH: You—those of you here tonight from Joplin, Missouri—

AUDIENCE: *[Cheers and applause]*

RUSH: You may not know it yet, but you are the essence of what the Founding Fathers had in mind.

AUDIENCE: *[Applause]*

RUSH: You are the epitome. You are the people who make this country work. What happened here is something that you are going to erase. You'll never forget it from your memories, but you are going to build it back. It is going to get fixed. It is going to be rebuilt. It is going to be better than it ever was. You are going to show the rest of the country how it's done, because . . .

AUDIENCE: *[Cheers and applause]*

RUSH: You represent the best of what this country has to offer. You understand the principles of hard work and self-reliance. You understand the difference between "self-interest" and "selfishness," and you are not selfish. You are all going to be working in your own self-interest to rebuild your lives, and in the process, everybody else's lives will be rebuilt right along with yours. American exceptionalism is simply the result of our Founding Fathers' understanding that our government is not to determine the equality of outcomes in life because we're not all the same. Our country was determined to provide equality of opportunity, and what you do with it is your business.

AUDIENCE: *[Cheers and applause]*

RUSH: You are showing the world how it's done. I am honored—I am really honored—to be here. You can be the best you can!

AUDIENCE: *[Wild cheers and applause]*

RUSH: Go for it—and I'll see you there! Thank you all very much, and have a great Fourth of July!

✳ ✳ ✳

RUSH: Jerry in St. Louis, as we go back to the phones. Great to have you with us, Jerry. Hi.

CALLER: Thank you, Rush. I appreciate that. Mega dittos.

RUSH: Thank you.

CALLER: First thing I want to do is I want to thank you for taking my call and thank the call screener for allowing me to talk to you. I actually called originally about—I was at the rally yesterday, I guess you'd call it, the party in Joplin. I drove from St. Louis across the state to Joplin just to see you, and it was worth it for the ten minutes, I want to tell you that. I've been listening to you since 1992; I actually found you by accident. And I feel as if we're friends, because I've been listening to you so long, and I actually talk to you while you're on the radio—"Yeah, Rush, that's right," that kind of stuff, so—

RUSH: Ah, you're making my day. I know what you're talking about. The remarkable thing about this program for me, what it's meant to me as a person, is that the relationship between my staff here, me, and the audience, you, is familial, it's like a family.

CALLER: Yes.

RUSH: There is a deep connection there. You drove across the state. Tell people how long a drive that is from St. Louis to Joplin.

CALLER: That's three hundred miles.

RUSH: So you drove three hundred miles. Well, God bless you.

• • •

To Democrats, America's heartland is "flyover" country. They don't know, or like, the Americans who live there, or their values. This election won't change that! —Rush Limbaugh

• • •

A FELLOW BEVERAGE SMALL BUSINESS OWNER

The Rush Limbaugh Show, July 24, 2012

RUSH: Stafford, Virginia. Shannon, thank you so much for waiting. Great to have you on the program.

CALLER: Oh, thanks, Rush. I'm actually calling as a small business owner here, holding on to the kite strings of the American Dream. Going back to what you began your hour with, you know, this is a war on small business. And the demonizing of the 1 percent and their willingness now to invest in the American Dream and help others realize it because of the hostile environment of this administration toward the American Dream and toward small business.

RUSH: That's a good point.

CALLER: *[Laughs]* I'm living it. I know it. *[Laughs]*

RUSH: *[Laughs]*

RUSH: What is your product? You say you're in a small business. What is your business?

CALLER: It's BRAT diet drinks, based on the age-old prescription of the BRAT diet: Bananas, Rice, Apples, and Toast.

RUSH: Wait, wait, wait. Wait a minute. Brats? Like bratwurst diet drink?

CALLER: *[Giggles]* No, like BRAT diet—Bananas, Rice, Apples, and Toast—when you've got an upset tummy and you need to rehydrate?

RUSH: Oh! Oh, oh, oh, oh, yeah. Yeah. You know, Shannon, I myself am in the beverage business: Two If By Tea. I am also Mr. Tea! I am in the beverage business, and my objective is to wipe people like you out.

CALLER: No, we need to team up! *[Laughs]*

RUSH: *[Laughs]*

CALLER: I'm a wife of a retired Marine Corps officer. I launched this with my family. You know, we believe in the American Dream, and I'm telling you, Rush: Until I know there is no chance for it, we're gonna keep fighting for it.

RUSH: And people like you are gonna be the reason we triumph. This is what happens. The genuine entrepreneurs and the people that make the country work!

"Making the complex understandable each and every day."

—Rush Limbaugh

BILL MAHER REVEALS WHAT LIBERALS
REALLY THINK OF US
The Rush Limbaugh Show, February 26, 2019

I had something in the Stack yesterday I didn't get to. Bill Maher had a monologue on his Friday-night program on HBO, and I thought it was fascinating. He said the red state–blue state divide is really nothing more than the red state being jealous of that. He said we don't hate the left. We want to be the left. They have Chef Wolfgang Puck. We have Chef Boyardee.

And he went on to insult life in flyover states, states that vote Republican, and portrayed blue states where leftists hang out as the crème de la crème and the elites of the elite and said the real problem in America is not that we on the right think the left is destroying things [but] that they're the cool kids, they're the hipsters, and . . . we really want to be invited to their party but we know we never will be, because we're nerds or we're kooks or we're hicks or we're freaks, and we know it.

He had some funny lines in it, but you know what it did? It unveiled a lot of the thinking about people who are among the elite, who think they are in the elite. And it revealed a lot about the way that they think. And at the top of the list, they really do consider themselves elitists. It's unusual for this to be admitted to, because most elites try to tamp that down. They try to blur that line. They don't like being called elites because that's a minority of people. Therefore, it's not a majority of thought, not a majority of behavior, it's not a majority of belief, and that's because they're elites.

And I don't know that the jokes and the making fun of red-state voters and conservatives and Republicans was all there, but the end result was that the guy ended up confirming the idea that there are a whole lot of people out there who, just because they're liberal, think they are much better than all the rest of us and much smarter than all the rest of us and that they do talk down to us and that we're not offended by it, we're jealous. We want in. We want to be in that big clique. It's almost like high school never ended. They remain the cool kids, and we're not.

NINETEEN YEARS LATER, SUCCESSFUL CALLER
RECALLS A PEP TALK FROM EL RUSHBO
The Rush Limbaugh Show, February 11, 2009

RUSH: Sean in Middleburg, Virginia, you're up first as we go to the phones today. It's great to have you with us on the EIB Network. Hello.

CALLER: Hey, Rush, how are you? First-time caller, longtime listener. It's actually Pennsylvania, but I started listening to you in Chico, California, back in 1990. However, you made an impact on my life. You told me—you told everyone—be your own man. Never rely on government for anything in your life. Get up, go to work every day, work hard, make a difference, and, you know, it will happen. I remember you saying your grandfather never cashed Social Security checks because he never wanted money from the government. And I believe that everybody goes through a level of prosperity in their life, but if you work hard every single day and make a difference, you move up those levels of prosperity, and things will come true. It's the American way, it's Newton's Law in this country, and why liberals want to create a utopian dream when it already exists.

RUSH: Well, not to them, because they're not in charge of it.

CALLER: I know. *[Chuckles]*

RUSH: But, you know, I want to thank you. You remember nineteen years ago, he said he remembers me saying, "Don't depend on the government or anybody else for anything. Make it yourself. Don't be obligated to anybody." I almost feel like I ought to apologize to you, now, though.

CALLER: *[Laughs]*

RUSH: Because you went out there and did that, now you're a target of the very government I told you not to pay any attention to!

CALLER: That's right, and I was eighteen years old, and I'm furious. I'm an investing advisor, and I'm saying, "Invest [in] Roths because you better pay your taxes today, because we're going to pay for it down the road. There's no question about it."

RUSH: Well, no. See, not everybody has to pay taxes now either.

CALLER: That's true.

RUSH: At least not on time.

CALLER: That's true.

RUSH: *[Laughs]* Anyway, look, Sean, I appreciate the call. That's really nice. Nineteen years ago, he remembers me. You know, I do these pep talks frequently. You know, you start depending on government, you look to Washington for what you want, you end up like that poor Henrietta.

*   *   *

His generosity allowed the Broadcasters Foundation to continue its mission of helping colleagues in acute need across the country. We are grateful for the support he provided. America has lost one of its most preeminent broadcasters and charitable individuals. —Scott Herman, Chairman, Broadcasters Foundation of America

*   *   *

PART 3 — HIGH TAXES DESTROY SMALL BUSINESSES

After being audited year after year, Rush finally had enough and decided to escape the high taxes of New York City. He opened the Southern Command Studio in Palm Beach, Florida, with the help of his longtime engineer Brian Johnson and a small radio team. When a close friend, who happened to be a lifelong New Yorker, asked him at a cigar dinner party why he ever left New York, Rush replied, "You try being audited every year and let me know if you stick around. The taxes in New York are outrageous, and I am target numero uno."

THE MOST TELLING MOMENT OF OBAMA'S PRESIDENCY: "YOU DIDN'T BUILD THAT"
The Rush Limbaugh Show, July 24, 2012

RUSH: Let's go back, because Obama will not let this go. This is perhaps the [most] telling moment of Obama's presidency and his campaign. This little fifty-second blurb from Roanoke, Virginia, on Friday, July thirteenth.

OBAMA: Look, i-i-if you've been successful, you didn't get there on your own.

FOLLOWERS: That's right!

OBAMA: You didn't get there on your own. I'm always struck by people who think, "Well, it must be because I was just so smart!"

FOLLOWERS: *[Laughter]*

OBAMA: There are a lot of smart people out there. "It must be because I worked harder than everybody else." Let me tell you something. There are a whole bunch of hardworkin' people out there!

FOLLOWERS: *[Cheers and applause]*

OBAMA: If you were successful, somebody along the line gave you some help!

FOLLOWERS: Yeaaaaaah!

OBAMA: There was a great teacher somewhere in your life.

FOLLOWERS: Yeaaaaaah!

OBAMA: Somebody helped to create this unbelievable American system that we have that allowed you to thrive. Somebody invested in roads and bridges! If you've got a business, you—you didn't build that!

FOLLOWERS: Yeaaaaaah!

OBAMA: Somebody else made that happen. The Internet didn't get invented on its own. Government research created the Internet so that all the companies could make money off the Internet.

RUSH: Okay, I'm gonna put this Internet thing in perspective and to bed once and for all on today's program, because the government did not develop the Internet. They sat on it! It was the private sector that developed the Internet. The private sector turned it into a commercial enterprise. The government didn't have the slightest idea what they had. They sat on it. I'll get to that in just a second. The real thing to grasp here from this bite is what Obama is really saying. As I've mentioned a bunch of times, he's literally saying to this audience and to the people he hopes are a majority of the country: "The people who've succeeded and the people who've achieved and the people who have wealth don't deserve it. They did it stealing from you. They used work or labor from you that they didn't pay you for, not fairly. Or they ran businesses that cheated people or overcharged. Or they made too big a profit. They're no smarter than you are, and I'm here to get it back for you! I'm here to equalize this. I'm here to balance this out." This roads-and-bridges stuff is just liberal claptrap. What he's doing, what he's setting the stage for is trying to socialize profit so that he can claim it. What he wants people to conclude is that profit was not possible, is not possible, without government first making it possible. And, therefore, government owns it. It's government's profit. He wants to socialize the profit, and that's then the vehicle for going after everybody's money via higher taxes, a wealth tax, or whatever technique that he tries.

* * *

The power to tax involves the power to destroy.
—Chief Justice John Marshall

* * *

THE PRIVATE SECTOR MAKES WHAT THE GOVERNMENT TAKES
The Rush Limbaugh Show, January 24, 2014

I got an email during the break, and our first call somewhat related to this. But I got an email. "Rush, are you against the government building roads? How else do you think it's going to happen?"

There are certain things to me that are self-evident, that are common sense, that maybe are not to others. So let me spell it out. I'm not against the government building roads. That is a legitimate government function. But I am very much against the government claiming that their building the road is the reason somebody on the road is successful. I'm deeply resentful—I don't care where you find it in life—of people trying to claim credit for the achievements of others. That really rubs me raw.

But as far as legitimate government functions—building schools, building roads and bridges—those are perfectly acceptable and fine government functions. . . .

Now, redistributing wealth, that is not a legitimate government function. Nationalizing industries and taking them over, that's for people like Hugo Chavez, but not us. Destroying industries, targeting industries for destruction, picking and choosing winners and losers in the private sector . . . that's not a legitimate government function. You add the top federal marginal rate to the top state marginal rate, and then you throw in property taxes—and then you add FICA, Social Security, and Medicare taxes—and there are a lot of Americans who are having the government confiscate over half of what they earn. That's not a legitimate government function, and if that's what government must do in order to be big and good, then you can leave me out. . . .

So you want to stack all that up against building roads and bridges, and that's how you want to defend Big Government is they build roads and build bridges? I'll concede that. Fine. Build all the roads you want. Build all the bridges you want. Legitimate. But none of the other stuff is. You libs, let me ask you a question. Do you use toilet paper, or do you use leaves? Government doesn't make toilet paper. The private sector makes the toilet paper. Procter & Gamble, Kimberly-Clark. Government doesn't run 'em. Do you

315

use toilet paper, Chuck-U? Mr. President, do you use toilet paper? The government doesn't make it. Senator Schumer, do you like to eat? I happen to know he does. I've been to dinner with Chuck-U. Chuck-U can pack it in, by the way. He's one of these guys that doesn't gain weight. He just can pack it in—and, you know what?

The private sector produces the food.

The government doesn't feed anybody, not until they take the food that's already been produced and give it away. You leftists, do you like your clothes? The private sector makes clothes. Government doesn't make your clothes. Government makes roads and bridges? Big whoop. How about the car you drive? Outside of General Motors, the government doesn't make the car you drive.

> Over the years, Rush was inundated with requests for interviews and to appear on media programs. He did not often accept, as he knew it would be stepping into a lion's den. On occasion he decided to take the career risk and appear on late-night shows like David Letterman and Jay Leno. Rush disarmed the hosts with his humor, humility, and charm. Rush was also regularly featured on popular television shows and news programs.

RUSH EXPLAINS GOVERNMENT SPENDING ON THE *TONIGHT SHOW WITH JAY LENO*
The Rush Limbaugh Show, September 28, 2009

An amazing story. What was it? Just last Thursday night I was on Leno, and I had a little discussion with him about Social Security and Medicare. Jay is a nice guy, don't misunderstand here. But he is an example of the kind of people who think if the government's giving people checks, that it's compassion, that it's really good. And he was saying, "What's wrong with it?" I said, "Jay, they're bankrupt! They're bankrupt, and they're destroying the future." So we get this today: "Big job losses and a spike in early retirement claims from

laid-off [seasoned] citizens will force Social Security to pay out more in benefits than it collects in taxes the next two years." First time that's happened since the 1980s. "The deficit's $10 billion in 2010, $9 billion in 2011 will not affect payments because Social Security has accumulated surpluses from previous years totaling $2.5 trillion," which is BS.

There is no Social Security surplus! "It will add to the overall federal deficit. Applications for retirement benefits, 23 percent higher than last year, while disability claims have risen about 20 percent. The recession hit many older workers suddenly. They found themselves laid off with no place to turn but Social Security. 'If they were younger, we'd call them unemployed,' said an economics law professor at University of California Berkeley, 'which means that the unemployment numbers are higher than are being reported.'" So job losses and early retirements hurt Social Security.

Capitalism is also what enables brilliant people to answer the question: "Okay, President Reagan, Cold War: What are your thoughts?" "Simple. We win; they lose."

EXCESSIVE REGULATIONS SQUASH THE ECONOMY!
The Rush Limbaugh Show, September 29, 2014

CALLER: There's so many regulations and rules that increase the cost of labor, that increase the cost of doing business. An employer is not going to pay a ton of money for an employee that's not gonna be insanely productive for them. Because they have to pay that money out in other avenues for regulations, for things like that.

RUSH: That's exactly right. Employers have work that needs to be done, and they will pay to get it done. If it's specialized work, they'll pay even more to get it done, and if somebody is willing to show they can do it and is willing to work hard—the formula is still there, and it still is applicable. But I'll tell you, you're right, there's so much pressure on, for lack of a better term, the private sector. I think that term turns people off, but I'll stick with it just for the sake of this call. I think there's so much pressure in the private sector with all the regulations, now Obamacare and the vast unknown that it is in terms of the cost of doing business, it's really challenging. And it's all because, or maybe not all, largely because the government has interceded in so much of the private sector. What kind of law do you practice? Because the one thing that the Democrat Party has made sure of is that trial lawyers are making out like bandits.

CALLER: [Laughs] Well, I haven't been able to practice law, because the legal market was one of the markets to take the biggest hit during the downturn in the economy.

* * *

Hey, by the way, it was just pointed out to me that the left does understand how raising taxes reduces economic activity. How about the desire for increasing cigarette taxes, soda taxes? What are they trying to do? Get you to buy less. They know. They know that higher taxes reduce activity. It's real simple. If you want more of an activity, lower taxes on it. If you want less of an activity, raise taxes. So if you want more jobs? [Chuckles] *It's very simple. You lower payroll taxes. If you don't want as many jobs, then you raise corporate taxes. It's that simple, folks.* —Rush Limbaugh

* * *

TRUMP FOLLOWS RUSH'S LEAD, EXITS NEW YORK!
The Rush Limbaugh Show, November 1, 2019

So I heard, like everybody else did, the tweet from President Trump last night that he was leaving New York—that he was making it official, he was going to relocate and establish—in fact, he's already done it—his residence will be right here in Palm Beach.

I can remember, I played golf with President Trump long before he was president. I played golf with him at Trump International here, and this is some years ago now. I left New York in 1997. I had come down here to Florida. It's kind of a long story, but let me give you the brief of it. When I started the radio show in 1988, just constant work, building the network, starting from fifty-six stations up to six hundred in four years.

In the first four years I wrote two books, and then the *Rush Limbaugh* TV show started. And all of my broadcast partners feared I had not taken any significant vacation time 'cause I was loving it. I was so into what was happening, it was a success track unlike any I had ever experienced. But my broadcast partners began to get worried I was gonna burn out if I didn't take some time just to get away from it.

Roger Ailes had a condo in the vicinity here, and they got together, arranged for me to come down here on a weekend in February. It was around the middle, February fifteenth, Valentine's Day or some such thing. And in order to get here I had to beat a New York City snowstorm. There was a fourteen-inch snowstorm on the way. And it started about two o'clock in the afternoon. My program ended at three. So I had to hightail it to the airport and try to beat that snowstorm to get down here. And I did.

And I got down here and it was eighty-five degrees for the entire weekend. This condo's on, like, the twenty-fourth floor right on the ocean. I'd never been in a place like that. I'd never stayed in a hotel on the ocean, I mean, really, really on the ocean, where you could hear the waves, you could see the sharks, I mean, twenty-four floors up. And I decompressed like I didn't ever remember decompressing. And by that, I mean relaxing.

I was out on the deck day and night, I was reading this and reading that, I was puffing away on cigars, it was just two or three days. I liked it so much I started coming back. Then I ended up purchasing a little place down here, intended it to be six weeks a year. And there was no way it was only gonna be six weeks a year.

And finally I made the call, once it all made sense to me on taxes. I was paying through the nose in New York; state, city, federal, unincorporated business, whatever they can hit you with, they do. So sometime in the middle of 1997, I made the decision to move to Florida permanently. And my primary reasons were two: lifestyle and climate and escaping taxes.

I got audited the next twelve years. The New York State tax authorities audited me, and I ended up having to prove—and, folks, this is not an exaggeration: every audit was for three years' worth of returns. I had to prove where I was every day of the year fourteen different ways: credit card receipts, computer IP addresses, flight and travel records, hotels.

And even at that, they thought I was lying and making it up. In tax disputes you automatically are guilty and you have to prove your innocence. They were subpoenaing employees and sweating them, trying to get them to say, "He doesn't really live in Florida. He lives in his New York condominium." "He just has that place to try to escape, right? He's here all the time, right?" "No. No. He's not." But they were called in as witnesses. New York demanded to visit both of my residences to see which one was really the most lived in. And it went on for twelve, maybe thirteen years.

Two greats—golf legend Arnold Palmer and Radio's G.O.A.T.

No, I did not spend in legal fees as much as I would have spent had I just stayed there and paid New York taxes. And I don't know when the next audit's gonna be, but they always happen. I think states like New York have divisions in their tax departments that follow people who move to no-income-tax states. So if you move to Texas, if you move to Kentucky, if you move to Florida, I think they follow you.

My only point in telling you all this is once again, folks, your host, El Rushbo, is on the cutting edge. I was playing golf with Trump at his golf course back—oh, I don't know—ten years ago, fifteen years ago.

And he's asking me, "Why did you leave? Why did you really leave New York? 'Cause, you know, Rush, I'm hearing more and more people say they gotta get out, they gotta get out," and I told him exactly what I told you. He said, "It's incredible."

• • •

It's typical. John Kerry—who, by the way, served in Vietnam— went out and bought a seventy-foot sailboat, and he docked it in Rhode Island and avoided paying taxes in Massachusetts. You know, Democrats ought to move to where it is the most expensive for them to live in accordance with tax law. —Rush Limbaugh

• • •

INSPIRATIONAL CALL FROM BLIND CPA GOLFER
The Rush Limbaugh Show, November 29, 2007

RUSH: Here's James in the Bronx. Nice to have you, sir, on the EIB Network. Hello.

CALLER: Rush, a pleasure to meet you. Mega dittos from a conservative lonely guy in the Bronx. I wanted to, first of all, say the debate last night, I thought was a complete joke, and I finally turned it off out of disgust. But the one point that they haven't mentioned is our economic progress and the tax situation in this country, that's really fueled our economy, and nobody has ever really mentioned it to the extent it has.

RUSH: Well, see, that's another great point. They chose questions that had nothing to do with reality here, just conservative clichés.

CALLER: That's right.

RUSH: You are exactly right. Economic growth for the third quarter estimated at 3.9 percent a month ago—

CALLER: 4.9 percent.

RUSH: 4.9 percent, revised upward by the Bureau of Economic Analysis today.

CALLER: May I make another point, too?

President Trump hosts Jack Nicklaus and Rush at Trump National in Florida.

RUSH: Wait just a second. Wait a second.

CALLER: Go ahead.

RUSH: All during this period, the Drive-bys are predicting a recession.

CALLER: That's right. They're full of baloney. The other thing is, I happen to be a practicing CPA. I lost my sight a while ago, but I still have my business, thanks to your encouragement, so I have no problem with that. But as far as changing the tax code, it's not going to happen, because there are too many lawyers and CPAs that would die if they ever changed the tax code. They got too much of an interest in it—believe me, and I know because I've been a CPA since '56, so I know what goes on.

RUSH: Let me ask you a question here.

CALLER: Sure.

RUSH: James, I'm fifty-six years old. You've been a CPA since 1956. Is that right?

CALLER: Correct. That's correct.

RUSH: In the course of your life, how many presidential campaigns have you heard either candidate, either party, independent or whatever, third party, "We've gotta do something about the tax code. We've gotta reform it. We've gotta revise it. We're going to have to scrap it and start over." How often have you heard that said?

CALLER: Never. Only by, maybe, Reagan, but that's about it.

RUSH: No, I hear it every campaign season is my point, but nothing ever happens.

CALLER: Because they're full of baloney. They just like to hear themselves talk. Come on, Rush. Let me tell you—

RUSH: No, it's not that—they're fooling people into thinking they're actually going to be able to do something about it.

CALLER: There was no conservative candidate on that panel last night, and I don't think we have one. Believe me. And it's very upsetting and very disconcerting. Can I say one other thing?

RUSH: Yeah, go right ahead.

CALLER: I happen to be a blind golfer, by the way, and I enjoy the game immensely, even though I'm blind, lost my sight ten years ago—

RUSH: I have to ask you a question about that.

CALLER: Sure.

RUSH: Most people can't relate. First of all, blind CPA, that's numbers.

CALLER: Right. I have equipment that enables me to do my work, special speech equipment.

RUSH: Okay, but part of the fun of playing golf, James, is when you cream the ball, when you hit it on the screws, it's almost orgasmic to see the thing sail down the fairway 250 yards. How do you replace that, since you can't see? Do you know when you've hit a good shot by how it feels?

CALLER: Yes. Yes, first of all, I've been playing for a lot more years, number one. Number two, when I hear the click of that ball, I can tell by the impact where that ball is going. And then, of course, my friends yell, "My God, look where he hit that ball!" So I get that same thrill, believe me.

RUSH: Okay, so you're going up, let's say you're twenty yards short of the green, and the pin's plus ten, they give you the distance, and they use the—

CALLER: I use my number ten wedge or whatever and I pop it right on.

RUSH: And putting?

CALLER: Yeah, putting was good. The last game I played, believe it or not, I shot a ninety-nine, which I think is respectable.

RUSH: *[Laughs]* Respectable? There are people who have been playing twenty years that can see who haven't ever broken a hundred.

CALLER: It takes practice, Rush, practice. And, by the way, I gotta thank you for your inspiration. When I was down on my luck, I listened to you back in [the] nineties, and it helped, it really helped.

RUSH: I appreciate that. You're an inspiration. Glad you called.

Many of you will remember "the Hutch," a close friend who played football professionally before becoming a reverend. We were honored to have Ken Hutcherson and Steve Limbaugh Sr. officiate our wedding.

Almost every year, around the Super Bowl, Rush and the Hutch would make their predictions during the program. As you know, Rush was an avid sports fan and loved the Pittsburgh Steelers ever since his early days there as an up-and-coming deejay.

SUPER BOWL TRADITION: THE HUTCH
The Rush Limbaugh Show, February 4, 2011

RUSH: We welcome now to the program the Hutch, the Reverend Doctor Ken Hutcherson, from Seattle.

THE HUTCH: How you doing, my brother?

RUSH: Very well. I was just sitting here thinking that all this talk about the Packers coming out with four wide receivers or five wide receivers and spreading the field, with all this talk, they'll probably come out and try to run the ball.

THE HUTCH: *[Laughs]* Well, you know, that's probably one of the weakest points of the Packers is their running back and fullback situation. But they got a lot of the guns, they got Rodgers back there.

RUSH: They do have Rodgers, but this James Starks guy, he's a rookie, and he popped out of nowhere in the Philadelphia playoff game.

THE HUTCH: Yeah.

RUSH: The Steelers have the number-one run defense in the league anyway. But if they want to run the ball, they've got personnel to do it, good personnel grouping, but—

THE HUTCH: I think they're balanced. They didn't get to the Super Bowl because they got lucky. They have done some things very well, and this is the year of the upset, so that's why I think you gonna be crying Sunday night.

RUSH: No, no, no. The upset would be the Steelers winning.

THE HUTCH: The way the news has been, man, everyone thinks that the Packers are gonna lose. I'm just really surprised at that thinking. But one thing I want to get straight before we get into football and get some of these names and stats—

RUSH: Yeah, right.

THE HUTCH: I want to know what the Pittsburgh Steelers is gonna do for you.

RUSH: What will the Pittsburgh Steelers do for me?

THE HUTCH: Yeah. I mean you've been the biggest fan ever. You've given them more free time than Van Camp's got pork and beans. What size ring do you wear?

RUSH: You think they gotta get me a ring? *[Laughs]* Listen, they don't call you old Captain Excrement Stirrer for nothing.

THE HUTCH: Well, we know they ain't gonna win, but they should—

RUSH: *[Laughs]*

THE HUTCH: *[Laughs]*

RUSH: You know what?

THE HUTCH: But if they do, they better get you a ring.

． ． ．

El Rushbo! Al Michaels here, wishing you a happy, glorious twentieth. You know, the world's greatest iconic athletes are exalted because they perform at the highest level year after year after year. You are the radio equivalent of these legends. For two decades you've always been prepared, and when I turn on the radio, I know that you'll be topical, informative, interesting, thought-provoking, and funny. You are an everyday treat, an unusually important figure in this country. And on a personal level, Rush, having gotten to know you over the years, you are a man whose friendship I am extremely grateful for. Your loyalty knows no boundaries, and your friends are the lucky beneficiaries. Rush, here's a toast to the past twenty years, to twenty more, and to twenty more after that. Cheers, skol, lehayim, *and congratulations to you in a hundred languages.*
—Al Michaels, Hall of Fame broadcaster

． ． ．

Chapter 6

PEACE THROUGH STRENGTH

TRIBUTE
by Prime Minister Benjamin Netanyahu

Friends,

Rush Limbaugh was a great American, a true friend of Israel, and a firm believer in the US–Israel alliance.

Rush understood with outstanding clarity what unites America and Israel. He valued the fact that Israel and the United States are vibrant democracies that will staunchly defend the freedoms both countries cherish.

He knew that Israel and the United States are both nations inspired by our founding pioneering ethos and by the biblical heritage we revere.

He appreciated that both our societies share a spirit of rugged individualism that celebrate those who overcome the odds and succeed.

Rush recognized that Israel and the United States are stronger when standing together, and he stood by Israel through thick and thin. Always firm. Never wavering.

He realized a crucial truth: that America has no better friend in the world than the State of Israel, and that Israel has no better friend in the world than the United States of America.

In his passing, America has lost a great patriot, Israel has lost a staunch supporter, and I have lost a friend.

I will miss him greatly.

Benjamin Netanyahu
Jerusalem, Israel

What is Netanyahu, among many other things? He's fearless.
Right? It shows you, it illustrates, there's no reason to be afraid.

—Rush Limbaugh

PART 1 — OUR MILITARY, TRUE HEROES

GREATEST FORCE FOR PEACE IN THE WORLD
The Rush Limbaugh Show, August 18, 2008

RUSH: This country, without any question—this, ladies and gentlemen, is inarguable—the United States of America is the greatest moral force in the world. We not only eliminated slavery in our own borders, we defeated mass murderers in the Third Reich, Imperial Japan, the Soviet Union, and thousands of other places. In fact, the most significant human force against evil in the world is our country: the United States of America.

The American left doesn't think so. There is not another group of people on the history of this earth living together as a nation that have done more for the moral rectitude of the world, for the moral ability of nations to treat citizens properly. There's no nation that's done more to rid the world of evil.

* * *

The older I get, I am more and more in awe of people in the military, and I am just indescribably in awe of the founding of America and the miracle for everything that happened just to take place at the right time when it did. I think it is a miracle, and I think we're blessed. —Rush Limbaugh

* * *

AN AMAZING EXPERIENCE IN WASHINGTON, DC
The Rush Limbaugh Show, November 17, 2006

RUSH: I had the most amazing day and a half in Washington. . . . [I went] to the Walter Reed Army Hospital itself for a visit to the wing where amputees are undergoing rehabilitation, both occupational rehab and therapeutic rehab. Folks, I'll tell you, it was my first time, and these men and women that

335

Rush with Medal of Honor recipient James E. Livingston at a MC-LEF gala in New York.

are in the United States Armed Forces—and I've always known this, but—
they're just a different breed.

They are such a cut above. I walked in there, and my first glance around
I got a lump in my throat, and I am not exaggerating. I walked in that room,
and we had about five or six in our group, and here are people who have lost

336

both legs above the knee, one leg and one arm, shrapnel wounds all over their bodies. Every darn one of them was smiling. . . .

These people are anywhere from late teens to mid-twenties, and they were all just smiling, and I asked every one of them I talked to, "Have you got what you need?" and they looked at me kind of surprised. "Oh, yes. Yes, sir. We have everything that we need."

Many of them are listeners of this program, as are their family members. I walked in there and I almost felt unworthy to go in this room, and I feel that more and more when I'm around people—veterans of combat in the US Armed Forces. I felt like I'm not good enough to be in this room. These people have lost significant parts of their bodies defending the country and protecting the country and performing their orders and missions. To watch 'em all smiling and laughing and going about their work was just beyond touching.

But you talk about inspiration and motivation. . . . Any time I start getting down in the dumps, and it happens to all of us, I just think about what I saw in Afghanistan, think about what I saw yesterday, it tends to put it in perspective. . . . But it was just one of the most meaningful periods of time that I have ever spent.

* * *

The profound impact of freedom on billions of lives is impossible to calculate. So, too, is freedom's cost. The hardships and sacrifices that American veterans have borne, their innumerable individual acts of valor and compassion, are known only to the ages. No other nation in the history of this world has given so many sons and daughters to defend the freedom of others, too often without thanks from those they liberate. So to our American veterans, each one of you—and to the memory of those who came before you— thank you, and from all of us, God bless you. —Rush Limbaugh

* * *

LETTER FROM SERVICE MEMBER IN IRAQ

Dear Mr. Limbaugh,

I am a soldier that was serving my second tour in Iraq with the 101st Airborne Division of Fort Campbell, Kentucky. May seventh of last year, my vehicle was hit by a roadside bomb; the explosion instantly severed both of my legs. I have been recovering and going through therapy at Walter Reed Army Medical Center for almost nine months.

Sir, I listen to your program every day; I even try to schedule my therapy and appointments before noon or after 1500 so I don't miss any of it. On behalf of my fellow soldiers, and myself, I would like to thank you for standing up, and bringing the truth to Americans. I want to thank you from the bottom of my heart for your continued support of the ideas that are America.

Once I complete my therapy and am medically retired from the army, I am returning to my hometown of Clinton, Missouri. I will be running for State Representative in 2008, and hope that I can begin to bring the ideas and the morals that founded this amazing country back to our elected officials.

Thank you for your time again, sir, and please continue the amazing job. America is counting on you to continue bringing the truth to her people.

Your fellow American,

Christopher R.
SGT, United States Army

OUR COUNTRY IS DOING THE LORD'S WORK: RUSH VISITS TROOPS IN AFGHANISTAN

The Rush Limbaugh Show, February 28, 2005

Now, ladies and gentlemen, as you know, I was in Afghanistan all week, and I don't know how many of you had a chance to hear . . . I have such—and this happens every time I travel, folks. I don't care where I go. I go to Europe, go to any foreign country, I come back here and am so proud and ecstatic and happy to be an American.

Folks, a twenty-three-hour plane trip back, and I didn't sleep on the plane. . . . I didn't sleep . . . I don't know how many time zones. It was nine and a half hours, is the time difference. It is, like, for example, right now it's 9:45 p.m. in Afghanistan.

The main reason that I went over there was to visit the troops, and I had four troop visits, and one that was scheduled that didn't come off, which was scheduled for Friday morning at Bagram Air Force Base. That didn't happen because, as we were leaving Kandahar, which is the one spot that real combat still goes on, overnight there was mortar fire that we could hear and see both in and out of the base camp.

We left there, or tried to leave there, I guess it was eight o'clock on Friday morning, and just as we lifted off, we lost an engine, the number four engine on the C-130. No, I was not scared. This is exciting. I've always wanted to fly in a C-130.

They have four engines on the C-130, and the number four engine is the far-outside starboard engine on the right side of the wing, and they just had to feather it, because they didn't know what happened. There was no fire or any of that. So we did 360s. We flew in circles turning to the right for what seemed like eight, ten minutes at eight thousand feet, trying to see if something could be done to force fuel back into the engine.

Nothing could, so we had to turn around and go back, and we were on the ground there probably for five and a half hours waiting for another flight, and by that time it was too late to go to Bagram; had to go back to Kabul. . . .

I have more respect and awe and admiration for the people that wear the uniform of this country in Afghanistan, and I'm sure around the world, than I had even before I left, and I didn't know how I could appreciate them any more. . . .

* * *

I was taken to the camp, by the way, where we launched those cruise missiles, the empty training camps of Osama bin Laden. It's near Kandahar. I saw Tora Bora, saw the caves that we turned to two thousand degrees. Yeah, saw all this stuff. . . .

We also have government aid workers out there, which are teaching literacy, teaching Afghanis how to teach literacy and other things; women are voting now in record numbers, so it's all kinds of great progress that's taking place.

It's all oriented toward the notion that a free people working [in] their own self-interest will develop themselves and their own economy in a prosperous fashion—it's going to take some time—while at the same time increasing our own security, and I think the efforts of all Americans over there in this regard are to be applauded and appreciated. . . .

* * *

I have to tell you, folks, our country is doing the Lord's work in Afghanistan and that whole region. I tell you, this makes me want to go to Iraq. I want to see what's going on in Iraq. Now, admittedly, Iraq is still a daily combat battle zone.

Afghanistan has slowed down because there's victory there, but now putting Afghanistan back together and bringing it up to speed in the twenty-first century and securing it as a government that is functioning on the part of free people equaling the additional security to the United States is just a massive project.

You cannot believe the amount of work to be done to put this country back together. But there are people there doing it step-by-step, each and every day; they are patient, and they've chosen it as their life's work, and that's what they're doing. I ran into Americans who live there, have lived there now for two to three years. They've made it their life's work to build this country back.

＊　＊　＊

America's military power must be secure, because the United States is the only guarantor of global peace and stability. The current neglect of America's armed forces threatens its ability to maintain peace.
—Dr. Condoleezza Rice, sixty-sixth US Secretary of State

＊　＊　＊

THE LEFT AIMS TO DESTROY THE US MILITARY
The Rush Limbaugh Show, February 15, 2007

The left had a propaganda campaign designed to convince the American people that people such as your sons only join because they have no future. "The economy and the country [are] horrible; they can't get into a decent school. You're poor. You probably live in a trailer park somewhere, and the military is your kid's only way out," and so that's why I say there are no stories about the valor of the military in this country.

There are no stories about the heroism that these people engage in. All we get are the stories about how they're a bunch of dummies. They have no future because America sucks economically. They have no way out of the ghetto in which they live and so forth, and they're raised to become killers and they go over there doing things they'd really rather not do—and there aren't any movies made of heroism of US military men these days, and there certainly aren't any stories in the Drive-by Media. That's why people have a misunderstanding of what particularly soldiers in this war are all about.

● ● ●

I cannot, or will not, take the freedoms this country offers for granted. But these freedoms have come with a price so many times. The sacrifices made by our veterans are reminders to us of this.
—First Lady Melania Trump

● ● ●

THE FATHER OF A FALLEN SOLDIER
The Rush Limbaugh Show, October 19, 2007

RUSH: Bob in Colorado. Nice to have you, sir. Welcome to the EIB Network.

CALLER: Yes, sir. I'm calling to let you know that not only does your program and your opinions serve to interest people in the truth and get interested in the military and give them a reason to join—excuse me—*[Crying]* my son was killed April this year over there, and what you do and say gives us a reason, as survivors of people who made that sacrifice . . . a reason to believe in what they did, because we know he believed in it. It was his second tour. And it does a lot to comfort us and make us know that it was just worthwhile. It's tough to say that, but it is.

RUSH: I appreciate that. I can only try to relate to your loss. It's something that—losing a child is something that nobody expects to happen. It's not the way things are supposed to happen. But this happened in a duty of honor. He was doing it for his country, which is entirely honorable. The thing, if I may say so, Bob, that infuriates me is in the midst of all this, your son giving his life and others in Iraq and Afghanistan, while this is going on, we have politicians in this country who want to just quit, bring 'em home, render their loss meaningless by saying that what we're doing is meaningless; that what we're doing is based on a lie; that it has no business taking place; that there's nothing to fight for, it's just a civil war, we can't win. I can't imagine how that infuriates you, and it is not honorable. It's the exact opposite. It is dishonorable, and this has been going on for far too long, and it's happening precisely because a political party thinks it needs to do this and say these things in order to get elected to the White House. It's disgusting, it is sickening, to me, it's almost indescribable. Which is why, for me, it is a privilege and an honor to continually sing the praises, both morally and spiritually and courageously, speaking of the courage of people like your son. It's a courage and a bravery that a lot of Americans don't have, and that's not a criticism. It's a special thing that your son volunteered to do. I know you're as proud as you can be, even though you're still in pain over the loss, and I can totally understand that. But I'll speak on behalf of everybody in this audience. If we could come to your house and thank you in person and share your grief with you, we would do it.

CALLER: Well, thank you, sir. We owe you a debt that we can't repay, but—

RUSH: No, you don't.

CALLER: —keep up the good work.

RUSH: You know, this is really hard for me. I appreciate—I'm trying to get better at receiving. I'm not going to reject what you said. I appreciate it. It just humbles me to be compared to what your son did. I've told this story a couple times. I'll tell it again. *National Review*'s fiftieth-anniversary dinner was at a little museum in Washington. They invited some wounded troops from Walter Reed to come for the evening, and the troops at Walter Reed have suffered severe injuries. One of the guys that I spoke to lost an eye, was wearing an eye patch; some were without an arm, and a couple of them came up to me, I was told that they wanted to meet me, and they came up to the table where I was sitting with Mr. Buckley, and they started thanking me for what I was doing. I felt three inches tall. I mean, look who I'm talking to. I said, "Look, I really appreciate this, but I'm flapping my gums. You guys, look what you've given up here for our country." "Stop it, sir." They always call everybody "sir." He said, "We all have our roles to play." We all have our roles in this. When I toured Walter Reed, I was there mere moments after Senator Kerry had left, and heard much the same thing. And I saw the serious injuries. This was the amputee rehab wing that I went to visit. It was the day I spoke at a theater in Washington on the Rush to Excellence Tour later that night, and toured the Fisher House, which Max Fisher and his family have built a number of these homes near military bases where recovering wounded soldiers who . . . no longer require hospitalization can stay. It's sort of like a Ronald McDonald's house for the military, and they call it the Fisher House. And these guys were

Rush's father was always fascinated with aviation from his younger years as a World War II pilot.

working really hard in the swimming pool and the exercise machines, doing rehab, learning to walk again and so forth, and they were just all—I didn't see any misery. I did not see any doom and gloom. I'm sure they feel it. They have to. But they were all in a good mood, and they would happily discuss their service. They would tell you what happened if you asked. They were speaking excitedly about their future, once they'd gotten well. It's inspirational to talk to people who do these kinds of things, like your son. I wish more people could meet them personally because, especially in the climate that we're in now, it would slap people into a sense of reality as to what people are actually doing. They're volunteering to do it because they believe the threat that we face is real, and they want to defend and protect their country. It's really a special thing, and it's been an honor for me to be associated with it, in however which way, all of us here are. So, Bob, thanks for the call. I appreciate it.

* * *

The attacks of September eleventh were intended to break our spirit. Instead, we have emerged stronger and more unified. We feel renewed devotion to the principles of political, economic, and religious freedom, the rule of law, and respect for human life. We are more determined than ever to live our lives in freedom.

—Mayor Rudy Giuliani, Opening Remarks to the United Nations General Assembly, Special Session on Terrorism, October 1, 2001

* * *

THOUGHTS ON 9/11—AND PATRIOTISM
The Rush Limbaugh Show, September 11, 2013

RUSH: It is also 9/11, the anniversary of 9/11, and I've been watching it on television today. I don't know about you, but I can't help but be stirred and profoundly moved. I think like everybody, I was remembering where I was, which happened to be in the air. I had taken off around eight o'clock for Omaha. It was the last Warren Buffett Charity Golf Tournament. It was my second or third year to be invited to play in it.

I was, at the time, experiencing very severe hearing loss, and I had not yet lost enough hearing that would permit me to qualify for cochlear implant surgery, so I was getting by with hearing aids. They just weren't doing the trick. I was able to hear noise, but I wasn't able to comprehend speech very well. So I guess about an hour, hour and a half into the flight, the pilot comes back and says, "The World Trade Center has been hit, and we have to set down. . . ."

The fact that we were ordered down out of the sky—and everybody else was, too—indicated it was very, very bad. We finally rolled in here at around 2:30, 2:45, with maybe a half hour, twenty minutes left in the program, and that is the first time, when I got in here, I had seen pictures. So it was, I don't know, five hours after it happened. I was . . . I mean, I was shocked. I had every emotion: anger, sorrow, sadness, disbelief, curiosity, everything. All these emotions were firing off instantly.

I sat down here and I was trying to make sense of it. I did the last twenty minutes of the program from the guest host that day. . . . The next morning, I'm driving in to work here, and I'm driving on the Ocean Coast Road with the Atlantic Ocean on the left, just after dawn. I couldn't sleep much, so I was driving in here, and it's just an absolutely beautiful dawn here. It's just the kind of day it was in New York that day. It was a little warmer, but in terms of blue sky, sunshine, it was a clear, beautiful day. The ocean was calm driving in, and it was serene. I was one of the few driving around. I remember looking out over the ocean, out the car window driving in, trying to imagine why anybody would want to do what they did. . . . The pictures were in my mind as I'm driving out, looking out over this beautiful sea, the sun coming up. . . .

* * *

Every car I saw had an American flag waving on it. Everywhere you went in the immediate aftermath, you saw American flags. You couldn't buy them. They were sold out. Jewelry featuring the American flag was made. There were bumper stickers that were slapped on people's cars. Do you remember how unified this country was in the aftermath of 9/11? I will never forget, folks. . . .

* * *

It wasn't long after 9/11 that no matter where you went, every automobile had and was proudly flying an American flag somewhere. A bumper sticker, whatever. Jewelry. You couldn't find American flag bumper stickers anywhere. Bumper stickers were left and right. There was a renewed patriotism that we hadn't seen in the country a long, long time . . . and the country was unified. There was patriotism. Patriotism had broken out everywhere, and it was being displayed. You didn't have to hear anybody talk to know it existed. They were flying flags. They were using any symbol they could to express their pride. Everybody in this country was.

Even on the freeways of California, you'd see American flag after American flag. It was a beautiful sight, by the way. We were united as a country, and it was patriotism everywhere. Even amid all the sorrow, there was a great comfort in that. . . .

ONE OF THE MOST TOUCHING CALLS EVER
The Rush Limbaugh Show, June 1, 2007

RUSH: Here's Amy in Fort Eustis, Virginia. Amy, thank you for calling and waiting. Nice to have you on the program.

CALLER: Thank you so much for taking my call, Rush. I'm very excited to be talking to you. . . . I grew up an air force brat. My father did not retire until I was a freshman in college. Then, when I was twenty, I married a man who had just finished up flight school in the army, and that was almost fifteen years ago. So my whole life I know the military lifestyle, that's about all I know. Along with that comes moving around . . . all the time. I'll be thirty-five years old this year. I am in my twenty-first house in my life—

RUSH: Whoa ho-ho-ho! . . .

CALLER: I had this realization that no matter where I have lived, especially over the past ten years or so, I have had Rush Limbaugh. We have the radio everywhere, and I can just turn it on, and I wanted to thank you for being, I guess, my stability and my home, especially for the past ten or twelve years.

RUSH: Wow. I don't know what to say. That is so sweet. That's so nice.

PART 2 — NATIONAL DEFENSE

Rush believed unequivocally in President Reagan's idea of "Peace through Strength." He maintained that the United States simply cannot be a superpower by bowing to terrorists, tyrants, and bullies who want to destroy our people. "They do not like us and never will, no matter how we try to appease. We stand for democracy and freedom," Rush said. He opposed the entire notion of apology tours and argued that our leaders cannot go around the world begging for forgiveness in hope that we will prevent evil that way. Rush always said our country is the greatest fighting force for peace in the world.

In 1994, Rush visits Israel and is welcomed as a foreign dignitary by then Prime Minister Yitzhak Rabin.

WHEN DID WE BECOME A PACIFIST NATION?
The Rush Limbaugh Show, January 3, 2007

RUSH: This is Jason in New Braunfels, Texas. You're next, sir. I appreciate your patience. Welcome to the EIB Network.

CALLER: Hi, Rush. Happy New Year to you.

RUSH: Same to you, sir.

CALLER: I've always thought something. I wanted to ask you this question. You were talking about toughness in the first hour, and I knew when people didn't flock out to see the movie about United 93 that we were going to lose the election in November, for many of the same reasons you outlined—just the general, overall loss of toughness, and I wanted to ask you if you think it would have been better if the Americans had defeated the Russians militarily versus politically in the Cold War. Because I think a lot of this Oprah-fication of America began when we didn't have to go mano a mano with the Russians back in the day.

RUSH: You know, I hadn't thought of that, and rather than just give a knee-jerk answer that would appear on liberal websites, I would like to think about that, because it is an interesting point. It's dangerous to play the "if" game. We don't live in a TiVo world. We can't rewind it back then and change the outcome. It is what it is, but it does give thought. . . . I always love explaining motivations, or understanding them so I can explain them. . . . So to try to explain why the American people, to get back to your original point, why the American people to me have become a nation of pacifists: I think there's so many factors that it would be difficult to go back and say, "You know, if we had really achieved a big-time military win over the Soviets, then we'd be a little tougher than we are today," and I know what your point is, that we won the Cold War without firing a shot, and we did it with words and doctors and nurses and clean water, but we didn't. We did it with deterrence and we did it with a robust and strong military and a president who everybody feared had the will to use it. This is still a world governed by the aggressive use of force, and it always will be. But we have a country, God love it, that is so affluent, with so much opportunity for prosperity every day, that people who don't want to realize and deal with the fact that we face an enemy that would like to wipe us out don't have to. They're not needed to win it, and if they don't think they're needed, it may as well not be that big; it might as well not be that large a matter. But I think it's a cumulative thing that has been creeping up on us for years and years and years, and I think, as Shelby Steele has written, one of the things that's hap-pened—and it has been a slowly creeping thing, too, ever since even prior to [the] civil rights movement. But the multicultural curricula in all the schools today [have] successfully imposed a bunch of guilt on the American people. We are guilty because we're a majority. We're guilty because we're the biggest. We're guilty because we're the most powerful; we're guilty because we're the richest, because what did we do to become all that? "Well, the first thing we did was kick the Indians off their own land! Why, they were at one with nature, and then we imported racism and sexism and bigotry and homophobia and we destroyed the environment! We're destroying the planet with global warming. We deserve a comeuppance! We deserve to lose in Iraq! We deserve to lose everywhere else! We need to get ourselves cut down to size!" All of this guilt is what allows illegal immigration to go unchallenged by a whole lot of people, just a number of things. So to cite one example as the primary cause would be a difficult thing to do, but I appreciate the call.

◦ ◦ ◦

To be prepared for war is one of the most effectual means of preserving peace. —George Washington, First Annual Address to Congress, January 8, 1790

◦ ◦ ◦

TRUMP VOWS TO REBUILD THE MILITARY
The Rush Limbaugh Show, September 7, 2016

RUSH: Trump is speaking in Philadelphia today on military matters. He's doing quite well. I want to join a little bit of this in progress, just to give you a flavor for how Trump is sounding today. Looking great, too.

TRUMP: We have to create that strength, and sometimes we have to reduce bureaucracy. It just gets in our way.

AUDIENCE: *[Applause]*

RUSH: Getting a lot of applause here, announcing military reforms and upgrades. It's a really good speech.

TRUMP: Early in my term I will also be requesting that all NATO nations promptly pay their bills, which many are not now doing.

AUDIENCE: *[Applause and cheers]*

RUSH: His tie matches the American flag background.

TRUMP: Only five NATO countries, including the United States, are currently meeting their minimum requirement to spend 2 percent of GDP on defense. They understand it. They know they have to do it. They can afford to

• • •

Rush Limbaugh made conservatism popular with the entire nation and revolutionized conservative media. He will be missed by all of his "Dittoheads," this one included. Our country has lost one of its most important voices. —Mike Pompeo, seventieth US Secretary of State, Tribute to Rush, 2021

• • •

do it. They have no respect for our leadership. They have no respect for our country. They will do it. They'll be happy to do it. They will be happy to do it.

AUDIENCE: *[Applause]*

RUSH: They'll be happy to do it. It's a very well-received speech, I have to tell you.

TRUMP: Additionally, I will be respectfully asking countries, such as Germany, Japan, South Korea, Saudi Arabia, to pay more for the tremendous security we provide them.

AUDIENCE: *[Applause]*

RUSH: It's a very substantive speech on reforming and rebuilding the military, folks.

TRUMP: Using these new funds, I will ask my secretary of defense to propose a new defense budget to meet the following longtime goals.

RUSH: Here we go.

TRUMP: We will build an active army of around 540,000, as the army's chief of staff has said he needs desperately and really must have to protect our country. We now—

AUDIENCE: *[Applause]*

TRUMP: We now have only thirty-one brigade combat teams, or 490,000 troops. And only one-third of combat teams are considered combat ready. That's not good for our country. I actually don't even like saying it because plenty of countries are watching us right now, but we'll get it shaped up very quickly.

AUDIENCE: *[Applause]*

RUSH: It's a teleprompter speech, very reserved, very substantive, serious.

TRUMP: We will build a Marine Corps based on thirty-six battalions, which the Heritage Foundation notes is the minimum needed to deal with major contingencies. Right now we only have twenty-three.

RUSH: Not good.

TRUMP: We will build a navy of 350 surface ships and submarines, as recommended by the bipartisan National Defense Panel. We right now only have 276 ships, and it's not enough. And we will build an air force of at least 1,200 fighter aircraft, which the Heritage Foundation again has shown to be needed to execute current missions. We now have 1,113. Not enough. We will also seek to develop a state-of-the-art missile defense system.

AUDIENCE: *[Applause]*

RUSH: Oh, you hear that applause for that? Star Wars!

TRUMP: Under Obama-Clinton, our ballistic missile defense capability has been degraded at the very moment in the United States' history, and its allies . . . we are facing the strongest, most heightened missile threat that we have ever, ever had. You look at Iran, you look at North Korea, you look at terrorists, we don't even know where to look. We don't know where to look. But believe me, you can look all over, so we are going to do that. We need a form of shield. We want to protect our country.

AUDIENCE: *[Applause]*

RUSH: We had six hundred ships, a six-hundred-ship navy under Reagan. We're down to two hundred now.

SENATOR BIDEN GUARANTEES WORLD CRISIS UNDER OBAMA WITHIN SIX MONTHS
The Rush Limbaugh Show, October 20, 2008

Hey, folks, how about our boy, Joe Biden? Hey, stand up, Joe, tell us again what's going to happen when Obama gets elected. You hear what Biden said? ABC is reporting that Joe Biden is warning now of an international crisis. The world, multiple nations, will test Obama just as JFK was tested the first six months of his administration.

Biden is guaranteeing trouble under Obama. We can also assume that McCain would not cause such a test to occur from leaders around the world, but Biden is out there saying to multiple countries; he said, "Your influence within the community, to stand with him. Because it's not gonna be apparent initially, it's not gonna be apparent that we're right," in how we deal with whatever it is. And he said, "I could give you five or six scenarios."

Love Joe Biden. He says it would be patriotic to pay higher taxes and that this country is going to face an international crisis or two only if Obama is elected. We will not face an international crisis, according to Biden, if McCain is elected. See, under McCain what we would get is lower taxes and, apparently, a far more peaceful world. McCain's been tested; no one will screw with him, according to Biden.

You know what a gaffe is, is when a politician tells the truth. What's amazing to me about Biden's statement, ladies and gentlemen, is I thought the election of Obama was going to make the world love us again. I thought we're going to repair this busted image that we have all around the world, and the moment Obama is elected—we don't have to wait 'til he's inaugurated—from the moment he is elected, the world is going to *[kissing sound]* love us again.

They're going to want to kiss us everywhere they can. They're going to be so happy, and here's Biden saying—paraphrasing—"Oh, yeah, get ready, folks."

TV NETWORKS IGNORE BENGHAZI HEARINGS
The Rush Limbaugh Show, May 8, 2013

What a shock. What an absolute shock, ladies and gentlemen. It looks like no other news network, not even cable news, is covering the Benghazi hearings except for Fox News. We live in an upside-down world, ladies and gentlemen, where most everybody is going to ignore what happens here in these hearings, and, when it's over, they're going to say, "What's the big deal anyway...?"

But let me make a prediction here. When these hearings are over, no matter what's revealed about Benghazi, the mainstream media is all gonna say, "What difference does it make now? There's nothing to see here. This isn't Watergate." And it isn't Watergate. Nobody died in Watergate. Four people died in Benghazi. Nobody died in Watergate....

Was it because of a protest or was it because of guys out for a walk one night who decided they'd go kill some Americans? What difference, at this point, does it make?
—Hillary Clinton, sixty-seventh US Secretary of State

I mean, the cover-up, the attempted ways in which this was swept under the rug, all of it's fascinating. Now, the Situation Room is the government's nerve center for intelligence and crisis support, deep down under the White House. Five thousand square feet. It has the most sophisticated high tech. It has sensors to prevent bugging. It has the ability to monitor situations anywhere in the world. It has seating that accommodates the National Security Agency, Homeland Security, the White House chief of staff, the official White House photographer.

On May the second, 2011, fifteen officials and the White House photographer watched the killing of Osama bin Laden in the Situation Room. On September eleventh, 2012, no one was there, apparently. The Situation Room was not used. Nobody went there, apparently, evidently, [when] four Americans were killed. You know, the old saying is that success has a thousand fathers, and failure is an orphan.

RUSH: Eric Nordstrom. This is this morning at the Benghazi hearings. A portion of his opening remarks.

NORDSTROM: What happened prior, during, and after the attack matters. It matters to me personally, and it matters to my colleagues—[chokes up] to my colleagues at the Department of State. It matters to the American public, for whom we serve, and most importantly—[clears throat] excuse me—it matters to the friends and family of Ambassador Stevens, Sean Smith, Glen Doherty, and Tyrone Woods, who were murdered on September eleventh, 2012.

RUSH: That's the response to Mrs. Clinton saying, "What difference does it make? What difference does it make now?" Eric Nordstrom, former regional security officer in Libya. That's who he is. Eric Nordstrom: "It matters to my colleagues." He was breaking down. He was crying. He was sipping water. He was choking up here. "It matters to the friends and family of Ambassador Stevens, Sean Smith, Glen Doherty, and Tyrone Woods, who were murdered on September eleventh, 2012." What difference does it make now anyway, though? Why do we care?

OUR FREEDOM THREATENS THE WORLD'S TYRANTS
The Rush Limbaugh Show, September 24, 2015

Most of the world's leaders are tyrants. That's another reason that we are special and why we are so hell-bent opposed [to] and frightened of tyrants. We don't want dictators, which is what most people live under. Most people were born to tyranny and bondage and dictatorship, and most, to this day, are still subject to it in one way or another, or in many ways.

Those people, the tyrants and the dictators, and many others who seek to run and rule countries, do not want a free people. Do you think Fidel Castro wants his people to be free? Do you think Raúl Castro wants his people to be free? Do you think Stalin, old Joe, wanted his people to be free? Or Lenin? Do you think Hitler wanted his people to be free? How about the ChiComs? Do you really think they want their people to be free? No. They want them to be controlled.

The leaders in these tyrannies and dictatorships do very well economically. They are literal thieves. They plunder and steal the national wealth of the countries they lead, à la the Castros, à la the Soviet leaders. Look at the oligarchs even today there, Putin and his buddies. The thing that stands in the way of that is a free people and a runway economy. A growing economy with prosperity for all. That's, again, what explains, illustrates, defines the specialness or uniqueness of the United States, and it really is a rarity.

My question was, all of these leaders that I'm talking about, these tyrants and dictators, if you listen to them, what are the names of their countries? The People's Republic of whatever. The people don't have a say in anything in these countries. The leaders who claim to be for the little guy, who claim to care about the oppressed, who claim they're gonna get even with the rich, claim they're gonna get even with those who have their jackbooted thugs on the necks of the little guy, don't mean it.

If they did, they would be trying to emulate the United States, and they would attempt to seek the stature and credit one would attain from founding, establishing, leading such a nation, such a prosperous nation. But that's not who these people are. They're dictators. They're tyrants. They rule by the use of force and intimidation and imprisonment.

And that is the story for most of the people in the world. And in light of that fact, it infuriates me even more when I have to listen to people both in this country and visitors to this country blame us for the problems in the world.

It really steams me. It really ticks me off when they start going down this road of climate change and how we're destroying the world and we are destroying the planet. I can't tell you, I get so insulted, I get so angry when I hear this. Anyway, I appreciate the call, Alan. I really do.

● ● ●

Bill Clinton did everything in the world he could to fight terrorism and confront and defeat those guys—with subpoenas. —Rush Limbaugh

● ● ●

TRUMP'S HISTORIC MIDDLE EAST PEACE DEAL
The Rush Limbaugh Show, September 15, 2020

So the signing ceremony is about to begin; the whole ceremony has begun at the White House, Donald Trump and the Israeli prime minister, Benjamin Netanyahu. This is truly historic, and it is, I don't think, going to get anywhere near the proper weight and coverage that this event deserves.

My whole life this has been a major political initiative that every new president tackles. Every new president, my entire life; every new president, every new term has made Middle East peace an objective. . . .

Donald Trump, Mr. Bull in the China Shop, Mr. Stupid, Mr. Dummkopf, Mr. Outsider, Mr. Illegitimate, Mr. "He Stole the Election Working with the Russians" has come along and achieved something every American president since the 1950s has been attempting to achieve. And how did he do it? He did it by going at it an entirely different way. . . . And, lo and behold, it worked. We now have peace in the Middle East, and it's just beginning. United Arab Emirates, Bahrain. You watch.

PRIME MINISTER NETANYAHU DELIVERS EPIC SPEECH BEFORE US CONGRESS
The Rush Limbaugh Show, May 24, 2011

Benjamin Netanyahu gave an epic speech today before a joint meeting of Congress. It's a lesson in commitment. It is a lesson in confidence. It is a lesson in statecraft and leadership. This was an epic, epic speech. There was nothing partisan in the speech whatsoever, other than his obvious love and support for his nation of Israel. But it was filled with humor, it was filled with goose bump seriousness. It ran the emotional gamut, it ran the intellectual gamut. The timing was flawless. Just a fabulous speech. The lesson that is there for people is to say what you mean, to say it confidently, to be fearless, and don't feel the need to excuse what you think or make excuses for how you feel.

He made it very clear he understands what's needed for peace, made it very clear that Israel is willing to compromise again—and thereby putting the onus back on the Palestinians. Where is compromise on their part? . . . The reason I'm spending time on it, folks, is words mean things. One of my earliest philosophical pronouncements from the earliest days of this program: Words mean things. We live in a time when many politicians utter words that are meant to beguile and fool, not communicate properly.

I, in a small way, as a conservative, relate to Israel. Surrounded, mischaracterized, blamed for things I'm not doing; blamed for things I don't think. Racist, sexist, bigot, homophobe. Israel is blamed for starting wars in the Middle East, all this stuff. Plus, I've had the good fortune of meeting Benjamin Netanyahu.

I have described in great detail a couple of times my five-day trip to Israel in 1993, where I met Netanyahu, Rabin, Shimon Peres; three-hour private, personalized bus tour of the new settlements in the West Bank from Ariel Sharon, who built them.

Also in the nineties, back when he was prime minister during his first stint, I remember it was a Sunday, I was returning to New York from—I think I'd been out on a Rush to Excellence appearance somewhere. Netanyahu was in New York, and they were staying at the Essex House, and I received an invitation to come by and have a cigar. So I went by, and Netanyahu's office had taken up residence somewhere in the Essex House. By the time you went through security and got through there, it was a labyrinth of a maze that you had to go through to get to where he was.

We sat in there, maybe an hour and a half, just discussing Israeli affairs and the United States during the Clinton years and smoking cigars. So I have a personal affection for Netanyahu. I think he's great, and he's getting better, he's maturing. He's plainly spoken. He's just good at what he does, and I've often said one of the greatest perks of my success, one of the greatest benefits of my success is that I've been able to meet people who are the best at what they do, who have reached the pinnacle of their profession. That's a rare opportunity, and it's inspiring in and of itself. And he's got an impossible job.

He runs a country that, not just the Middle East but people all over the world wish didn't exist. He runs a place that is under constant fire. And, you know, in fact, the Jewish people for me, you look at their world history, wherever they've been, people have tried to wipe 'em out, exterminate 'em. And yet as a culture, they have not crumbled. Their values have remained strong and solid.

One of Rush's all-time favorite parodies and nicknames was Ali Limbali, live from beautiful midtown Kabul. Rush said to the troops in Afghanistan on his visit, "There's this guy that's sending in tapes now and then that's undermining the Afghan operation, trying to pass himself off as the Rush Limbaugh of Afghanistan, Ali Limbali. See if you can find the cave he's broadcasting out of and eradicate him, and they promised to do it."

FROM THE GREATEST PARODIES HITS ROSTER . . .

ALI LIMBALI

ANNOUNCER: Now, live from high atop the second floor of the EAB building in beautiful midtown Kabul, it's the most dangerous man in Afghanistan—Ali Limbali.

ALI LIMBALI: Thank you, Omar Sunibaugh. Hardly recognized you without the beard *[chuckles]*. That's right, I am Ali Limbali—talent on loan from Allah—in the newly liberated Kabul. I'm here, I've been waiting all day and night to talk to you people. I'm holding in my hand the latest Taliban update: Joe Taliban on the run, scurrying south on their vaunted riding mowers, vacuums, even their paper gliders. You just have to love it. Oh yes, Osama and Mullah Omar know their days are numbered, folks! Courtesy of the Yankee American bombs, which fall with precision and vengeance. It is a great day, people. Let's go to the phones, find out what you people think. Let's go to Zaif on a cell phone in Herat. You're on with Ali Limbali.

ZAIF: I give you no hummus and much Hamas, Ali Limbali.

ALI LIMBALI: All right.

ZAIF: Listen to you. You sit there while infidels disembowel our country. We are regrouping, Ali Limbali. . . .

ALI LIMBALI: I'm quaking in my sandals, Zaif, quaking.

ZAIF: The Taliban will be back, don't you forget it. We will be seeing you very soon. Don't go shaving your beard just yet, Ali Limbali!

ALI LIMBALI: Hey, Zaif.

ZAIF: Yes, infidel.

ALI LIMBALI: Just one question. What are your coordinates? I wanna be sure that the American navy delivers a special gift for Ramadan in your cave.

ZAIF: Well, let me tell you something! I am not . . . *[goes off on a screaming rant]*

ANNOUNCER: You're listening to the EAB network, 2001.

As conservatives, we are very used to being labeled anti-immigrant simply because we care about enforcing our borders. Rush asked, "Why should we allow people to break the laws that are designed to protect American citizens and our country's way of life?" He would push back against the typical liberal slander of conservatives being "anti-immigrant" by pointing out the difference between legal and illegal immigration. Rush noted that the United States has welcomed legal immigrants from the time of our founding and that our country has the most diverse population in the world.

CONSERVATIVES DON'T HATE IMMIGRANTS!
The Rush Limbaugh Show, December 16, 2014

It dawned on me yet again that people do not understand principled opposition to amnesty. There's nothing personal about it. It has nothing to do with these particular 15 or 20 million people. It has nothing to do with that. It has everything to do with borders. It has everything to do with preserving the country as we know it with a distinct and proud of it, damn it, American culture, which is why every immigrant in the past has wanted to come here.

There's not a person I know that wants to deport, try to round up 15 or 20 million people and send 'em packing. It isn't practical. It isn't going to happen. What everybody wants is the border secured, with active limits on the amount of immigration so that the flow is two things: economically acceptable and productive, and that something that used to happen automatically begins to happen again; that's assimilation.

Every time I tell people that there was no immigration in this country for over forty years, from the 1920s to the 1960s, seventies, they're shocked. You'd be amazed at the number of people that do not know we totally closed the borders after the wave of European immigration in the 1920s. And we did it for one reason: That mass arrival of immigrants needed to be assimilated. Now, they wanted to be. They wanted to become Americans. They had to learn English. They learned American customs. They became acquainted with American holidays. They studied for citizenship. All of this they wanted. And it took that many years to assimilate. All the opposition to amnesty is not personal to these 15 million people. It is, (A), rule of law. If we lose the rule of law, that's all we've got. We are seeing how really precariously structured this country really is.

We've got a document, the Constitution, that is the law of the land, and we've now got a president who, when he doesn't like it, pretends it doesn't exist. There is no mechanism other than censure or impeachment to deal with that.

And the Republicans have taken both off the table. So there's no signal that he must stop. If this continues, the United States is not gonna be what it was founded and [what] the Constitution spells out. Somebody asked me on the phone recently, "Is it the honor system, Rush? Is that how it's worked for two-hundred-plus years—the honor system?"

What the caller meant was, was it just high elected officials, presidents, are just duty-bound to obey the Constitution? Well, partly, but it was respect for it, but it was also respect for the law. There was a reverence for it. Now, there's always been opposition to it. Since the days it was written there have been people opposed to it. I don't mean to present a Pollyannaish picture here, but it is precariously balanced. If any given president or succession of presidents just decides to pretend it doesn't exist, and if the other two branches of government aren't gonna do anything about it, then it won't exist, and this country—there will always be an America, but it won't be what was founded. Who knows what it will be, but it won't be. That's what people are worried about.

They're not worried about being overrun. It's nothing personal here. It's a desire to hold on to America and make it a beacon, keep it a beacon. Stand for something. We're losing our economic stature and status to the ChiComs now.

There's a reason for this. And when you realize that amnesty and open borders is a weapon used by the anti-American left, that's reason enough to

USAF veteran Vitor and Thelma—longtime EIB listeners and proud immigrants to the United States.

oppose 'em. When you realize who wants open borders, when you realize the political and ideological motivation behind it, you are duty-bound—talk about the honor system—you're duty-bound, I would think, to stand up and oppose it.

It isn't personal. It has nothing to do with ethnicity or race whatsoever. And, by the way, don't go crazy crediting all these amnesty people with love of humanity. They don't want these people to ever be self-reliant. They want these people to be voting as dependent incompetents.

The political powers that be that are trying to make this happen see a wave of potential registered voters who are unskilled and uneducated and will never be self-reliant—therefore, they are always going to need support from government. They are seeking dutiful, respectful, appreciative dependents.

The open-borders crowd has no love for these people. That's the thing that really bugs me. These people are pawns, and there is no desire for these people to come here and become the best they can be. That's not gonna serve the purpose of the political class. The value of these people is as future voters.

The Democrat Party needs a permanent underclass, and as people in the old days, not so much true right now, but in the old days, as people worked hard and moved themselves out of the lower quintiles of poverty and up until the middle class and beyond, they became less and less dependent on government. The Democrats had to replace them. And so Ted Kennedy thought, after forty years of no immigration, well, let's open the borders.

That's what it was all about. It's inhuman, if you ask me. And these people get away with getting all the credit for compassion and caring and big hearts. The people pushing this, in my mind, are the people who have the least real human concern. These are just pawns.

It's offensive in every which way you can think of. That's why, whenever you hear people talk seriously about this, border security is always the first thing required before anything else in a deal to take place, provable, demonstrable. That would mean years of border security before we do anything on amnesty.

You can't just promise that you agree with securing the border and then we make 'em legal. You gotta show three years that you're serious about securing the border. Then we do it. There has to be some value attached to this or it all becomes meaningless. Which, sadly, way too much of what used to be important is now becoming meaningless as the political class corrupts as much as they can for their own power.

RUSH ANSWERS A THIRTEEN-YEAR-OLD'S QUESTION ON IMMIGRATION
The Rush Limbaugh Show, November 15, 2018

RUSH: We have from Ohio, I guess, it's Delia, and she is thirteen years old. Hi, Delia. Welcome to our program.

CALLER: Hi, Mr. Limbaugh. Thank you for having me.

RUSH: You bet.

CALLER: So, I attend a Catholic school in Strongsville, Ohio, and every Friday we have a current event topic, and we pick a side, and we debate about it. So this week our topic is whether or not it should be easier for immigrants to become US citizens. . . . So I was wondering if you could help me with this problem.

RUSH: Well, I could tell you what I think about your question. Could I ask you a question first?

CALLER: Sure.

RUSH: How is it you're not in school today? I mean, it's 1:30 in the afternoon.

CALLER: I knew that was gonna come up. I'm sick today.

RUSH: Ah. I didn't get away with that very much. I tried. Well, I hope you're not too sick. You sound good. . . . Have you been given a side to take in this, or can you take any side you want based on what you really think? Or are you supposed to research this and find out somebody else's opinion? What is your assignment here, if there is one?

CALLER: So we're supposed to pick a side and we're supposed to get statistics about it, but I don't understand how I'm supposed to get statistics for this topic, because there's nothing really to get, except what the American people think about it.

RUSH: Well, in researching—this is a problem, I think, with the Internet in general, is finding untainted, you know, just straight objective news. . . . It can get pretty complicated. I can give you the overall theory of immigration that has always governed the subject in the United States. And, in a nutshell, when you attach the question "Should it be difficult to become a citizen," yeah, it should be. There is no country in the world like the United States, not even free Western democracies. We are the only country in the world with a Constitution that limits the government, that provides for the primacy of the citizen over government. We do not have a Constitution that limits what people can do. We have a Constitution that limits the government. That had never been done before in the history of the world. Most people, Delia, even today, most people alive today live under some form of dictatorship or tyranny and have nowhere near the freedoms that we in the United States have. They don't have anywhere near [the] economic freedom and liberty or prosperity that we have, which is why we're such a targeted destination for people. We stand out. And it's precisely because this country was founded on the basis that human freedom and human liberty and the human mind unfettered lead to exceptionalism and greatness. Not that we're better than any other people on the earth, but because we have fewer restraints and restrictions on us, that we are freer to reach our potential as individuals and as a population. Well, this led to the establishment of a distinct American culture. And by culture I mean [the] rules and regulations and morality by which the citizens of America live. And this culture was itself rooted in the premise of individual liberty, where you could pursue happiness while living your life unafraid of what you think, unafraid of what you say, unafraid of where you go, because your government does not have the power to penalize you for it. So this kind of unshackling of the human being led to untold innovation and progress, economic prosperity. In order to preserve this country, it ought to be a very specific task for somebody [who is] not a citizen to become one. If they come here via legal immigration, they do have to take a test. And those who endeavor to become citizens and pass the test, it's one of the most proud days of their lives. If you've ever been to a naturalization ceremony or ever seen one televised, it's one of the proudest days of their lives to become, quote unquote, an American. They learn the language. They become familiar with the customs. They do not sacrifice their nationality. If they arrive here as Italians, they're still Italians,

Italian Americans, but they become Americans. It's a good thing to become an American, to be a participant in this unique, distinct culture. Well, what's happening is that that unique, distinct culture is being diluted and watered down by record numbers of illegal immigrants who want to become citizens but do not want to have to do anything required to become a citizen other than show up. And that's why so many of us feel the country is at risk and threatened. The bottom line is that America is so valuable to the world, America is so important, preserving the culture that led to this exceptionalism is worth preserving, and it ought to be hard. It ought to take some effort to become an American.

CALLER: Thank you. I just wanted to say, my parents have been listening to you for over twenty years, and our family is a huge fan of yours, and my dad was able to get on your show once, and now I was able to get on your show once. And our family is just really happy.

RUSH: Well, you've made my day. I appreciate it. You asked me a question that actually means a lot to me. It's why I continued and maybe said more than you wanted to hear. But once I get going on this, it matters so much to me that I end up desiring and wanting to be persuasive. And I'll admit that. So I appreciate your patience and tolerance, and I hope that—did it help or did it confuse you?

CALLER: It definitely helped. I mean, I'm in a school where there's a lot of liberal teachers who aren't afraid to give their political opinions. Like, for example, yesterday I had a teacher that was saying that President Trump is going to attempt to change the Fourteenth Amendment. I mean, it's hard to have conservative beliefs when you're in such a liberal school.

* * *

RUSH: Mark in Chicago. Great to have you with us, sir. You're next here on the EIB Network. Hi.

CALLER: Hey, Rush. Thanks for taking my call. I really appreciate it. Hey, Rush, your articulation and explanation to that little schoolgirl was absolutely amazing. It was over-the-top. I was so impressed with it. Just briefly, my dad's parents, they immigrated here legally in 1923 from northern Italy, they settled in Illinois, had to learn English, had to have a job, they worked hard, never asked for anything. And they had three sons, one was

my dad, my two uncles, they've all passed. But during family parties my uncles and my dad would always refer to him as Pa, and he said, "You know what? Pa always wanted us just to be good citizens." And you articulating that is exactly what his vision was for them to become Americans, and I have instilled that in my kids. As I hold my grandkids today, Rush, what you talked about forty minutes ago is exactly what I try to communicate to my grandkids. Keep that legacy going of hard work and really under-stand[ing] what becoming an American really is. I gotta tell you, Rush, I think that was just a reset for a lot of us. It was a reset for me. You gave chills up my back.

RUSH: Wow. Here I thought I was being too verbose when I was talking.

CALLER: Rush, everything you talked about is why this country is so great, and there's nobody that articulates it better than you. And again, it was emo-tional listening to it 'cause that's exactly why my grandfather came here in 1923 from northern Italy. It's just special to keep hearing somebody talk about that, because that's something you will not hear in schools, and it's up to us as parents and grandparents to continue to educate our kids so this country stays on the right path.

•   •   •

Ask yourselves, if our country is such a horrible, unjust, racist, flawed-beyond-compare society, then why on earth do so many people want to come to the United States to become American citizens? —Rush Limbaugh

•   •   •

WHO DOES THIS SOUND LIKE?
The Rush Limbaugh Show, September 6, 2016

RUSH: There's one other thing I want you to hear. It's all the way back on Jan-uary 24, 1995. Bill Clinton in the State of the Union address, January 24, 1995. I want you to tell me who this reminds you of.

CLINTON: All Americans, not only in the states most heavily affected but in every place in this country, are rightly disturbed by the large numbers of illegal aliens entering our country. The jobs they hold might otherwise be held by citizens or legal immigrants. The public services they use impose burdens on our taxpayers. That's why our administration has moved aggressively to secure our borders more by hiring a record number of new border guards, by deporting twice as many criminal aliens as ever before, by cracking down on illegal hiring, by barring welfare benefits to illegal aliens. In the budget I will present to you, we will try to do more to speed the deportation of illegal aliens who are arrested for crimes. It is wrong and ultimately self-defeating for a nation of immigrants to permit the kind of abuse of our immigration laws we have seen in recent years, and we must do more to stop it.

RUSH: Sounds exactly like Donald Trump, doesn't it? Now, Mr. Snerdley, have you heard this Clinton sound bite? Do you ever recall hearing Clinton say this back in the nineties? I mean, you should have seen people's eyes on the other side of the glass listening to this. They don't recall ever having heard it before, even though we all watched it. When I found the bite, I was stunned like you probably are. I remember all the Clinton similarities going after Osama bin Laden and Iraq that George W. Bush had said. But this—this is no different than what Trump is talking about. Here's Bill Clinton in 1994 talking about deporting all of these illegal aliens we could find, stopping their welfare benefits. And you have a standing ovation in the House chamber.

* * *

So I checked the email during the break. It's typical. This guy says, "So what's the big deal what Clinton said back in 1995? Clinton says the same thing on immigration in '95 as Trump; so what, Rush?" I'll tell you so what. He got a standing ovation for it in 1995. How many years ago is that? Twenty-two? Twenty-two years ago.

The American people were so fed up with illegal immigration that the president of the United States was echoing their sentiments. We had to start mass deportation. We had to stop welfare benefits. We had to secure the border. And it was roundly supported and applauded.

Nothing happened.

The American people pay attention. This issue affects millions of people, and has for longer than twenty years. And all these politicians have come along, and they've said they're gonna do something about it, including President Bill Clinton back in 1994, and nobody has. So you skip forward to 2016, here comes the Trump—2015, actually. Here comes Trump. And they believe him on it.

My point is, do not—if you are, do not underestimate the power of this issue, in terms of motivating people and turning people out, and causing people who haven't voted in a while to maybe show up and vote. It's that big. And the establishment totally misses this. Obviously they miss it. Because they have yet to take it seriously. And, in fact, they've done everything they can to make sure what Clinton was advocating, what Trump's advocating, never happens.

* * *

Rush, please know how revered and appreciated you are for your ever-faithful work to inform the American public and inspire love for God and country and fellow citizens! You have spoiled us for any other radio show! No voice is so comely and hilariously right on and yet so timely truthful [as] Rush's voice is! We LOVE you, RUSH!

—Clifton and Linda, members of the audience

* * *

FLASHBACK TO 1991: RUSH INTERVIEWS "POP" ON HIS ONE HUNDREDTH BIRTHDAY
The Rush Limbaugh Show, September 27, 1991

RUSH: Greetings to you, folks, all across the fruited plain. From Kansas City today, this is the Rush Limbaugh program on the Excellence in Broadcasting Network, and we welcome you to an essential edition of the program today.

I am opening the program today with an amount of pride that is difficult to describe. Today, ladies and gentlemen, my grandfather, Rush H. Limbaugh—I am actually Rush H. Limbaugh III—turns one hundred.

The entire Missouri Bar meeting this year is practically devoted to his achievements as a lawyer, celebrating his seventy-fifth anniversary in the practice of law today.

POP: I am the one that I should think is more like you have described, in your own condition. I'm delighted to be here. Thank you for your introduction. You have expressed praise that's beyond what you should have said.

RUSH: No, no, no. It's Missouri.

POP: Because I'm just a country boy—

RUSH: Here we go.

POP: —that came up from the country when there wasn't anything else to do where I lived.

RUSH: Well, I was gonna ask you about your boyhood. You grew up, you were born in Sedgewickville, Missouri, which is in southeastern Missouri, in 1891. What was your boyhood like when you were growing up, and when did you leave home to start out on your career?

POP: Well, I was born not in Sedgewickville. Sedgewickville was our post office. It was four miles away from the place of my birth. I was born in a farm home on a little creek called Muddy Creek, and I was the last of eight children. And the family into which I came, when I was born, we lived in the usual farm home at that time, all of us working together.

RUSH: You followed a horse on a plow, right?

POP: Oh, yes.

RUSH: I mean, you plowed fields.

POP: Oh, yes.

RUSH: For how long did you do that?

POP: Well, I was at home regularly until I left home to go to Millersville High School when I was fourteen. Up to that time, I had spent all my life on the farm where I was born, with the exception of the time I was in school. I went to a one-room school about a mile from our home when school time was on, and we had a six-month school period.

RUSH: Mmm-hmm.

POP: The rest of the time I was working on the farm, did all kinds of farmwork. I plowed and all.

*   *   *

I think of you as my second dad. You've taught me so much, inspired me, and [given] me hope. Thank you so much for all you've done for this country. May God continue to bless you and your family. —Cara, member of the audience

*   *   *

Chapter 7

UNWAVERING PATRIOT

TRIBUTE
by Supreme Court Justice Clarence Thomas

Rush was a fabulous man and a wonderful friend. Rush embodied the American Dream. In those early years, he reinvigorated the AM radio stations across the country, and it was fun to listen to him as he added station after station.

I first heard of Rush when I arrived at the Court. I received hundreds and hundreds of letters, and one of the letters asked me whether Rush Limbaugh was a friend of mine, since he spent so much time on his radio show defending me and supporting me. I had not heard of him.

During the following summer a friend of ours, a very dear friend of ours, brought her radio to me as I rested and said I should listen to him. I started listening to Rush, and I would listen regularly to him for the next quarter of a century. He became a very, very important part of my life. It's probably hard to think of those years now or remember them. But those were very difficult years for my wife and for me. I often think of those years as a dark night of my soul, but Rush was that beacon of hope, that beacon of light that brought joy.

Days would be dismal or difficult, and I would listen to him and the music, and his jokes, and his upbeat attitude—even about serious things— and it would change my attitude, it would sort of help me through it. He treated others—I watched him around people who worked in restaurants or who worked around him—he treated them the way he would have wanted to be treated if he were in their position, and the maxim "Do unto others as you would have them do unto you." He was an honorable, good man. When he gave his word, he kept his word.

*What a godsend for the court and for America Clarence Thomas
has been. Not just has been but is. His legal mind and his
brilliance are on display with every opinion he writes or concurs
with or dissents from. He's a genuine treasure.* —Rush Limbaugh

PART 1 — COURAGEOUS AND LOYAL

Rush thought it was absolutely hilarious that some non-listeners thought he would walk into an event and start shouting his beliefs across the room. He was highly entertained by this idea and would laugh while pretending to pound his fist on the table in rage. He would say, "I think it is hysterical that some people actually think I will go to a reception and have a total fit." Rush was, in fact, the exact opposite. If he ever felt a friend or even someone he had never even met was being unfairly treated, he would be the first to speak out forcefully in their defense on the radio. Throughout his career, Rush took it upon himself to always protect conservative and American principles. He was a fiercely loyal friend and warrior for all of us, even in times when it was not popular to be.

WE DEFEND WHAT WE HOLD DEAR EVERY DAY ON THIS SHOW
The Rush Limbaugh Show, March 30, 2015

RUSH: You know, this is a great example of what we do every day on this program, and I've mentioned this countless times previous. Every day we're minding our own business here. We're bothering nobody, just going about our business. We wake up every day, start getting ready for the day, and we find out that people or things or institutions that we love, respect, and hold dear are under assault. So I come here and defend them, and that's exactly what's happening here today with this business going on in Indiana.

I'm attacking nobody. I'm impugning nobody. I'm simply reacting to a bunch of lies, dis-, and misinformation in the Drive-by Media in what is probably a meager attempt, meager effort at getting the truth out there against this avalanche and assault of lies, half-truths, distortion, and propaganda that the Democrat Party and the media are responsible for. That's what we do. This is a classic illustration. We were minding our own business.

We don't come here with the idea of attacking people every day. We just watch what's going on, see ourselves under assault (for the most part daily), and see the need to defend it. . . .

It's a total misrepresentation, misinformation, disinformation campaign designed to totally screw with people's emotions, not tell 'em the truth about what's going on, not give them any kind of historical context, all for the express purpose of not just advancing the Democrat Party agenda but destroying the opposition agenda's conservatism, Republican Party, what have you. Somebody's gotta stand up and defend it, and that's what we do here.

And I say this in reaction to the charge that I simply get up every day and decide who I next want to attack. We don't attack here. Well, I mean we do now and then. But the vast majority of time is spent like it is here today. The Drive-bys and the Democrats start lying about something, and somebody has to tell people the truth [and] in the process defend traditions and institutions that we all hold dear, and that's a great example of it.

FLASHBACK TO 1991: RUSH ON CHARLIE ROSE DEBATING CLARENCE THOMAS AND ANITA HILL
The Rush Limbaugh Show, October 15, 1991

In 1991, CNN was the only cable news network, and this show . . . was it. There was no blogosphere. There was no Fox News. There was nothing.

So it's October 15, 1991, Charlie Rose's show on PBS. It aired at eleven o'clock at night, live, on PBS back then. He had me on with the executive director of the New York Urban League, whose name was Harriet Michel. We're talking about Thomas's appointment to the Supreme Court. Charlie started by saying, "What should the Senate Judiciary Committee have done if somebody comes to their attention and raises the issue of sexual harassment? What should the committee have done?"

RUSH ARCHIVE: The thing that has to be done is the American system of jurisprudence has to be consistent in focusing. I kept hearing people talking about "the seriousness of the charges." The seriousness of the

"Justice Thomas has the most infectious, hearty laugh." —Rush Limbaugh

charges is irrelevant. The nature of the evidence is what's relevant. The presumption is always with the accused, and just 'cause someone comes forth at the last moment and claims that something happened, her accusation cannot be regarded as evidence. And, if there's nothing to corroborate it, there is no way—just because she charges it—any weight should be given it.

ROSE: All right, it's evidence but it doesn't have corroboration, but—but—

RUSH ARCHIVE: No, it's not evidence! An accusation is not evidence. It can't be evidence.

RUSH: It can't be! An allegation is never evidence, it cannot be evidence—and, notice, back then they didn't care. It was evidence. It was the seriousness of the charge. They didn't care about it being corroborated, just like today. Her lawyer is saying, "It's not her job to corroborate the charge. The charge is enough! The allegation is enough. When we say it, that's what happened." That's their cock-certain, arrogant attitude. "When we say it, it happened, and it's up to investigators to prove that it didn't."

Why hasn't the woman come forward before now? Why has she not accepted the invitation to come to the committee? F. Chuck Todd's out there saying, "Do you people who think that a woman of her age would destroy her life by coming forward like Christine Blasey Ford is now, you don't understand left-wing . . ." What do you mean, destroy her life? Has Anita Hill's life been destroyed, or has she become a hero? Anita Hill's become a heroine! They still make books about her. . . . Right, and this kept going. The next sound bite here is . . . Let's see, what is it? I asked Harriet Michel of the New York Urban League if she believed Anita Hill.

[Archive clip begins]

RUSH: Do you believe her?

MICHEL: Do I believe her?

RUSH: Why do you believe her?

MICHEL: Yes, I believe her.

RUSH: Why would you believe her? Can I ask you why you believe her?

MICHEL: I—I—I believe her—I be—

RUSH: She offered no evidence, Harriet. There was no—

ROSE: You asked the question. Let her answer.

MICHEL: That's exactly right. I believe that for everybody to make this assumption that Clarence Thomas, the public persona, cannot possibly—under any circumstances, in a room one-on-one with a female—be gross and be obnoxious is out of their minds.

RUSH: Wait a minute. What's dangerous is assuming he did it with no evidence.

MICHEL: I don't—I don't assume that he did it. I believe—

RUSH: If you believe her, you have to.

MICHEL: I believe that it's possible that he did it, and I believe that four—

RUSH: So we convict him on that?

MICHEL: —lawyers coming forward—

RUSH: We convict him on the possibility?

MICHEL: This wasn't a trial, though!

RUSH: Oh, it was. . . . No evidence. No reason to believe her. She just chooses to believe her.

[Archive clip ends]

Those sound bites of me on Charlie Rose are twenty-seven years ago, folks. That's twenty-seven years. And you'll notice that what I believed and stated back then is identical to today, rock-solid, because my core is my core. My core beliefs are not calculated daily or weekly or monthly or annually. They are what they are. You'll also notice that nothing changes with the left. It's the same things that motivate 'em and animate 'em, and it's the same strategies and tactics that they use.

• • •

This is a circus. It's a national disgrace. It is a high-tech lynching for uppity Blacks who in any way deign to think for themselves. And it is a message that unless you kowtow to an old order, you will be lynched, destroyed, caricatured by a committee of the US Senate rather than hung from a tree. —Justice Clarence Thomas, 1991 Senate Confirmation Hearings

• • •

HOW DO DECENT PEOPLE DEAL WITH SUCH DASTARDLY ATTACKS?
The Rush Limbaugh Show, September 17, 2018

I was so mad, and I didn't hide any of my anger. During the heat of the moment here, I had a Rush to Excellence Tour appearance in Tulsa, I believe. It was either Oklahoma City or Tulsa. I'm pretty sure it was Tulsa. And I spent the entire, almost 90 percent of the two-hour stand-up that I did on Anita Hill–Clarence Thomas. I was looking at people's faces in the audience—and there were thousands, five or six thousand people there—and I could tell that some people were not even aware what I was talking about. Most were, but some weren't.

But I just remember being so livid, and I remember devoting every ounce of energy I had every day on this program to exposing what I knew was a pack of lies about Clarence Thomas. I did not know Clarence Thomas at the time. I had not met him. I only know who he was. I knew friends of his. I knew people that vouched for him. I knew that no allegation like this had ever been made about him. What I learned about Anita Hill, what I learned about all this, was this was just a Democrat trick.

LEFTISTS TRY TO INTIMIDATE THE SUPREME COURT
The Rush Limbaugh Show, July 12, 2005

DEMOCRAT SENATOR PAT LEAHY: I worry when they're an activist judge, uh, who almost reflexively votes down laws passed by the Congress or by the states and creates laws of their own, substitute. The two most activist judges we have right now are Justice Thomas, uh, and Justice Scalia.
RUSH: *[Laughs]* The two *least* activist judges are Thomas and Scalia. What you just heard Senator Leahy do here—remember: words mean things—Senator Leahy is twisting the word "activist" around and applying it to originalists like Scalia and Thomas. This other gibberish about, "Well, they're divisive because they've taken positions that show they're almost monolithically in favor of just one group, like they'll just only rule in favor of business,

they'll only rule . . ." Everything with these people apparently is class envy, and the court is there to balance the economic scale, guarantee equality of outcomes or sameness of outcomes or what have you. But regardless, I just think this is pathetic. I think these people . . . *[sighs]*. They don't have the ability to be embarrassed. . . .

I know. It's frustrating. It's frustrating to a lot of people. But you know what's frustrating about it? I've always thought—just in interactions with people—we all have various personality types that rub us the wrong way. Whether it's these guys in politics or whether it's the neighbor, whether it's a coworker, and, speaking for me because I can only speak for me, the personality traits that have rubbed me wrong the most are arrogance, condescension, and lying—and insulting my intelligence, people telling me things I know are untrue, as though they think I'm an idiot and will believe it.

That's all wrapped up into one bundle when you get these Senate Democrats. They are all arrogant. They are all condescending, and they think that all of us are absolute blithering idiots and the country can't run without them in charge, and their birthright as Democrats is to run this country, and we have gotten in the way; and they think very little of us for that, and they're going to get even one way or the other. If they can't persuade us to vote for them, then they will do their best to get the people we vote for thrown out of office or thrown in jail. If we don't vote for them, then they will see to it that what they believe should happen to the country will be implemented by a bunch of activist judges where we can say nothing about it. But here, when they have gone down to humiliating defeat in the House and Senate over the last—well, since '94, it's ten years, ten, eleven years—when they are losing their percentages in both bodies and the margin of victory for the Republicans in the presidential race continues to expand, these guys act like they win. They act like they're the winners and should have won. "So, since we should have won, we're going to act like we did." Just the whole arrogance here of Schumer demanding a summit, Camp David, dinner at the White House; Leahy lying through his teeth about who activist judges are, "always defending just one group of people." Yes, it's frustrating, but it's also indicative, folks, of a party in the midst of its last gasp. One more bite from Candy

Crowley. She said, "I know you know that Republicans have a different definition of what an activist judge is, Senator."

LEAHY: Well, it's the same definition they've always used for, uh, Democrats.
They said Democrats who would strike down a law passed by the people and
substitute something of their own. I'm just using their—by their own definition, the two most activist judges there right now are Antonin Scalia and
Clarence Thomas.

RUSH: What he's basing this on is a recent poll that showed Scalia and
Thomas have voted most often lately to say that a law passed by Congress is
unconstitutional. That's not what we mean by "activist," and he knows that.
Activist judges are judges that don't interpret the Constitution. Activist
judges are judges that actually don't want there to be a Constitution. If we're
going to have activist judges, folks, we don't need a Constitution. It's just like
if we're going to let in anybody in the country that wants in, we don't have a
country. We may as well not have a border. If we're not going to enforce the
border, we don't have a country. Well, if we're going to have judges that will
not look to the Constitution, we don't have a Constitution, and that's what
we get with activist judges.

We get activist judges who take their personal policy preferences to the
bench, and then they decide cases on the basis of those personal policy preferences, and they call that "law." So their personal policy preferences become
constitutional. Well, they're not. You can say something is constitutional all
you want, but it is only constitutional if it is. If it's not constitutional, it's
not—and these are, you know, not matters of debate. That's why "originalist"
is a key word. You go back; you look at the original intent. You can find it. It's
there. *Federalist Papers*, numerous discussions, the document itself. But look
at this takings case in New London, Connecticut.

The Fifth Amendment to the Constitution is clear, but the US Supreme
Court three weeks ago said, "Ah, we think it means something else." So now
we have a bunch of states and the US Congress thinking of writing a law that
basically says what the Constitution already says. So we're having to rewrite
the Constitution because we've got a bunch of judges who are ignoring it,
plain and simple. That's the definition of an activist judge—and in this case,

Thomas and Scalia are not activist. Basically, let me make it as simple as I can: An activist judge is a liberal who believes liberalism should become institutionalized in the courts. You want a great definition? To show you how out of whack Leahy and his comments are, you look at the eminent domain decision out of New London, Connecticut. That was a bunch of liberals. Liberals are said to stand for the little guy. That's what Leahy just [said]: They stand for the little guy against the big guy.

What did the Supreme Court just do? Just stood for a local government over a little guy and said the local government can say to the little guy, "You don't own that property that you actually own. We're going to take it away from you. We're going to give it to this other private citizen because he's going to generate more tax revenue for us," and so a lot of people have to get it through their heads now. The US Supreme Court, the liberals of this country, do not stand for the little guy. They'll sweep the little guy out of the way as soon as he gets in the way. They have to. What's paramount is big government. Be it local government, state government, federal government, it's gotta be big. It's gotta be big and all-powerful.

* * *

They can't believe . . . They can't believe that this court's now 6–3 conservative. They can't believe that Justice Roberts has been eliminated now as the power behind the court to fix things. It's 6–3 conservatives now with Amy Coney Barrett. So their only reaction is they're going to pack the court. They're gonna get rid of her influence. They're gonna negate her confirmation if they win the presidency by packing the court, minimum 13 justices on the Supreme Court. They won't admit it, but they've been caught flat-footed saying it. —Rush Limbaugh

* * *

R ush was always at the tip of the spear, fighting for those he respected and felt were being unfairly treated, including General Michael Flynn.

ONE OF THE MOST GIGANTIC POLITICAL SCANDALS OF OUR LIFETIME
The Rush Limbaugh Show, February 13, 2018

One year ago on this program I offered up opinions/feelings about some of the stuff going on. At the time, one year ago, Michael Flynn was the big thing. We find out from Byron York the FBI didn't think Mike Flynn had done anything wrong!

Do you know that Comey testified to Congress that he didn't think Mike Flynn had done anything wrong, didn't think he had lied? And yet that investigation was pursued, and now we've got this indictment from Mueller where a plea deal and people say, "If he didn't do it, then why did he settle?" 'Cause they were driving him bankrupt! Flynn was broke. He was worried about the effect this was having on his family. But we've got on the *Congressional Record* that James Comey of the FBI told members of Congress on a committee that Flynn had not lied to anybody.

It takes us back to the actual FBI interview of Flynn anyway. It was not set up as an interview. Flynn is the incoming national security adviser. That means there's frequent contact with the FBI and the CIA. They called over to the White House and said they wanted to come talk to Flynn. Flynn said, "Okay, come on over." He thinks it's gonna be a consultation. Instead it turns out to be a full-fledged interview that he wasn't aware of. But Byron York in the *Washington Examiner* has a really, really great piece today on all of this, and I just want to kick it off with my comments on this from one year ago almost to the day.

RUSH ARCHIVE: To show you just how lame the media is and how little they've got, they're already asking, "What did Trump know, and when did he know it?" and that's not the question. The question is, what did Barack

Obama know, and when did he know it, and what has he engineered here? This all happened with Flynn back in December. Trump had not even been inaugurated yet. And it's still mysterious to me what really happened. Even if—even if Flynn, as the incoming national security director, had called the Russian ambassador to talk, so what? That's not hard to imagine. That's not a big deal. It really isn't a big deal.

RUSH: Not a big deal. It'd be standard operating procedure. We're talking about the Russian ambassador here, and the new administration reaching out, familiarizing themselves with various representatives of other countries. It wasn't just the Russians that Flynn was talking to. The Russian ambassador, remember, was being surveilled. Standard operating procedure. Also, we wiretap foreign officials. This guy's phone call to Flynn, therefore Flynn was unmasked. Susan Rice, hi! Flynn's unmasked. It's reported what he and Kislyak talked about, and bammo!

LIEUTENANT GENERAL MICHAEL FLYNN CALLS RUSH
The Rush Limbaugh Show, June 24, 2020

RUSH: I'm told that we have General Flynn on the phone. Michael Flynn, you are here on the EIB Network, is that right?

FLYNN: How about that, Rush? Yeah, this is Mike Flynn. How you doing?

RUSH: I'm great. I'm a little stunned.

FLYNN: Well, I want to just tell you, first of all, you got a lot of prayers coming from the Flynn family for you and all the things that you're going through, so just know that. And I just want to say from the bottom of our hearts, you know, you've been right from the beginning. And we can't thank you and your listeners enough for all the support that they have given us through this fight. And, you know, obviously the fight's not over, as you've been highlighting for not just today but for a long time. And the decision today is really, it's a good thing for General Flynn, it's a good thing for me, it's a good thing for my family, but it's really a great boost of confidence for the American people and our justice system, because that's what this really comes down to, is whether or not our justice system is going to have the confidence of the American people. And, boy, your listeners know this.

RUSH: You had to have your doubts in it for the longest time. I can't imagine what it's been like.

FLYNN: *[Laughs]* Well, I'll tell you what, maybe there will be another time that we can get into the details of it, but I will just tell you that I have always believed and fought for our rule of law. The most important thing that we have in this country, bar none, is that. And we have to make it work whether we like it or not, and it has to work with the right people and the right leaders and the people of our country to step up to the plate. You know, and elections matter, right? Voting matters. So, anyway, I just wanted to get my two cents in with you today and tell you that we think about you often and we pray for you, and that we are so happy with the decision, not only for our family but for our country.

RUSH: Well, it's been an honor, General Flynn. And everybody is so happy for you here. It's actually justice deserved and justice served. We only wish the best for you and your family, sir, and God bless.

PRESIDENT OBAMA SAYS I'M HIS PROBLEM
The Rush Limbaugh Show, January 23, 2014

Well, ladies and gentlemen, it looks like I continue to live rent free in the head of the president, Barack Obama. It seems that the *New Yorker* has just posted more from their eighteen-page Obama interview. I don't know if the whole thing has been on the Internet. I didn't read the whole thing. It may have been up there all the time. But here is what the president said, the *New Yorker* interview with David Remnick that they have just posted.

"Another way of putting it, I guess, is that the issue has been the inability of my message to penetrate the Republican base so that they feel persuaded that I'm not the caricature that you see on Fox News or Rush Limbaugh, but I'm somebody who is interested in solving problems and is pretty practical, and that, actually, a lot of the things that we've put in place worked better than people might think. And as long as there's that gap between perceptions of me within the average Republican primary voter and the reality, it's hard for folks like John Boehner to move too far in my direction."

So it's me again, and Fox News. We are the reason Obama can't advance his agenda, because Boehner is afraid to move too close to Obama because I have made you—along with Fox News has made you—think Obama is something that he isn't. And it's such a shame. I have so distorted who the real Obama is in your mind that it is paralyzing our government. It is paralyzing the Speaker of the House, who really, really, really, really wants to go in there and really, really work with Obama, but he just can't. It's hard for people like Boehner to move too far in my direction because of the misperception of me, Obama says, created by Fox News and Rush Limbaugh.

And greetings, my friends. Welcome. Great to have you.

US REPRESENTATIVE BARNEY FRANK BLAMES YOUR HOST FOR THE DEATH OF COMPROMISE IN WASHINGTON
The Rush Limbaugh Show, March 25, 2015

RUSH: Once again, ladies and gentlemen, your host is being blamed partially or totally for the lack of compromise in Washington, DC. Last night on some website—and Larry King now has a show. The name of the website is Ora. TV. That's where Larry King is hanging out, and he had Barney Frank as his guest, the former congressman from Massachusetts, and Larry King said, "The art of compromise is dead, Barney; what happened to it?"

FRANK: Part of it is the ideological rigidity of this Tea Party group. But there's another factor. They live in parallel media universes. The left is over here listening to their programs, MSNBC or the *Huffington Post*, the right's watching Fox News and Rush Limbaugh. If you are trying to compromise with the other side, your supporters say to you, "Why are you giving in?" And you say, "Well we don't have the votes to do what we want." And they say, "Oh, how can you say that? Everybody I know agrees with us." People on the left and all the people on the right, they only talk to people and hear from people who reinforce them. So if somebody from their position says, "You know, we need to work with the others," they see it as a betrayal, because they believe they're in the majority.

RUSH: I understand why Barney Frank thinks that. It's a popular misconception of people on the left, because they don't listen to us. They don't know what we believe. They think they do, but they have never endeavored to really understand it. They've tabbed it as extremism. See, the left, if you can understand this—and this is true—the left thinks that we are ideological [and] they aren't. Liberalism to them is not an ideology. Liberalism is just what is. They call themselves pragmatists. They think that they look at things issue by issue and decide based on what's best, and they think they'll go along with anything as long as it's best. But they discount totally and automatically conservatism, 'cause there's no pragmatism there. It's all ideology, in their mind, and therefore it's disqualified. Ideologues are extremists, they're wackos, in their view, and they don't see them that way. Now, you who listen to this program know that what Barney Frank just said may apply to some, but not to me. You learn more about liberalism on this program than you will watching MSNBC.

US SENATE DEBATES RUSH LIMBAUGH
The Rush Limbaugh Show, November 8, 2005

RUSH: Let's go to the audiotape. We're going to start with the Harkin floor debate on me and this program. Our nickname for him is Tom "Dung Heap" Harkin. I've forgotten why we named him that. He said something once about a dung heap, called his opponents dung heaps or something, so we've turned it back around on him. This is a portion of his remarks. They're debating the Defense Authorization Bill, but Harkin is upset that I dominate so much of [the] Armed Forces Radio Network and that so few "progressives" have a chance to be heard.

DUNG HEAP HARKIN: What they actually get is nothing on the—on the progressive [liberal] side. But they get 100 percent of Rush Limbaugh; 2,460 minutes a week? That's balance? That's fair? That's not balance, that's monopoly. . . .

RUSH: By the way, my program was put on the Armed Forces Radio Network during the Clinton administration. . . . It was popular demand . . . they took a poll, and I was a write-in candidate of all the troops, and they put my program on. That's right! They took a poll, and my show was not listed. They put out a list of programs and let the armed forces members around the world vote—and my name was not on the list that you could vote for. They wrote my name in, and I got more votes than anybody else, and that's why they put the program on. . . . Here's more of what he had to say, talking about when he brought this effort up last year. . . .

DUNG HEAP HARKIN: I said, "Well, typical of Rush Limbaugh. He doesn't understand what's happening." You know, he wouldn't know the truth if it hit him in the face. So all I gotta do is stand there and say, "What I wanted was balance. What Rush Limbaugh wants is monopoly."

RUSH: Yeah, right . . . You have a US senator personally berating a citizen of this country, and I'm, on the other hand, honored to be the citizen. I am honored to be the citizen berated as a small mind by Tom "Dung Heap" Harkin on the floor of the Senate, and I sat here. I walked out yesterday. . . . My dad would not believe this, just wouldn't believe it.

* * *

Rush Limbaugh had unrelenting boldness to proclaim the truth. Watching his wit, passion, and willingness to hold the media accountable informed my entire career. Growing up in Plant City, Florida, my dad would always play the Rush Limbaugh program in his pickup truck. My fellow classmates from my all-girls Catholic school knew if they rode in my car, we would be listening to Rush Limbaugh. I am the definition of a "Rush Baby," and it's not just me. There are tens of thousands of us all across the conservative movement. He has built a legacy that will endure for many generations to come and will continue to inform our country. Thank you, Rush, for all you have done for this nation. The United States of America is better because of you.

—Kayleigh McEnany, White House Press Secretary, Tribute to Rush

* * *

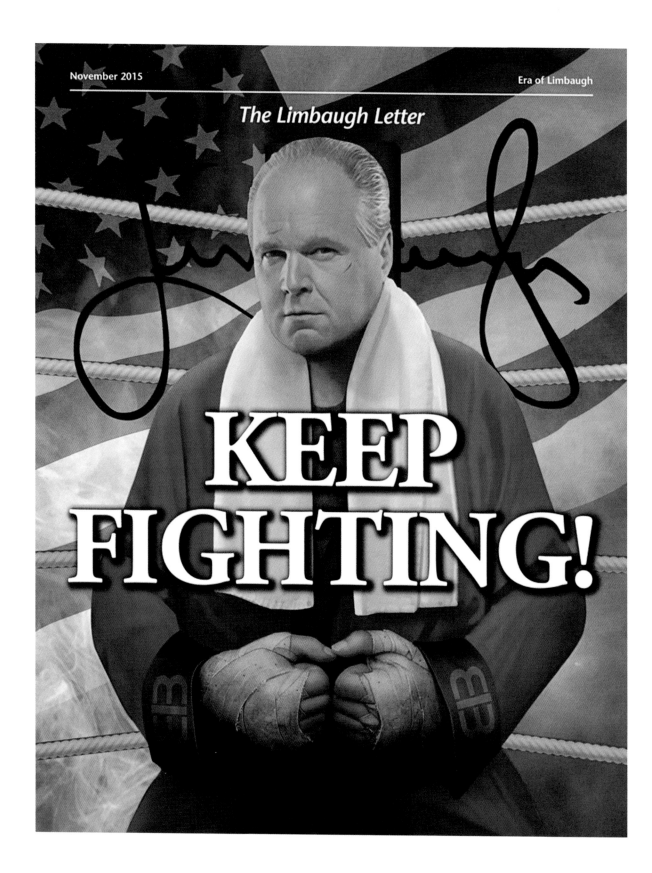

PART 2 — THE DRIVE-BY MEDIA

RUSH REFLECTS ON LEARNING TO BE HATED
Personal Recording in the Hospital with Kathryn, Boston, Fall 2020

One of the toughest things I had to learn is rooted in the truth that nobody wants to be hated. Nobody is born wanting to be hated, and nobody is raised to be hated. Everybody wants to be loved. You know what I had to do? I had to learn, psychologically, to take being hated as a measure of success. Now, think about that. Nobody is raised to do that, and I had to—if I was going to stay anywhere near confident and sane—I had to learn to take being hated or disliked as a measure of success, as a measure of effectiveness.

And it wasn't hard to do; all I had to do was stand by my convictions. The things that I say I believe, I meant. I didn't ever make it up. I didn't say outrageous things just to get people's attention or to make news. I only, and to this day, say what I actually believe.

And there have been efforts—the media has tried for over thirty years now to damage me and to ruin me, and they failed. And you know why? Because they had nothing to do with making me. When I said earlier that I want to be a legitimate number one, not a buzz PR number one—I want to be able to prove I've got the audience—I am a legitimate number one. And they are there because of me, not because the press told them the show is whatever it is. They didn't make me.

But if the media does make you, you see this in Hollywood and other entertainers all the time. If the press has anything to do with making you, like creating big buzz about you, running puff-piece stories about you, they can destroy you just as easily as they made you. But they can't me, because they had nothing to do with making me.

The minute I started to make noise and making a move toward success in the radio, they started trying to damage me and harm me. They didn't help me keep climbing up. So, it's a very proud moment, because my success is totally, 100 percent genuine. There is nothing artificial about it.

• • •

Being Prime Minister is a lonely job. In a sense, it ought to be: you cannot lead from the crowd. —Prime Minister Margaret Thatcher

• • •

PRESIDENT OBAMA: GET RID OF RUSH AND GO BACK TO CRONKITE
The Rush Limbaugh Show, October 15, 2020

RUSH: Democrats have a little half-baked podcast out there they think is the greatest thing under the sun. It's called *Pod Save America*. One of the cohosts is this radical leftist little guy named Tommy Vietor, and he's got former president Barack Hussein O. on as a guest. Here's the question:

"There's this debate about whether Trump is an aberration or whether he's the next phase of a Republican Party that's been built on racial grievance, built on cruelty [to] immigrants and Fox News conspiracy theories. Now, we all hoped the Republican fever would break after the 2012 reelection. Clearly it didn't. Things have gotten worse. Do you, Mr. Obama, have a view on this debate about whether Trump is an aberration?"

OBAMA: I did well in a bunch of white, evangelical counties, rural counties that I think, it's fair to say, there's no way right now that I could get those votes, right? And the reason is because they see me only through the filter of Fox News, Rush Limbaugh. Those folks right now are just being fed what's coming through that filter. If they were watchin' Walter Cronkite, then you could, in fact, have just the normal debate—and in that circumstance, democracy works. Trump is expressing or mirroring—and in some ways, explicitly exploiting and took on—the crazy that was being pumped out through these venues each and every day.

RUSH: So, there's crazy here on this program, and Trump has kind of taken it on. *[Summarizing]* "If we just had Walter Cronkite! If we just had Walter Cronkite back, then none of this would matter. If we had Walter Cronkite back, then we would have a media monopoly as well. If we had Walter

Cronkite back, there wouldn't be Rush Limbaugh; there wouldn't be anybody to criticize us. There wouldn't be Fox News out there criticizing us." This is what they want, folks. They're telegraphing what they're gonna do if they win. They're setting up a one-party everything. Good-bye, individual liberty and freedom on everything. This is drastic!

• • •

It's hilarious. I live rent free in President Obama's head.
—Rush Limbaugh

• • •

UNLIKE THAT INSENSITIVE RUSH, SHOW YOU CARE WITH A #HASHTAG
The Rush Limbaugh Show, May 12, 2014

If you're a regular listener here, you know that I love tweaking the media, and it's very easy to do because the media doesn't listen to this program. Ergo, I see the picture of Mrs. Obama in the diplomatic reception room, and I'm sure it took a bunch of different takes to get her facial expression just right, the proper mixture of solemnity and concern and deep caring with the sign, the hashtag, #BringBackOurGirls.

And I knew when I pointed this out that the Drive-bys were going to have a fit. That once again they would all be talking about the insensitivity of Rush Limbaugh and the backwardness and the, just, refusal to adapt to a changing world. Rush Limbaugh just doesn't understand things. And, lo and behold, it's happened.

So somebody is holding members of their group prisoner somewhere, and they want their brothers back, and when they get their brothers back, they supposedly will return our girls. But if you in any way represent the administration, the United States, the government, and you do this hashtag, I mean, it's pathetic. It's absolutely pathetic, and it's inconsequential. It's not gonna matter a hill of beans except in one way: It's all about intentions and showing that you care. These phonies on the left get behind their Twitter hashtag campaign and they get credit for caring. "Oh, Rush Limbaugh, he doesn't care. He's coldhearted and mean-spirited. He doesn't care." Right. So all I would have to do to care is get behind this Twitter hashtag. What would it accomplish? Nothing. Nothing toward the objective.

• • •

When people meet me in person, some of them are genuinely shocked. They're expecting me to be whatever they've heard the media portray me as. —Rush Limbaugh

• • •

LIMBAUGH LIFE LESSON: DON'T WORRY ABOUT WHAT PEOPLE THINK ABOUT YOU
The Rush Limbaugh Show, December 13, 2013

You know, if I could wave a magic wand and change people, it would be "Don't worry about what people think of you, particularly people that don't know you." People that don't know you, it doesn't matter what they think. You and what you think of yourself is what matters, and if somebody thinks things about you that aren't true, forget it. Nothing you can do about it, and it's a total waste of time to try to change that.

I occasionally get emails from people: "Rush, don't you care what they're saying about you on X? Why, it's outrageous what they're saying about you!" Yeah, sometimes I do, but most of the time I don't. It happens too much to get worried about it and be affected by it. But I did an NPR interview. One of the questions that the reporter from NPR asked me was, "You use terms like 'feminazi.' You throw these things around. Don't you worry about it bothering people?" This is the answer that I gave.

RUSH ARCHIVE: The fewest number of words you can use to convey a point, the more power the point has. Now, I understand people are going to be offended, but I've had a policy all my life not to worry about offending people, because it's going to happen. It's a daily part of life. I think way too many people are way too sensitive, walking around just waiting to be offended, and I think a bunch of people claiming they're offended is really an attack on free speech. It is the root cause of political correctness, which is nothing more than silencing things you don't want to hear when uttered by others—so, "That offends me! I will not sit here and put up with that!" I don't grant people that much power to offend me. Things said about me or the things I like . . . I'm not going to waste time being offended by it. Life's too short, and it's just words!

THE MEDIA OBSESSION WITH RUSH LIMBAUGH, TRIBAL CHIEFTAIN
The Rush Limbaugh Show, January 9, 2019

RUSH: Grab audio sound bite number one—for three weeks now they have been doing this.

DON LEMON: If he doesn't do this, the Rush Limbaughs and the other conservative media will go nuts.

CHRIS MATTHEWS: The *[cross talk]* president of the United States is a Dittohead. He's doing literally what Rush Limbaugh calls his people, those who "ditto" everything.

JONATHAN CAPEHART: It's about keeping Rush Limbaugh from criticizing him.

HOWARD FINEMAN: . . . Tribal chieftains like Rush Limbaugh.

RUSH: "Tribal chieftain"?

ROBERT ZIMMERMAN: Rush Limbaugh took the president on and started attacking him.

JOE LOCKHART: He said he'll sign the bill, and then Rush Limbaugh told him not to do it.

JAMES CARVILLE: Rush Limbaugh went crazy, and he had to change his mind.

ANA NAVARRO: . . . President of Ann Coulter and Rush Limbaugh—and, look, he has allowed these right-wing conservatives to take him hostage.

RUSH: Right. I thought I was "a guy in Palm Beach with a golf shirt." Now I'm a "tribal chieftain." For three weeks, these clowns!

● ● ●

He's extremely articulate. Rush Limbaugh is . . . I guess to the left, he is sort of like an aching tooth—they can't stand him, but they can't leave him alone—and to the right, he's like cotton candy: They just keep gobbling him up. —Ted Koppel, *Nightline*

● ● ●

DRIVE-BYS STILL DON'T GET THIS SHOW; HERALD "DEMISE OF RUSH" AGAIN
The Rush Limbaugh Show, February 4, 2008

RUSH: I got the sound bite roster from Cookie at about ten minutes prior to show time, and the first twenty sound bites are about me, and most of them are from the Sunday shows; some are from last Friday. I didn't watch any of the Sunday shows yesterday, so I didn't know any of this, and nobody had sent me emails. I guess it's so common now that I get mentioned all over the Drive-by Media that nobody sent me any email. So I'm reading the roster here today, and I'm literally stunned at all of the questions that McCain and Huckabee and some of these other people, the Russert roundtable, that are about me.

There was such glee on Fox and on the *Meet the Press* roundtable over my demise—all of this means my demise. I've had a lot of requests over the weekend, since last Thursday and Friday, from TV people, from newspaper people, from website people to grant an interview, to appear on election-night coverage tomorrow night. I've turned 'em all down. I have a friend of mine running for city council here in Palm Beach. . . . I want to get to these sound bites; there are a lot of them. I'm trying to space them out because they're all about me and I'm trying not to make the show about me. This is Bill in Sioux City, South Dakota. Hello.

CALLER: Hey, Rush, great talking to you, and it's a great show from my perspective today, too, by the way.

RUSH: Thank you.

CALLER: I agree with you that the Drive-bys do not get you and do not understand why you do this show, and I agree that your audience is generally very intelligent and thinks for themselves, and that you do not give them marching orders and stuff like that. But I do think that there is something important, maybe, that, you know, you have missed about why it is that the Drive-bys are so anxious to decide whether you've got any relevance anymore, and that's because your natural humanity—and you have some, I know, I've listened to you long enough to know what you do regardless of what some callers may think, and that is that you overlook what it is that you have accomplished and where you find yourself at this stage in your career. I mean, when you started out in AM radio, it was dead. I mean, there was nothing there. You have single-handedly caused a complete revolution in AM radio to the point where today you have, on local stations, national, syndicated talk show hosts who are all there because you paved the way. And, frankly, all of them are going to themselves, "God, I wish I could be Rush Limbaugh when I grow up." They look to you and say, "That's what I want my career to look like someday," and because of where you've gotten, you are, whether you intend to or not—and I don't think you intend to—but whether you intend to or not, you are something of a conservative Republican kingmaker, whether you intend that to be the case or not. I mean, how many other talk show hosts will routinely have the vice president of the United States on the air? You don't get to be where you're at without having a fair amount of influence, at least in terms of articulating conservative values and conservative ideas.

RUSH: Well, that's true. I'm not going to deny that. That's one of the objectives here. That's why I called this the Limbaugh Institute for Advanced Conservative Studies. The objective here, when you take the business objectives out, and this is a business, and this is one thing that nobody—the left or right—when they examine this program, none of them do so in terms of the career aspect of it. They look at me as a political figure who happens to be on the radio, while these other political figures are in the newspaper, and some of them are on television, and that's just fine, because the longer they go not understanding what I do and how I do it—and, by the way, folks, don't worry about any of this, because the media did not make me. If the media doesn't make you, they cannot break you.

* * *

There is total glee out there, folks, anytime the Drive-by Media think I am on the way out! They actually have roundtable discussions. "Limbaugh really stepped in it this time. He's done, finished, get him off the air." It is hilarious. —Rush Limbaugh

* * *

CNN'S CHRIS CUOMO, NICKNAMED "FREDO" BY RUSH, CAN DISH IT, BUT HE CAN'T TAKE IT!
The Rush Limbaugh Show, August 13, 2019

RUSH: This is hilarious. This turns out to be one of the biggest inside jokes in the country. The Drive-by Media still doesn't know—they still don't know the origins of Chris Cuomo being affectionately called Fredo. They still don't know, folks. Yet they claim I'm responsible for the El Paso shooter and I'm responsible for all of the lack of gun control. I'm the guy that's gonna prevent Washington from doing it.

And they do not know that the reason a guy approached Fredo Cuomo at some bar in New York last night and said, "Hey, Fredo, can I have a picture?" is because they don't listen to this program. Yet they have assigned all of this evil to me. If they had listened to this program, if just one of the Drive-bys ever listened to this program, all of this would have been understood the moment that it happened last night.

Anyway, folks, just our own little private joke here, and it has blown up, and, man, is it delightful. And now we got Fredo running around claiming that it's a racial slur. Everything to these people on the left is racist. Hey, you know, people have forgotten: Remember when the Covington kids were confronted by the elderly Indian banging on the drum?

You remember what Fredo said on CNN? Fredo said the kid should have walked away. Fredo said the kid should have not stood there in the Indian guy's face and provoked the incident. He should have walked away.

Did Fredo walk away last night? Fredo did not. And, you know, this is totally innocent—the guy that walked up to Fredo and asked him for a photo really thought his name was Fredo. The guy listens to this program! *[Laughs]*

MAN #1: *[Background noise]* I thought . . . I thought that's who you were.

FREDO: No! Punk-ass bitches from the right call me "Fredo." My name is Chris Cuomo. I'm an anchor on CNN.

RUSH: All that happened was a guy walked up to him and said, "Hey, Fredo, can I get a picture with you?" That's all that happened, and Fredo lost it— and Fredo sounded like Fredo. He sounded like Fredo! He sounded like Michael. He sounded like a bunch of them rolled into one here. Now, these people, folks, they all think they're Walter Cronkite. *[Fredo impression]* "I'm an anchor! I'm an anchor at CNN!" Yeah, that nobody watches. "I'm an anchor at CNN. My name is Chris Cuomo! I'm gonna throw your ass down the stairs," whatever else he was threatening to do there. But, you know, it's a fascinating case study. These people can dish it out. They can talk about Donald Trump all day long. They can spread lies. They can slander and libel people left and right. They can spread false conspiracy theories and hoaxes, and they can try to pass them off as real. They can try to overturn the results of an election! They can join a silent coup. They can join in the attempted destruction of anybody who is on the right simply because they don't agree with them. But, man, they cannot take a single little bit.

. . .

I have been shocked (pleasantly so) to see some in the Drive-by Media recognize our Al Gore countdown clock at RushLimbaugh.com. Back in 2006, Al Gore said that we had ten years remaining. Ten years. Humanity had ten years left to save the earth from what was then called global warming. —Rush Limbaugh

. . .

LATE NIGHT TV SHOW HOST CONAN O'BRIEN RIPS OFF THE EIB MEDIA MONTAGE

The Rush Limbaugh Show, January 2, 2014

RUSH: Yeah, yeah, yeah, the Conan rip-off. I've got it here. I'll get to it here in just a second. I mean, I'll tell you what it is. We were the first to discover and document how the media, all of them, will use the same word or phrase in covering a story. We put together a montage. When Bush chose Cheney to be his vice-presidential running mate in 2000, the media used the word "gravitas" to discuss and describe Cheney and the move.

We put together a montage of at least twenty different media people all using the phrase, all using the word, and whenever we have found it happening again, we've put together another montage. Well, I guess last week sometime Conan did the same thing, as though it had never been done before, and the media is talking about what a brilliant comedic bit it was, and the media's talking about, "Oh, my God, look at what Conan's discovered!" The media is out there, "My gosh, this is incredible, what Conan's discovered about the way the media operates," and I will bet you that the twenty writers that Conan O'Brien has will each win an Emmy for this, even though our gravitas thing . . . When did we first air this? It has to go back to 2000. It has to be fourteen years ago now, and we've been airing it a lot since. . . .

Here's what we're talking about. Go back, Mike, grab sound bite number three. This is it. You remember this. We put this sound bite together starting in July of 2000. This is a montage [of] when George W. Bush decided to choose Dick Cheney as his vice-presidential running mate.

AL HUNT: He meets all of George W's weaknesses, lack of gravitas.

JUAN WILLIAMS: We see the son, who is seeking some gravitas.

JEFF GREENFIELD: We're to use the favorite phrase, gravitas.

LESTER HOLT: This is a vice president who brought gravitas.

WOLF BLITZER: This will give some gravitas, add some credibility.

SAM DONALDSON: He displayed tonight a certain gravitas.

MARIO CUOMO: I think gravitas is the word. Unfortunately for the governor, you can't graft gravitas. He has gravitas.

RUSH: Is it possible that all of these people independently thought to describe this choice as "gravitas"? That's a hard thing to believe, and there have been countless other instances of this since 2000, and we've documented them each and every time. . . . Conan is introducing and playing a montage of various news anchors from around the country all saying the same thing and thinking he's onto something big.

O'BRIEN: Judging by local news—and I've been looking at a lot of local news—there is an even bigger story that's sweeping the nation right now.

LOCAL ANCHOR: Who are you really shopping for this holiday season? It's okay. You can admit it if you bought an item or two, or ten, for yourself.

LOCAL ANCHOR: Well, it's okay. You can admit it if you've bought an item or two, or maybe ten, for yourself.

LOCAL ANCHOR: It's okay. You can admit it. You bought an item or two, or ten, for yourself.

LOCAL ANCHOR: It's okay. You can admit it if you bought an item or two, or ten, for yourself.

LOCAL ANCHOR: It's okay. You can admit it if you bought an item or two, or ten, for yourself.

LOCAL ANCHOR: It's okay. You can admit it if you bought an item or two, or ten, for yourself.

RUSH: That's it. Now, this goes on for another minute. Now, obviously, what happened here is that these are local anchors from around the country—if this is legit. I don't know if they produced this. If it's legit, it's clear that some consultant who consults all of these local stations told the anchors to do this. All the news anchors are robots these days. Consultants dictate what's said to relate to people via focus groups and so forth. Well, but it's lazy, people doing the news. But, I mean, this is verbatim. So this is obviously from a consultant, a consultant firm that consults all these stations.

DRIVE-BY MEDIA CLAIM OBAMA PRESIDENCY WILL BE GOOD FOR RUSH

The Rush Limbaugh Show, November 4, 2008

RUSH: Let's go to the audio sound bites. We'll start out just at the top of the list. This is this morning on *Squawk Box* on CNBC. Joe Kernen, Carl Quintanilla, and Becky Quick discussing a possible Obama win, and then Joe Kernan, one of the hosts, says, "Well, who wins if Obama wins?"

QUICK: Limbaugh has done better when there are Democrats in—around, right?

KERNAN: Right! So Limbaugh . . . He just signed a new deal.

QUICK: Right!

KERNAN: What happens to the left? What happens . . . ? Is *Air America* still on?

RUSH: This is just laughable. People still ask me this in person. Last night at the football game, "You're secretly hoping, right? It would be good for you if Obama wins, right?" No. My job is to acquire the largest audience I can and hold [it] for as long as I can, regardless who's in office. There's always going to be liberals running around trying to destroy the country. But these people think that I only succeeded because of the election of Bill Clinton. I'm not even going to bother refuting it anymore. You've heard it over and over again. It's just BS, but this is an example of their template and how once they thought something, either in the Nexis database or in their narrative or template, you can't get it out, no matter how many times you tell them personally.

FLASHBACK TO 1992: BILL CLINTON "NO TRUTH DETECTOR"
The Rush Limbaugh Show, September 10, 2019

RUSH: Back in '92, '93, this show was it, folks. CNN was out there, but they were all on Clinton's side. There wasn't Fox News. There wasn't the blogosphere yet. And Bill Clinton went nuts with one radio show, a three-hour radio show; that's all the opposition he had, he went nuts about it.

He called KMOX in St. Louis from Air Force One to complain about this program and how there was no Truth Detector after it. There was nobody to set the record straight. Here's the note. "My name is blah, blah. I'm a reporter for the blah, blah. We're working on a story regarding a confidential document that we uncovered from the Clinton Library detailing White House involvement with the effort to train callers to call into conservative talk shows around the country. I know this is something Rush has always suspected, that he used to identify these trained callers—" That's right. They were seminar callers.

Here's my point. Bill Clinton went crazy—well, that may be a bit of a—Bill Clinton was totally bamboozled by one three-hour radio show. Blaming me for the Oklahoma City bombing, anything he could talk about. One radio show. And then, of course, there became more as Clinton's term began . . .

CLINTON: After I get off the radio today with you, Rush Limbaugh will have three hours to say whatever he wants—

BRENNAN: Would you like to leave a message?

CLINTON: —and I won't have any opportunity to respond, and there's no Truth Detector. You won't get on afterwards and say what was true and what wasn't!

* * *

You are listening to the EIB Network, the home of Industrial-Strength Ideological Purity. —Rush Limbaugh

* * *

And I have to tell you, people at the wedding on Saturday night had never seen me happier than while I was waiting at the altar for Kathryn. I'm hopping up and down up there at the end of the long aisle. And everybody said, "You never looked happier." Right, Snerdley? "You've never looked happier." —Rush Limbaugh

RUSH RECALLING THE BEST DAYS OF HIS LIFE: ELTON JOHN
The Rush Limbaugh Show, June 16, 2010

RUSH: You gotta hear this. There are a couple audio sound bites. I'm at home yesterday after the program, and I'm eagerly awaiting the arrival of Abbey 'cause I want to see Abbey get along with the new puppy. So I'm at the computer and I get this email that David Furnish, who is Elton John's partner, has spoken to *People* magazine.

They were in New York on Sunday—or I guess Furnish was—for the Tony Awards, and furnish was asked about Elton John appearing in performance at Kathryn's and my wedding. And Furnish said *[summarizing]*, "Ah, it was great. Elton had a wonderful time. He likes building bridges." It's at People.com. So on WABC-TV New York Eyeball 7, the entertainment correspondent, Sandy Kenyon, reported this about the latest development.

KENYON: Elton John's partner says the performer was a little surprised by an invitation to perform at Rush Limbaugh's wedding, because the conservative host has often opposed gay rights. But Sir Elton accepted because "life is about building bridges, not walls," to use his words. David Furnish couldn't attend the ceremony, but he tells People.com his famous partner saw it as a way to go where people wouldn't expect him to go. The Limbaughs were said to be very gracious. Gay activists very, very upset.

RUSH: They're just fit to be tied about this, because David Furnish actually said a lot more. He said *[summarizing]*, "Yeah, they're gonna come have dinner with us in England when they're flying through here, and Elton had a great time. We're very appreciative. Rush and Kathryn were just extremely gracious and kind. They had great friends that Elton met and so forth." So that just irritates them all the more.

RECALLING ELTON'S WEDDING PERFORMANCE
The Rush Limbaugh Show, December 23, 2014

RUSH: Chris, Newport Beach, California, great to have you on the program, sir, hello.

CALLER: Rush, you're a living legend. How are you, chief?

RUSH: Thank you, sir. I'm doing well.

CALLER: I've been listening to you since '85, first time calling in, and I can't believe I don't have a political question, but let's talk a little rock 'n' roll. Elton John at your wedding, and you kind of act like it's no big deal. Are you kidding?

RUSH: What do you mean, I act like it's no big deal?

CALLER: Well, I don't hear you talk about it. Let me ask you, who came up with the set list? Did you come up with the set list or did Elton?

RUSH: No, we worked with him on it, Kathryn and I. He gave us an hour.

CALLER: Oh, my word.

RUSH: Whatever number of songs we could squeeze into fifty-five minutes or an hour. Well, there were certain things he couldn't do; he needed an orchestra. I wanted "Circle of Life," but he couldn't. He needed an orchestra. He was just on solo piano.

CALLER: How about "Mona Lisas and Mad Hatters," one of my favorites?

RUSH: Oh, yeah. In fact, I'll tell you: Elton was fabulous. He was great. And he was shocked when he found out what some of our favorite songs were.

CALLER: Oh, wow.

RUSH: Not in an angry way. He was pleasantly surprised. It was a learning experience for Elton, believe me.

CALLER: I was gonna say, did he have Nigel Olsson with him, one of my favorite drummers of all time?

RUSH: No. He didn't. It was just him on the piano.

CALLER: Oh, boy.

RUSH: It was just Elton, and again, that affected the playlist. But again, the playlist, we got 90 percent of what we wanted. Maybe 100 percent of it. As I say, I would have loved to have "Circle of Life," but that was *Lion King* or Disney, and he needed an orchestra for that to work, but no, we picked it. I'll tell you this, since you seem to be desiring information. He talked to the audience. He talked to us between every tune and he explained why he was singing this next song. He told our guests that "Rush particularly likes this request" or "Kathryn, this was one of her favorites," and so forth. It was very personable. And we did a pretty good job of keeping his appearance secret so that most of the guests had no idea who it was. We filed into the big ballroom at the hotel, the Breakers, and all I did was, when everybody was seated and I

got the go signal, I just got on the microphone and said, "Ladies and gentlemen, Elton John." And the place erupted into a standing ovation. He didn't
know what he was gonna get. I mean, let's face it—there are so many clichés
about conservatives and liberals and so forth. He loved it. He just had a
bang-up great time, and we did with him. If you're an Elton John fan, Chris,
trust the fact that he was exactly what you would hope to be, if you had a
chance to meet him. Just a great guy.

RUSH EXPLAINS PUNKIN' THE CAT PROBLEM
The Rush Limbaugh Show, November 30, 2007

I got some good sleep last night. You know, I'm getting all kinds of advice on what to do about Punkin'. Wednesday night she started headbutting me right between the eyes, for like an hour and a half. I mean, it was a combination of headbutt and nuzzle. She wants me to get up and feed her. So people say, "Why don't you feed her before you go to bed?"

I guess I need to give you people the routine here so you understand what's so odd about this. I do feed her, whether it's midnight, two o'clock in the morning, eleven p.m., I feed her before I go to bed. I feed the cat three times a day, once when I get up, when I get home in the afternoon, and then when I go to bed. A bad habit has evolved. She will not eat out of the bowl. Sometimes she will, if she's really hungry, but she will not eat until she sees me pour something in the bowl, whether the bowl's [already] full or not.

Now, I put the food in these Ziploc bags, because there are two or three different kinds for urinary tract infections, to make sure she doesn't get them. Some days she won't eat one and wants the other, but I don't know that 'til I open each bag and let her figure it out. It's gotten to the point now where she won't eat except out of the Ziploc bag, so I have to open the Ziploc bag. I have to put it on the floor, open it up, and then stand there, make sure she doesn't strangle or suffocate in the Ziploc bag while this is happening. The cat is totally running my life here. I have a bunch of women emailing, "I want to be Punkin'." *[Laughs]* Not many, Dawn, but just a few. So anyway, I fed the cat, went to bed last night about 1:30 a.m., and I went up there, and she had not come down to see me all day.

From the time I got home yesterday afternoon until two o'clock in the morning, 1:30 a.m., whatever it was, I had not seen her. She generally comes down to the library and starts running around my feet and legs and so forth and demanding some attention. She didn't come down. I said, "Okay, she's mad."

I'm sitting here in the library, "Puuunkin', where are you?" just trying to get her, and she totally ignored me. So I got up there at 1:30 a.m., and she's just sitting there in her bathroom waiting. She has her own bathroom and sitting room, folks.

She's just sitting there waiting. So I went and I got the bag; she didn't want that bag, I had to go get another bag, open it up, bam, dug in there like crazy. Did not headbutt me today, but when I got up to feed her, bam, right back in the same bag. I know what you cat people are saying, that I've lost control here and the cat's running me. "Don't feed her all the time. Put the food in the bowl. When she gets hungry, she'll eat it." Yeah, but you're forgetting the headbutts at 5:30 or six o'clock in the morning.

LIMBAUGH SHEEPDOGS HAVE FELLOW SHEEPDOG FANS!
The Rush Limbaugh Show, December 3, 2010

RUSH: John in Indianapolis, you're next on Open Line Friday. Hi.

CALLER: Hey, Rush, golden retriever dittos from Indianapolis.

RUSH: Thank you very much, sir.

CALLER: I have a problem with the—

RUSH: Oh, speaking of which, golden retriever, you won't believe this. Two days ago I'm talking about my old English sheepdogs, Abbey and Wellesley, and they got a fan letter. They got a fan letter from another sheepdog named Garcia in the West Coast of Florida. And this sheepdog Garcia guest stars in a novel that's being written by Don Bruns. Anyway, I told Kathryn I'm gonna mention this, and she said, "Snerdley is gonna say you have been totally chickified if you start talking about your dogs having received a fan letter from another dog." I said, "Well, it happened." *[Laughs]* I'll read the letter Monday. I forgot to bring it in today.

Kathryn grew up all over the world due to her mother Penelope's career as a United States diplomat and father Richard's career as an international businessman and graduate of the Naval Academy. Both are brilliant and hysterical! They often drive their Mini Cooper across the country to visit the grand-pups. —Rush Limbaugh

The eldest sheepdog, and matriarch of the pet family, Abigail Adams Limbaugh.

PART 3 — UNWAVERING CORE BELIEFS

On the eve of Rush's birthday in 2020, we flew to one of our favorite destinations to celebrate the milestone. After we'd settled into the hotel suite, there was a loud knock. We opened the front door to find two of the hotel concierge team, whom we knew from previous visits, asking if we were available for a few minutes. They motioned for us to come out into the hallway. To our complete surprise, lining the long private corridor was an unbelievable sight: On either side of the hallway as far as you could see were representatives from the hotel—housekeeping staff, valet attendants, and servers dressed in their uniforms. There must have been sixty to seventy people. In unison, they all started clapping and cheering and broke into song, "Happy birthday to you, happy birthday to you, happy birthday, dear Mr. Rush, happy birthday to you!"

Rush was completely shocked. His eyes welled up with tears of disbelief. He went down the line shaking their hands. We started hearing shouts from all areas. An older housekeeper with a strong Cuban accent said, "Thank you, Mr. Rush. I immigrated here to the United States. I love you." Another gentleman said, "I listen to you every day. You are the reason I am working here today." The kindness demonstrated in that hallway was so symbolic and fitting. Rush treated everyone he met with respect. He was an unwavering patriot and a true gentleman. He deserves the title of American Hero because he impacted the lives of so many in the most positive way. Rush never wavered from his core beliefs and fundamental American values, and he inspired us with his conviction.

MY PRINCIPLES HAVE NEVER WAVERED
The Rush Limbaugh Show, August 1, 2017

RUSH: Nick in . . . where is this? North Carolina? Kernersville, North Carolina. How are you doing, Nick?

CALLER: Good, Rush. It's an honor to speak with you again.

RUSH: Thank you, sir.

CALLER: Congratulations on thirty years. So I'm thirty years old myself, and I've been listening to you for, I think, five or six years, and a few years ago my dad bought me your first book, which is *The Way Things Ought to Be.* For those in Rio Linda, you wrote that back in '92, and you're still using Rio Linda, which I love. But in reading it, I realized very quickly that you're exactly the same person today that you were twenty-five years ago, and as fast as things move today, I found that to be pretty cool—that over twenty-five years, nothing much has changed, principle-wise.

RUSH: Yeah, that's the key.

CALLER: Yeah.

RUSH: My principles and core beliefs haven't changed. You know, I don't change what I think with the wind just in order to perhaps attract more people. I am what I am, believe what I believe, and I say so. Now, we adapt to trends in media, broadcasting, and elsewhere in society. But the core—very perceptive of you. You're exactly right. That book still holds up today.

CALLER: Right.

RUSH: Just take Bill Clinton's name out, put [in] Obama's name, and it still works. Everything in it still works today. In fact, that book has been ripped off. You know, over in the Middle East there's a copycat host of me called Ali Limbali, and he wrote the book *The Way Things Ought to Become.* I was actually thinking of taking action against it, except I was flattered by it.

* * *

Just as you will not find in your library Great Moderates in American History, *you will not find* Great Pessimists in American Life. —Rush Limbaugh

* * *

RUSH'S FIRST THIRTY-FIVE UNDENIABLE TRUTHS OF LIFE

#1: The greatest threat to humanity lies in the nuclear arsenal of the USSR.

#2: The greatest threat to humanity lies in the USSR.

#3: Peace does not mean the elimination of nuclear weapons.

#4: Peace does not mean the absence of war.

#5: War is not obsolete.

#6: Ours is a world governed by the aggressive use of force.

#7: There is only one way to get rid of nuclear weapons: use them.

#8: Peace can't be achieved by "developing an understanding" with the Russian people.

#9: When Americans oppose America, it is not always courageous and sacred; it is sometimes dangerous.

#10: Communism kills.

#11: Neither the US nor anyone imposes freedom on peoples of other nations.

#12: Freedom is God-given.

#13: In the USSR, peace means the absence of opposition.

#14: To free peoples, peace means the absence of threats and the presence of justice.

#15: The Peace Movement in the US—whether by accident or design—is pro-Communist.

#16: The collective knowledge and wisdom of seasoned citizens is the most valuable yet untapped resource our young people have.

#17: The greatest football team in the history of civilization is the Pittsburgh Steelers of 1975–1980.

#18: There is no such thing as war atrocities.

#19: War itself is an atrocity.

#20: There is a God.

#21: Abortion is wrong.

#22: Morality is not defined and cannot be defined by individual choice.

#23: Evolution cannot explain Creation.

#24: Feminism was established so as to allow unattractive women access to the mainstream of society.

#25: Love is the only human emotion that cannot be controlled.

#26: The only difference between Mikhail Gorbachev and previous Soviet leaders is that Gorbachev is alive.

#27: Soviet leaders are just left-wing dictators.

#28: Abe Lincoln saved this nation.

#29: The LA Raiders will never be the team that they were when they called Oakland home.

#30: The US will again go to war.

#31: To more and more people, a victorious US is a sinful US.

#32: This is frightening and ominous.

#33: There will always be poor people.

#34: This is not the fault of the rich.

#35: You should thank God for making you an American, and instead of feeling guilty about it, help spread our ideas worldwide.

. . .

Whatever my radio program has meant to people, it doesn't compare to what all of you and all the friends I've made during these last years has meant to my family and my career, and I probably will never, ever find an adequate way to say thank you to everybody, so I try to do it as often as I get the chance and every chance I get. So, again, thanks to all of you who have helped me sustain what I need to do to be who I am.

—Rush Limbaugh

. . .

THE THINGS MENTALLY TOUGH PEOPLE (LIKE ME) AVOID
The Rush Limbaugh Show, December 13, 2013

Okay, now, mentally strong people, the things they avoid. Now, here's how *Forbes* gets into them: "For all the time executives spend concerned about physical strength and health, when it comes down to it, mental strength can mean even more. Particularly for entrepreneurs, numerous articles talk about critical characteristics of mental strength—tenacity, 'grit,' optimism, and an unfailing ability, as *Forbes* contributor David Williams says, to 'fail up.'"

Do you know people that fail up? I do. My brother knows some. It really irritates him. Do you know people that fail up? The Democrat leadership's a classic example of people that fail up. That no matter what, everything ends up going well for them. No matter how bad they screw up, some people just have that knack.

"However, we can also define mental strength by identifying the things mentally strong individuals don't do. Over the weekend, I was impressed by this list compiled by Amy Morin, a psychotherapist and licensed clinical social worker, that she shared [on] LifeHack," which is obviously a website. "It impressed me enough I'd also like to share her list here, along with my thoughts on how each of these items is particularly applicable to entrepreneurs."

Now, I'm not gonna read all that. I'm just gonna touch on it. And, again, they are compiled by Amy Morin, psychotherapist, licensed clinical social worker. The things mentally tough, strong people avoid. I don't know if they're in any order, but I'll share them with you in the order in which they are published.

Number one: They do not waste time feeling sorry for themselves. "You don't see mentally strong people feeling sorry for their circumstances or dwelling on the way they've been mistreated. They have learned to take responsibility for their actions and outcomes, and they have an inherent understanding of the fact that, frequently, life is not fair," and they don't get bogged down in the unfairness of life.

Let me tell you something: If these things are not in order, that is a great one to be at number one. I can't tell you. That one dovetails with not giving people the power to offend you. I think mentally tough people realize that they're not like most people, and to get all worried about being offended or, "Gosh, this isn't fair," it's beneath people that don't have time for something like that. The reality of life is that most people are not considerate. Most people are doing nothing but thinking about themselves all the time. So that's really, I think, a key element of toughness.

Number two: Mentally tough people do not give away their power. And that is part and parcel of not being offended all the time. "Mentally strong people avoid giving others the power to make them feel inferior or bad." Put up some boundaries and don't let that stuff affect you, especially if it isn't true.

Number three: Mentally strong people do not waste energy on things they cannot control. "Mentally strong people don't complain (much) about bad traffic, lost luggage, or especially about other people." They don't experience road rage. You don't know what's going on in that car that may be driving erratically and running red lights.

Number four: Mentally tough people do not worry about pleasing others. There it is again. That's a variation of not worrying about what other people think of you. The thing is, you can't please other people. Well, it's everybody else's responsibility to be happy. Somebody's happiness is not your job. Somebody being content and happy is not your responsibility. And if you let somebody throw that off on you, you're gonna be miserable. If you're in a relationship, romantic relationship, marriage, anywhere at work or whatever, and if you let somebody make you responsible for their happiness, your goose is cooked.

(A), you're dealing with somebody that can't be happy anyway. And (B), you can't do it. Happiness is an internal thing. Contentment is an internal thing, and it results from the pursuit of it. It doesn't just happen.

Number five: Mentally tough people do not fear taking calculated risks.

Number six: Mentally tough people do not dwell on the past.

Number seven: Mentally tough people do not make the same mistakes over and over again.

Number eight: Mentally tough people do not resent other people's success. That's a toughie, because human nature is such that—I mean, somebody that fails up, you're gonna resent them. That's a tough one.

Number nine: Mentally tough people do not give up after failure.

Number ten: Mentally tough people do not fear time alone. "Mentally strong people enjoy and even treasure the time they spend alone. They use their downtime to reflect, to plan, and to be productive. Most importantly, they don't depend on others to shore up their happiness and moods. They can be happy with others, and they can also be happy alone."

Number eleven: Mentally tough people do not think the world owes them anything.

And number twelve: Mentally tough people do not expect immediate results. I'm sure that Koko will find this story in *Forbes*. I've had it here since December the tenth. And it's written by Cheryl Snapp Conner, frequent speaker and author on reputation and thought leadership. She's got a newsletter you can subscribe to, but that's who the author of this piece is. So Koko will find it and put it up there. I heartily, as a really mentally tough guy, endorse this. *[Interruption]* What is so funny? Are you disputing my assertion that I'm a mentally tough guy? Okay. Okay. I endorse all of these. There's no question.

. . .

Three or four days ago, I called him just to find out—you know, his fight was very, very courageous, and he was very sick. And, you know, from diagnosis on, it was just something that was not going to be beaten, but you wouldn't know it. And he is married to an incredible woman, Kathryn, who really, every time I spoke to him, he would tell me how great she was, she took such great care. —President Donald J. Trump

. . .

MY FATHER ALWAYS SAID YOU CAN JUDGE A MAN'S CHARACTER BY HOW HE TREATS THOSE WHO CAN DO NOTHING FOR HIM
The Rush Limbaugh Show, June 21, 2013

RUSH: Here's Bob in Clinton, Connecticut, as we go to the phones on Open Line Friday. Hi Bob, nice to have you here.

CALLER: Hi, Rush. You're just a good friend I haven't met yet. Can you hear me okay? Well, the reason why I'm calling is, with your trip to Normandy and your tribute to Vince Flynn, you said something about fifteen years ago that had such an impact on my life. You talked about what your father taught you, and you stated that you can tell the character of a man by how he treats somebody that can do absolutely nothing for you.

RUSH: Oh, yeah. Yeah, yeah. That's exactly right.

CALLER: And when you said that, that just really struck me. Like I said, it had a profound impact, and I tried to live by that rule and raise my kids that way, and I just wanted to thank you for that. I mean, you said that a long time ago—fifteen, twenty years ago—and it's stuck with me all these years.

RUSH: I'm glad you reminded me of that, particularly in the context of Vince, because that was exactly the kind of person he was. Yeah, my father always said, "The best measure of the character of a man is to observe how he treats people that can't do anything for him." Everybody's gonna be nice to people who can do things for you. Everybody's going to go out of their way to be of service or to be nice if you think somebody can do something for you. But how do you treat people who can't do anything for you? That is the true measure of character and integrity, and I'm glad you reminded me of that, Bob, 'cause you're exactly right—especially, as I say, as it relates to Vince. Thanks very much!

. . .

In 1994, I held my first Night to Remember cigar dinner at the 21 Club in New York City. The dinner celebrated the cigar, and the proceeds went to prostate cancer research. In attendance were a notable number of cigar enthusiasts from all walks of life. During the dinner, we all got to know each other, and I especially remember two guests at my table: Gregory Hines and Rush Limbaugh. The evening conversation centered around the joy that a cigar adds to our lives and its ability to create and build friendships. Gregory and Rush were on different sides of the political aisle, yet through smoking a cigar they became instant friends with mutual respect. . . . In all of our time together at events and on the golf course, people would come up to him and tell him how much they love him, and he was always gracious with their requests for photos with him. He was truly a man of the people.

—Marvin Shanken, *Cigar Aficionado* and *Wine Spectator*

. . .

• • •

I want the listening public to know that the Marine Corps–Law Enforcement Foundation, which you've been such a tremendous supporter of over the years, Rush, you've been our biggest donor by far. I mean, ladies and gentlemen, this man has given millions and millions of his own dollars to the foundation, plus he's asked the loyal listeners, and they've donated millions and millions of dollars.

—Jim Kallstrom, Founder, Marine Corps–Law Enforcement Foundation

• • •

PART 4 — RUSH'S GENEROSITY

As you know, Rush was incredibly generous. He loved sharing both his passions and good fortune with so many. Throughout his life, Rush improved circumstances for countless individuals, families, and organizations. Many of these efforts were done quietly and never discussed. Rush not only contributed significant monetary donations, he often would provide his personal time to offer leadership, comfort, and support. He never sought recognition for these wonderful acts of kindness. He treated everyone with tremendous respect and empathy. In Rush's honor, we will continue our mission to improve the lives of others facing extreme hardships through the Rush and Kathryn Adams Limbaugh Family Foundation.

JUST A FEW EXAMPLES . . .

- Rush Limbaugh named one of most generous celebrities, *Forbes* magazine, 2008

- Hosted an annual cure-a-thon for twenty-six years for the Leukemia & Lymphoma Society, raising over $50 million

- Founding board member of the Marine Corps–Law Enforcement Foundation, an organization dedicated to providing scholarships and aid to the families of fallen US military members and first responders; over $5 million donated

- More than $5 million donated to the Stephen Siller Tunnel to Towers Foundation, an organization dedicated to providing homes for the families of fallen or severely injured first responders

- Gave to organizations focused on cancer research and cures, including Dana-Farber Cancer Institute, St. Jude Children's Research Hospital, and the Prostate Cancer Foundation

- Supported military personnel, police, first responders, and their families, including the Adopt a Soldier program, Toys for Tots, Support Our Heroes, the National Navy SEAL Museum, the Fisher House Foundation, and Back the Blue

- Assisted many organizations focused on children, including the Boys & Girls Clubs of America and Els for Autism

- Thousands donated in individual scholarships and college tuition

- Thousands of Adventures of Rush Revere series books, along with electronics and supplies, donated throughout the country to homeschool conventions, elementary schools, and the American Heritage Girls

YOUR HOST KICKS OFF THE TWENTY-FOURTH ANNUAL LEUKEMIA & LYMPHOMA SOCIETY CURE-A-THON WITH A $500,000 DONATION
The Rush Limbaugh Show, April 11, 2014

I want to give you another phone number and remind you of a web address. This is our twenty-fourth annual radio cure-a-thon for the Leukemia & Lymphoma Society of America. It's twenty-four years that we have done this, and you people have enabled records to be set in terms of donations. You have enabled research and progress toward cures of the blood cancers that are unparalleled.

As is the case most of the time, there simply isn't a proper way to extend thanks to everybody. All I can do is tell you how much it's appreciated by everybody involved, people that you'll never meet, people that you will never

know have the greatest appreciation for you. Even though they've not met you, they think that you are their friend.

They consider you a member of their family, simply by virtue of your generosity and your caring and your compassion. Twenty-four years of this Leukemia & Lymphoma Society cure-a-thon here on the Rush Limbaugh program. I want you to write down this number, because I'm gonna be telling you to call it for the next three hours. . . .

A dollar, anything. One thing I want to start off by telling people is don't not call because you don't think that whatever you can give or afford

Rush shares iPhone tips with "Golden EIB Ticket" winners in his studio.

• • •

Hi, Rush. This is Larry Vanderveen. Congratulations on twenty remarkable years of The Rush Limbaugh Show *and for single-handedly re-creating AM radio in the process. It's been a privilege to work with you for most of those years in your fight against the blood cancers for the Leukemia & Lymphoma Society. Your cure-a-thon broadcasts and your personal generosity have helped save thousands of lives. Your heart is truly as big as your talent, Rush.* —Larry Vanderveen, Broadcast Consultant, Leukemia & Lymphoma Society

• • •

matters. We're dealing with such large numbers here. Folks, this is the largest radio talk show audience in the country, by far. If every one of you simply phoned in one dollar, a new record would be set—and who knows? We might find cures. It's that many people.

The twenty-fifth year is next year, this is the twenty-fourth, but Kathryn and I are going to kick this off with a cool half a million.

* * *

You know, I just chatted with Larry Vanderveen, who is one of the head honchos at the Leukemia & Lymphoma Society. He's been there twenty-four years. You know, all these people at the Leukemia & Lymphoma Society, they're like my friends at the Marine Corps–Law Enforcement Foundation: They don't get paid anything. All of the money goes to helping. I mean, it's incredible. The pass-through is like 95, 96 percent. This is a labor of love for these people. They've all been affected by myeloma, leukemia. Every one of them there.

A FAVORITE GOLF STORY

The Rush Limbaugh Show, November 11, 2011

We're in Los Angeles, and I went out and played golf yesterday after the program with Joel Surnow, my friend who used to produce *24*. He was instrumental in the TV show *Miami Vice*. It was a real challenge to write a show about a drug bust every week for four years in Miami. And one of the guys, the Great Maurice, one of the head writers of that show, was also in the group. And Sami, who I'm told owns all kinds of land in Syria but can't sell it, obviously, because it's Syria.

I was not having a good hour. I told them I only had time for nine holes because I had a meeting last night, since we're leaving here earlier than I had planned. I had to move a meeting up, and it was last night, so only had time for nine holes, and this place was an hour and a half away from where I'm staying out here, so I had to get out after nine holes.

Everybody, when you go play golf, wants to bet. I'm the last to bring it up because I don't even think about it, just doesn't occur to me. So we're playing a twenty-dollar Nassau, and it's Surnow and me against the Great Maury and Sami, and I'm just horrible.

It's the third time I'd played golf since August. Saticoy is the name of the course, and the fairways are about five feet wide with trees lining. It's the second time I played it, and I said, "Look, I'm gonna be OB. I'm gonna slice to right. It's gonna take four or five holes here," because I just went right to the first tee from the car.

So it's gonna be four or five holes before I get warmed up, loosened up and all that, and they all think I'm sandbagging 'em. And first tee, three balls, OB, to the right; I just know, I'm lazy, I don't finish the turn. When Hank Haney is not around to berate me, I revert.

The point of this is that I'm playing horribly. Surnow is carrying our twosome, and we're down. In fact, we lose the front nine. We're dormie after seven holes. We can't win, but Sami and Maury are gambling pigs. When they beat us, they started betting the caddy on things.

So we go into the ninth hole, a par-three up the hill, 170 yards, I think. I said to Sami, "Sami, look, like I told you on the first tee"—and I did tell him this—"I don't carry anything less than hundreds. So the bet's gonna have to be large enough that if I lose, I can pay off with a hundred-dollar bill, because I can't make change."

I don't carry anything less than hundreds, I never do. His eyes widen, because I'm sucking here, I'm horrible. So ol' Sami's eyes widen up, so do Great Maury's, big-time. Turns out to be double or nothing on the whole front nine bet. So we go from losing to even with double or nothing on this last hole, and we all tee off, it's 160 yards, we all end up in a sand trap, not the same one.

I'm pin high to the left. The Great Maury and Surnow are a little bit long in a trap behind the green and to the left, and Sami is to the right side of the green in a trap. The green is like Augusta. You couldn't hold the green, and if you missed a downhill putt, it rolled off the green. I'm the closest to the pin, but that's not good coming out of a trap, and luckily I'm below the hole.

So I've gotta get it out of the trap and keep it below the hole for an uphill putt. Everybody else is looking at a downhill shot for a trap. If I could just execute one sand shot. I'm reminding them this whole time that all I got is a hundred dollars, I can't make change. They're all excited. And it turns out after we all take our second shots that I am closest to the hole; therefore, I go last. And they all missed their par putts.

Here I am, I haven't done a thing for eight holes. It's been horrible. I haven't done a thing for eight holes. Sami, the Great Maury are salivating, hundred bucks on the golf course is a big deal. Straight-in putt, back of the cup, plop, plop, and it was just a great ending. It just shows you, never quit, anything can happen.

And they knew, you could tell by the look on their faces, they were a little bit alarmed because I approached the putt with confidence, and—I don't know, because I didn't get paid off. The question was do they have hundred-dollar bills; I don't know, but they continued playing, those three continued playing, so I don't know what Surnow did with my winnings. He might have wagered 'em and lost it on the back nine with these sharks. So I don't know.

Anyway, it was fun. I got in the car and sped back an hour and a half for my meeting, and here we are, ready today, Open Line Friday. How did you like that, stick-to-the-issues crowd? Did you like that story? 'Cause I got more of 'em if you want to hear 'em. Clutch Limbaugh.

* * *

Rush had a certain shyness about him. And he didn't try to stand out in a crowd, but always he was the center of any crowd. People would come up to him at restaurants and golf courses and ask for autographs, ask for pictures, and Rush accommodated every one of those. He also listened to them, although that's an oxymoron because most of the time Rush heard chipmunks through his cochlear implant. So, he couldn't exactly hear them, but he made certain they all felt that he understood every word they said.
—David Rosow, Saturday Golf Foursome Leader

* * *

Chapter 8

HONOR OF A LIFETIME

TRIBUTE
by President Donald J. Trump

STATE OF THE UNION ADDRESS, 2020

THE PRESIDENT: Almost every American family knows the pain when a loved one is diagnosed with a serious illness. Here tonight is a special man, beloved by millions of Americans, who just received a stage 4, advanced cancer diagnosis. This is not good news. But what is good news is that he is the greatest fighter and winner that you will ever meet. Rush Limbaugh—

HOUSE CHAMBER: [Cheers and applause]

THE PRESIDENT: —thank you for your decades of tireless devotion to our country.

HOUSE CHAMBER: [Cheers and applause]

RUSH: This is the House Chamber at the State of the Union. My mom and dad would not have believed it. This kind of thing was not possible.

THE PRESIDENT: And, Rush, in recognition of all that you have done for our nation—the millions of people a day that you speak to and that you inspire, and all of the incredible work that you have done for charity— I am proud to announce tonight that you will be receiving our country's highest civilian honor: the Presidential Medal of Freedom.

HOUSE CHAMBER: [Sustained cheers and applause]

THE PRESIDENT: I will now ask the First Lady of the United States to present you with the honor. Please.

HOUSE CHAMBER: *[Hoots and applause]*

MAN: We love you, Rush!

HOUSE CHAMBER: *[Sustained applause]*

THE PRESIDENT: Rush and Kathryn, congratulations.
Thank you, Kathryn.

WHAT AN INCREDIBLE WEEK!
The Rush Limbaugh Show, February 7, 2020

RUSH: What a week. What an incredible week. I mean, from beginning to end. And it's still going. And there is still winning that's happening today. Just incredible. And I'm gonna tell you something, folks. One of the things I'm gratified about—you know, I don't like to brag, and I don't like to say "notice me." But everything happening to the Democrat Party today, if you go back and you look at excerpts of the award-winning broadcast, go to RushLimbaugh.com, you'll find that I predicted this implosion of the Democrat Party. And that's exactly what it is. I mean, you got people writing, "Well, what happened to the Democrats this week is unserious." It's worse than unserious. What happened to the Democrat Party is that they have lost their entire moral foundation. . . .

Despite living in the public eye, I really am a private person, for just a host of reasons, most of which that's just who I am. I want whatever I'm known for to speak for itself during these three hours and some other things. I'm not interested in being in the news all the time, for whatever reason. Of course, I can't help it—I am in the news all the time. But it's not something I seek.

Nevertheless, it has been one of the biggest blessings—you know, I understand now what Lou Gehrig, when he was diagnosed with ALS in the 1930s, he's announcing his retirement. This is after he has been the Iron Man, played in all these consecutive games, the record wasn't broken until Cal Ripken Jr. came along.

He's standing at home plate at Yankee Stadium, and he said, after having announced—the world knew—that he had ALS, everybody knew what it was, that it was fatal and there was no chance of recovery, and there still isn't, by the way. And Lou Gehrig said, "Today I consider myself the luckiest man on earth." I've seen that black-and-white film replayed numerous times in my life.

And don't misunderstand, I know he meant it. But the first two or three times I heard it I had trouble processing. How in the world can anybody feel lucky after having been told that you have a disease from which there is no recovery and that it's fast? And there was a part of me that said, "Okay. This is something that famous people are supposed to say. He's been very successful in life. He was uniquely talented to play baseball and all that." And I thought, "Okay. Clearly there is a portion of Lou Gehrig that thinks he has to say this."

And now I know that's all wrong. Now I know that there was nothing forced or phony or public-relations-related about it, because I feel the same way. I cannot thank all of the people that I have heard from since Monday, and they are still getting ahold of me. There are people I had no idea they knew how to get ahold of me. And the sentiments, the thoughts they're expressing are just incredibly nice and supportive.

And to have this kind of support and to know it, to be fully aware of it, yeah, it does make me one of the luckiest people alive. I'm trying to respond to everybody. I haven't even made a dent in it. I haven't had a whole lot of time to, but I'm going to try. Some people have written three or four times. . . .

Now, I know many of you want to know the story of the State of the Union address on Tuesday night and how that all happened, and someday I hope to be able to tell you the entire story. I can't tell you the entire story now without divulging medical details that I, frankly, don't want to give. I don't want to give people an opportunity to start investigating and writing about and pronouncing opinions and this kind of thing. People know enough about what I have.

It's late-stage. It's advanced lung cancer. But there's good news associated with the diagnosis and the treatment. So we are where I am to have the first procedure that will set up the beginning of treatment. This is Tuesday, and it is scheduled for five o'clock in the afternoon. We took no clothes, Kathryn and I. We just . . . We went Grub City with shorts, T-shirts. I mean, the whole week's gonna be in the hospital.

There's no reason to take a coat and tie. There's no reason to pack a whole bunch of stuff that you're never gonna use. "Light" was the byword. The procedure was gonna be five o'clock in the afternoon. I'd have to show up for it at twelve noon to do the prep, talk to the doctors, and so forth. At nine a.m., the phone rings. I've got the number in my address book. So it's the White House. I answered the phone, and they said, "Can you hold for President Trump?"

I said, "Yes."

"Rush! Rush! How you doing, buddy? Great to hear from you! Hey, look, what are you doing later today?"

I said, "Well, I have a serious medical procedure that's gonna start—all this—at five o'clock."

"Well, look, what's the doctor's name? I want to call him and have him delay it for a couple days 'cause I need you down here tonight."

I said *[chuckles]*, "Uh . . . *[chuckles]* Mr. President, um . . . I'm stunned."

He said, "Look, your health comes first; there's no question. But can't they just do half of what they're gonna do and then send you down here? Believe me, you don't want to miss this. It's gonna be great. It's gonna be great. You don't want to miss this."

Well, I don't know what's up. He told me he wanted me to be his guest at the State of the Union, that he was gonna mention my name, recognize me. I hung up the phone, and for the next hour and a half, I agonized—I literally agonized—over what to do. Kathryn and I are both sitting in the hotel room. As time is marching on, we're faced with the possibility of having to ask an entire medical team to broom their schedule and reschedule to accommodate this.

But we haven't told 'em yet. We're discussing the logistics. Now, there's something else. Earlier that day, I had sent EIB One to take my nieces from New York to Cape Girardeau, and it wasn't gonna be available to me until 4:30 in the afternoon. So I'm putting that in the equation. I mean, there's no way to even get there even if I want to, unless we charter. We could do that. But no clothes, no shirt, no tie, no socks, no dress shoes.

Zip, zero, nada.

Kathryn's saying, "You've got to do this! You can't not do this."

I said, "How are we gonna do it?"

She said, "Leave it to me. . . ."

So Kathryn . . . *[chuckles]* This was amazing, too. Kathryn got in gear and (again, without divulging too much) we went and met the doctor. We kept the appointment at noon to discuss what was gonna happen. We signed the papers, get as much of the procedure out of the way as we could, and then tell the doctor, "Hey, I have been summoned to Washington. Can this be moved to tomorrow?"

"Sure! It's not a problem. In fact, show up at 5:30 tomorrow morning before anybody else gets here. We'll get it started; we'll get it rolling." Everybody was just as cooperative and helpful as they could be. We get back from the meeting with the doctors in about two hours, and in our hotel room is fifteen sport coats of different sizes, four or five different ties, a bunch of shirts of different sizes, and all I had to do was try on various things and find an outfit that fit. I did have . . . I take it back. I did have a pair of slacks, 'cause it was cold where we went; so I wasn't wearing slacks and shorts, wasn't able to. But I did wear slacks. The slacks come from the suit. . . .

She had nothing, either, nothing that would be suitable for the House Chamber. Pardon me? Yeah, it was stuff off the rack. What are you gonna do? There was no time for a tailor. There's no time for a seamstress. Yeah. That's why there were fifteen different sport coats, Mr. Snerdley. That's why there are four or five different shirts with different neck sizes, sleeve lengths. . . .

And we arrived in Washington and were picked up and taken to the White House. We were met by Hogan Gidley in the communications shop, and went to the library in the White House, which is off the diplomatic entrance area, the elevator to the residence, where the First Lady was posing for photos with all of the people who were being recognized in the gallery that night.

And we were last in line on purpose, because after we posed for the photo with the First Lady, we were then escorted to the residence to meet the Trump family in the Yellow Oval. Again, that is a room in the residence. It's not far down the hall—if you keep walking past it, you run into the Lincoln Bedroom and the Queen's Bedroom. And it's the exact dimensions of the Oval Office in the West Wing. Teddy Roosevelt loved that room. He had it made for the residence, the exact measurements, with the predominant color being yellow.

So we were escorted into the room by Mrs. Trump, and we chat with her for two or three minutes, and then the Trump family began to come in, Ivanka, Donald Jr., Eric, their wives, spouses, and then the president came in and sat down and started talking about . . . how thrilled he was that we were able to make it. . . .

* * *

Okay. So the way they get everybody over—and I'm truncating this. They've got a couple of buses, minivans. They're very nice. Don't misunderstand "minivan." They put all the guests in, and the guests are the tail end of the caravan. It is a massive caravan, more SUVs than I've ever seen in a row, and we left the White House about 8:15 to get over there, and they hustle you into the gallery, and you sit down.

I've never been in the gallery. Oh, I have in the Senate, never in the House. I have seen the House Chamber from floor level. You're not allowed to go out there if you're not a member, and it was pretty full by the time we got there at 8:30, and all the Republicans are just . . . They're looking up and they're waving, thumbs-up. It was so inspiring and gratifying, and there was just a . . . If you can imagine an envelope or like a wave of warmth that just swept over me sitting there. Every Republican congressman, every senator, every . . . I'm looking down there. And then to see the Democrats not doing a thing, and they're dressed in all white and so forth. It was just a moving, moving night, and I'm sitting there. I can't believe we're there, can't believe it happened, can't believe it all came together—and then, it happened. . . .

THE PRESIDENT: And, Rush, in recognition of all that you have done for our nation—the millions of people a day that you speak to and that you inspire, and all of the incredible work that you have done for charity—I am proud to announce tonight that you will be receiving our country's highest civilian honor: the Presidential Medal of Freedom.

HOUSE CHAMBER: *[Cheers and applause]*

* * *

RUSH: For me, the highlight, though, was Sergeant Williams, brought back from Afghanistan. He hadn't seen his wife and kids in months. That moment that he came down those steps? You have to have been there to understand the power of that moment. . . . Go to sound bite number twenty-one. This is Howie Carr, who was on Tucker Carlson's show on the Fox News Channel on Wednesday night. And Howie Carr said, "Why not just say, 'I disagree with Rush Limbaugh'? Why does every disagreement have to be kind of per-verted into a race conversation? Okay, they disagree with Rush. Fine. Why

456

do they have to call everyone they dislike a racist every time?" That's Tucker Carlson asking Howie Carr.

CARR: That's the way it is with liberals. If they disagree with you, ergo, you are a racist. And it doesn't matter that Rush has raised millions of dollars for charities, leukemia foundations, with the Betsy Ross T-shirt more recently. He's done all that. He's an historical figure in American politics, I would say, and in the radio industry. I'll tell you one thing—he never rode around on Jeffrey Epstein's jet, unlike a certain former president of the United States. He never tried to cow Ronan Farrow into stopping his exposés of Harvey Weinstein like Hillary Clinton's people did. It's ridiculous. It's really loathsome.

RUSH: All of that is a good point. It's clearly, clearly a two-way street. And then the vice president—this [is] what I was looking for. This is the vice president, as I mentioned, he called me after the State of the Union on Tuesday as we were headed back to the airport. This is Wednesday morning on the Fox News Channel, *Fox & Friends*, and Doocy said, "You're a longtime friend of Rush Limbaugh. The president awarded him the Medal of Freedom. Rush didn't see it coming. It always happens in the White House, not Congress. So Rush didn't see it coming."

PENCE: I reached him shortly after he and Kathryn left the Capitol, and he was very moved, and told me that he was going to spend the rest of his life trying to earn it. And I said, "Rush, you've already earned it. Everything you've done to uphold the values and ideals that have made this country great." Rush told me last night that his wife said that God is working in all of this, and I believe that moment which—the president, we all found out about Rush, and then the president just had this thought to say, "I want to have you come to the State of the Union." But then he said, "I know you've got some medical procedures this week, but I'd like to have you there," but he didn't tell him he was gonna give him the highest civilian honor.

RUSH: Yeah. There were people when it happened, "Okay, you've got to turn to the right. You've gotta turn away from the First Lady." I said, "Okay." And it was a special night.

Members of Congress
and distinguished guests
cheer as Rush receives the
Medal of Freedom at the
2020 State of the
Union Address.

A BIG THANK-YOU TO CHRISSIE HYNDE
The Rush Limbaugh Show, February 18, 2020

MUSIC: "My City Was Gone"

This song that you're hearing is a looped version of the intro to a song by Chrissie Hynde and the Pretenders called "My City Was Gone." I'm calling attention to this because I haven't talked about this song in many, many moons, and I don't know how many of you know where the song is from. You so identify it with this program—understandably so, after thirty-plus years. But this song is used with the permission of one of the most legendary female performers in rock, Chrissie Hynde.

She was on PLJ in New York and they asked her about it. "I don't care. If Rush wants to use it, fine with me," which totally confounded her publishing company. So, we got the song back. The reason is that her dad was a huge fan of this program. Her dad's name was Melville. His nickname was Bud, and Chrissie Hynde says that her late father, Melville, would have loved Trump's presidency, would have absolutely adored Trump, and would have just been excited as he could be when Trump presented to me the Medal of Freedom at the State of the Union.

FROM THE REMCO CARAVELLE TO A HOUSEHOLD NAME IN ALL FOUR CORNERS OF THE WORLD
The Rush Limbaugh Show, December 23, 2020

Greetings and welcome back, my friends. It's great to have you here. This is Rush Limbaugh, the most-listened-to radio talk show in the country. You made it so. I have eternal, never-ending gratitude for all of you for so much. You have meant so much to me. You've meant so much to my family. You have meant so much to the happiness and joy that I have been able to experience.

You have been integral in my dreams coming true—my wildest dreams when I was a young kid pretending to be a deejay on the radio when I was eight years old. There was a device called a Remco Caravelle. It was a brand

name. Remco was the brand name; Caravelle was the name of their product. Somebody sent me one. We actually have one of these things back in one of the supply closets here, and it was the most amazing thing.

It's plastic. It was about three feet long and two feet high, and it transmitted over AM within the confines of—I don't know—a small house. The quality was horrible, but it worked. All you had to do was set it for a frequency that was open (in other words, there wasn't a real radio station in your town that was broadcasting on that frequency), and you could do it. So I pretended to be a deejay with this thing. My parents got it for me for Christmas one year. I pretended to be a deejay, and my mother actually had a radio; you could broadcast on a real radio. I mean, it was an amazing thing. I can't believe it was licensed to operate. We're talking here, folks, in the . . . oh, this would have been the late fifties, around the turn of the [decade] in 1960.

My mother would dutifully put a radio on her lap, and I would go upstairs where the bedroom was, and I would have my phono. . . . You had to have an external microphone to put near the speaker of the phonograph that you were playing records on. You had to move the microphone to your mouth when you were doing deejay stuff, and then you'd hold the microphone near the speaker for the phonograph to play the record.

And my mother would dutifully sit down there and listen to this. And the quality was just horrible. It didn't have a whole lot of power. It wasn't like listening to a real radio station, but it allowed me to pretend, it allowed me to get started on living out my dreams. And so many people have been a part of those dreams coming true. I knew what I wanted to do when I was eight years old. How did I know?

Well, you know the story. I hated school. It was prison. I just hated it. It was a room with windows, and I could see out the windows. I could see where I would rather be. Here I'm locked in this place, I'm having to learn about whatever you learn about in first grade—you know, how to paste things—and it was the last place I wanted to be. I just looked at it as denial of freedom.

But being out there! So every morning, getting ready to go to this prison, this school, my mother had the radio on, and she's listening to the guy, a local jock, and this guy sounds like he's having fun doing whatever he's doing. He's playing records. He's doing commentary—you know, weather forecasts—and he sounds like he's having fun. I said, "That's how I want my day to be. I don't want to begin my day in drudgery and something I don't want to do," but I had no choice. You have to go to school. Either that or the truant officer comes, and it's even worse for you. But that was how I decided I wanted to be in radio. I had a natural affinity for liking music and wanting to be the guy on the radio playing it for people and so forth.

But up until that point in my life, I had quit pretty much everything else that I had tried. Like, I was a Tenderfoot Boy Scout for a year. That's unheard of. You move on from being a Tenderfoot. You don't have to do anything. But I was a Tenderfoot. Whatever the least amount you had to do to stay a Boy Scout, I did. At the first campout, I got the Gold Brick Award. The Gold Brick Award went to the person least useful on the campout.

* * *

You are here in record numbers, folks. You are listening to this program in record numbers. It's a big deal. It's how success is measured in this business. It's one of two or three ways. And you are setting records. You're setting records in two ways. The numbers of you who are listening, and what is called time spent listening, how long you're listening. It's incredible. And so I owe so many people so much.

—Rush Limbaugh

* * *

IT DOESN'T FEEL LIKE THIRTY YEARS
The Rush Limbaugh Show, July 31, 2018

RUSH: Here is John in Rochester, New York. Great that you called. Glad you waited, sir. Hello.

CALLER: Hello, Rush. It's an honor and a pleasure to speak with you. I'm gonna get right to the point. It seems to me that you're about to end the last show of your thirtieth year and nothing has been said about it yet. So I want to be the one who congratulates you and thanks you on behalf of legions of Dittoheads and our Rush Babies, like my children. You have meant so much to me. I've listened to you since you started, and I'm nervous and choking up here. But thank you. Thank you, sir.

RUSH: I'm kind of—not choking up here, but scratching my eyes a little bit. I appreciate that. I hear from people throughout the year who say nice things like you have. It never ceases to hit me, affect me very deeply, you know. Thirty years; some of it seems like I can just imagine some of those days thirty years [ago like] yesterday. Some of those days twenty-five years ago are yesterday. Others it does seem like thirty years. On balance it doesn't, though. On balance it doesn't seem like anywhere near thirty years. I think it's because my attitude hasn't changed in thirty years.

CALLER: That's absolutely right. Even when I . . . There have been times I haven't been able to listen to you because of work schedules. When the opportunity came back to listen to you again, I always found you, as I used to say, right where I left you. You are that consistent.

RUSH: Well, you are very perceptive. I think you typify, you exemplify the exact way I imagine everybody in this audience. I think everybody listening here is involved and intelligent and aware, and thinks and shares a similar value system or value base. So what I mean by it is that I show up here like it's the first day in thirty years every day, and I have to prove it each and every day. That's just me and the way I was raised. But I appreciate it more than . . . I thank you very, very much, and I guarantee you, my feelings for all of you are identical. I've run out of time here, though. So we'll have to take a break. Thank you again.

465

• • •

Well, folks, I have to tell you, what red-blooded American kid growing up in the Midwest doesn't dream of being in the Hall of Fame someday? And yesterday I made it into the Hall of Fame in the state of Missouri, with a bust and everything. And it's a great bust. It's an awesome-looking bust. You would never make it to any Hall of Fame if you're afraid of failure. I'm next to Harry Truman, Mark Twain—I say this a lot. My parents would not believe my life. My mother and dad would not believe it. —Rush Limbaugh

• • •

MEGA MAGA! THE LARGEST RADIO RALLY IN HISTORY
The Rush Limbaugh Show, October 9, 2020

MUSIC: "God Bless the USA" by Lee Greenwood

[Crowd chants "We love you"]

RUSH: And greetings to you, music lovers, thrill-seekers, and conversationalists all across the fruited plain. Welcome to the Rush Limbaugh program. Mr. President, it is a distinct honor and privilege to have you with us. I want you to do something for me, sir.

THE PRESIDENT: G'head.

RUSH: I want you to imagine you have just landed in a gleaming, majestic Air Force One to the largest radio rally in history. Instead of thousands cheering as you walk up to the stage, there are millions and millions of patriots out there right now anxiously awaiting to hear from you. No doubt they're waving Trump flags, wearing their bright-red MAGA hats proudly. This, sir, is a MEGA MAGA rally. And we are all thrilled to be with you today. We are so glad you're doing better, and welcome to the EIB Network.

THE PRESIDENT: Well, I want to thank you, Rush. You're a fantastic man, a friend of mine, but before I really even knew you as a friend, you were like a supporter, and I said, "I know that guy, he's got a big audience," but I never

466

even knew the importance of what you do and what you say, and now I do very well. And it keeps us all in the game. . . .

RUSH: I have to tell you, from the moment that your appearance was announced, we've never had a response like this, sir.

THE PRESIDENT: Wow.

RUSH: I'm in my thirty-second year. We have never had a response like this. We have thousands and thousands of questions and comments for you. I hope you know how deeply loved you are by so many Americans who have invested their hopes and prayers for this country in you. . . .

THE PRESIDENT: Well, I appreciate it. And, you know, when you suggested this, I immediately jumped on it, 'cause your audience is the biggest. I mean, it's just incredible. . . .

RUSH: Mr. President, that's another thing. If you go back, 9/11, just nineteen years ago, not that long ago—this, to me, is a really sobering thing to real-ize—not that long ago, the police, the firemen, first responders were the heroes in our country. Go back after 9/11, athletes carrying the American flag on the field—

THE PRESIDENT: Absolute heroes.

RUSH TALKS TO ERIC TRUMP ABOUT HIS FATHER'S FIGHT TO SAVE AMERICA
The Rush Limbaugh Show, November 2, 2020

RUSH: A great pleasure and honor to have with us Eric Trump, joining us now from the campaign trail. Hey, Eric. Are you getting any sleep?

ERIC TRUMP: No sleep, Rush, no sleep. I've done about two hundred events in the last fifty-two days. We are burning the midnight oil. I'm actually going to meet my father in Scranton, Pennsylvania, as we speak, and I'm so proud of the guy. I know you are as well.

RUSH: You know, I want to ask you about that. And, by the way, Eric, let me say something just from my family to yours, Kathryn and myself. We really love and admire all of you. Your entire family obviously loves the country. I know you're eminently, profoundly successful, but you're sacrificing a great deal. You didn't need to do any of this. You're taking all of this heat for a lot

• • •

You know, you're rendering me speechless, and nobody
can do that, outside of Kathryn. –Rush Limbaugh

• • •

of us and for the country because I literally love the country, and you're willing to engage in all the fireworks that come with that. And I remember I met Ivanka for the first time at the rally in Cape Girardeau, Missouri, before the 2018 midterms. And I walked up to her and I said, "You have to be so proud." President Trump was addressing the crowd. I had just introduced him. I said, "You've gotta be so proud. If my father had been elected president, I would have just been so proud, I would not have been able to contain myself," and she said that every one of you were. And it's got to be an exciting thing for you. It has to be a big deal, and you're eminently part of it.

ERIC TRUMP: It is, because he did it against all odds. We ran against the entire media, the entire left-wing party, and everybody else who didn't give us a chance. And, you know, we did it as a family. We did it. My father, Ivanka, Don, myself, I mean, we did it as a family, we beat all odds. And it's because he was a better candidate, he had a better message. And people are sick and tired of seeing this country disgraced, sick and tired of seeing the American flag burned. They're sick and tired of seeing law enforcement, you know, harassed and defunded. People love this nation. They love their anthem. They love our Pledge of Allegiance. They love faith in society. And the radical left wants to take it all away. They want to take it all away, and people are sick and tired of it. That's why . . . I mean, you've been covering this longer than anybody. When was the last time you heard forty thousand people chanting "We love you!" to a politician? Normally, they do the exact opposite. They chant "We hate you!" to a politician. They're chanting "We love you," and that's because my father, I truly believe that he's saving this country. He's saving faith. He's saving society. He's saving our flag. He's saving our values and everything that we believe in. He's done a great job for the nation.

RUSH: Well, I think that he is doing all of those things. That's why people love him. That's why they're willing to say so. That's why forty thousand of them wait in line in freezing Pennsylvania today singing "God Bless America." There isn't—and, by the way, folks, I don't mean any of this to be [a] suck-up. I'm not . . . This is really phenomenal, what is happening out there. This degree of support . . . "The bond," I call it. The bond of connection between Trump voters and the president himself is unparalleled in American politics. I've never seen in my lifetime anything like this, and it's fascinating to watch your father react to it. He's humbled by it; you can tell. He's humbled by it, and his humility surfaces and you see him deeply moved by this love for him. And I think that has to even steel him even more for the job, to get it done, to accomplish all these things that he's accomplished and wants to add to the list.

DON'T GIVE UP

The Rush Limbaugh Show, December 21, 2012

RUSH: Jim in Indianapolis, hi, and welcome to the EIB Network. Hello.

CALLER: Thank you, Rush. Love your show. First of all, happy holidays to you, your staff, your loved ones, and listeners.

RUSH: Thank you very much, sir. We all appreciate it.

CALLER: I work sometimes six to seven days a week. I go to school full-time. I have a wife and two small boys. The reason why I do all this is because I need to be a role model for my boys and a man for my wife. That's my job, not the government's. The point I'm trying to make to your audience is: Don't ever lose your high morals and values. Don't ever give up, stay optimistic, and eventually it'll pay off.

RUSH: Well, I know exactly what you're saying. Don't give up. Like Churchill said, "Never, never, never, never give up." Right now, I don't think a lot of people want to quit. I think people need some time off. It's been an intense year. I always encourage people to try to stay upbeat and positive about things, because you only get one life. Life in general is gonna present you with lots of suffering. But you don't have to add to it. You don't have to invent your own. Life presents enough of it as it is. Despite what's happening in Washington or elsewhere, it shouldn't govern your life. I'm not talking to you specifically. Everybody in general. People need to seize this great gift of life, realizing it's the only one you'll ever have, and to try to do the most with it for yourself, for your family, however that manifests itself to you each and every day. That's the best you can do, and then let that influence others around you, and that's how I think this thing gets turned around. I do have ultimate faith, like you do, that it will. We're too great a country, we have too much at stake, and the world needs this country. Just like, folks, I need you in this audience. Every year at Christmastime is when I really get thankful, and I count my lucky stars and my blessings for the fact that we're here twenty-five years. You people have no idea what you have meant to me and my family, and I can't ever repay you or thank you enough for it. But I do thank you sincerely from the bottom of my heart.

ADVICE FROM THE MAHA RUSHIE: ALWAYS BE WHO YOU ARE
The Rush Limbaugh Show, March 17, 2021

BRETT WINTERBLE (Guest Host): There are many people I have run into in my life that remember exactly when they first heard this program. Rush always said, "I'm just a guy on the radio," but he was more than that to a lot of us. He was a father figure, a brother, a friend. This program was a gathering place. He's also that voice in our head when perhaps we doubted ourselves, faced a fear in life, or just needed some encouragement and motivation.

RUSH: I've learned a lot in life, and I hope everybody does as they grow older; it's the whole point of things. And I remember back to the first days and weeks and years when this show started, and there was no grand strategy to it. It had a big, overarching goal: Be great, be the best show, be the number one show documented by ratings and audience research, the number one. That was the objective. There was no plan on how to do it, and there wasn't any five-year plan, three-year plan, or any of this. It was just me being myself each and every day here on the radio. And then, as that happened, everybody began analyzing it. People that I worked with, people in the media. They could not avoid it. People were analyzing what I was doing. And I had to make sure to never read any of that and to never listen to any of it. The last thing I wanted to know was what I was doing so that I could consciously continue to try. Because once you have to consciously continue to try what you already are, you're gonna stop being what you already are and you're gonna start trying to copy what you think you are. The danger when you try to keep being who you are, you stop being who you are. Being who you are shouldn't require any effort at all. Who you are au naturel is who you are. The minute you start trying to be who you are—

The President of the United States of America

Awards this

Presidential Medal of Freedom

to

Rush Hudson Limbaugh III

Rush Hudson Limbaugh III is a leading voice of conservatism and among the greatest radio hosts of all time. He has displayed a penchant for excellence throughout his career. From behind his golden EIB microphone, he created national conservative talk radio, speaking to millions of Americans who felt forgotten and inspiring a generation to government service. Mr. Limbaugh has also touched countless Americans through his generosity and philanthropy for the families of fallen first responders and for wounded service members. The United States proudly honors Rush Hudson Limbaugh III for his tenacity, love of country, and his irreplaceable voice.

The White House
Washington, D.C.
February 4, 2020

Rush was deeply moved
to receive America's
highest civilian honor,
the Presidential Medal
of Freedom, in 2020.

I had to resist it. I mean, there were a lot of well-intentioned people that said, "Well, if you want to keep this up, you're gonna have to change. If you want to keep this up, if you wanna really be doing this a long time, you'll have to moderate this and change a little bit." Some of them [were] well-intentioned, some of them weren't, but it didn't matter, because none of it was right. And it's another reason why I've never listened to anybody else who does this. I don't want to even inadvertently start copying other people and not be who I am—and being who I am in the sense of what interests me, what doesn't. If I start trying to imagine, for example, every day what all of you want to hear, I'm finished. And I don't mean this humorously or . . . It's a decent thing. Loving yourself is very important, folks. Not bragging about yourself or being sick about it, but if you don't like yourself, if you're not comfortable with who you are, then you're gonna always try to be something you're not, and you're finished, 'cause everybody's gonna recognize you as a phony eventually. We've got a guy on the phone from Katy, Texas, who said the references I made to everybody being who you are, not what somebody wants you to be but remaining who you are, that's the big challenge. He said it's something Mozart said during his lifetime, and that therefore I am in great company. It's a very nice thing. Thank you, Spencer.

BRETT: Indeed, he's in Mozart's company.

A RUSH BABY THANKS HIS PROFESSOR
The Rush Limbaugh Show, June 5, 2009

RUSH: Matthew in Fresno, California, you're on Open Line Friday. Hi, sir.
CALLER: Hello, sir. Mega dittos. I just wanted to call to let you know that I just graduated from Fresno State as a political science major.
RUSH: Congratulations!
CALLER: Thank you, sir. I've grown up ever since second grade coming home and watching *The Rush Limbaugh Show* with my dad. I've had Rush Limbaugh around me my whole life. My wife bought my first *Rush 24/7* subscription when we got married, and I've used information from the *Limbaugh Letter*s and from the Essential Stack for at least 90 percent of all

papers written during my college career. I just want to thank you for everything that you've done, and much appreciated.

RUSH: You're making me blush here. Is my face getting red? Can you see it on the Dittocam?

CALLER: *[Chuckles]*

RUSH: That is so nice of you to say. You have made my day.

CALLER: I'm forever grateful for all that you do for the conservative movement, sir. My children right now are listening to you. They love dancing when the music comes on. I've got a two-and-a-half- and a one-year-old, and they just love listening to you.

RUSH: Well, thank you very much. That is just . . . In these times, to learn that people your age and your kids are somehow missing the exposure to that which would pervert their thinking is just great. You are doing a great job. I'm sure it's not easy for you out there bucking the trends of popular sentiment yourself.

CALLER: No, it . . . I mean, some of my classes, you know, I was probably one of three conservatives, and probably the only one actually speaking up in a lot of my classes. But, you know, armed with a lot of the information that you put out there, I've been able to defeat a lot of the liberal premises.

RUSH: Thanks, Matthew. Congratulations. I appreciate it more than you know.

SIXTEEN-YEAR-OLD CALLER TO THE HOST: THANK YOU FOR INSPIRING US

The Rush Limbaugh Show, November 24, 2020

RUSH: We have Logan, sixteen years old. He is in Florida, visiting from California. And it's great to have you, Logan. You're up first today. Welcome to the program.

CALLER: Hi. Thank you for having me.

RUSH: Well, you bet. It's great to have you here.

CALLER: My grandma and I, we've called so many times. And we're here in Florida. I'm here with her, and she's the one who turned me on to your show. We used to listen to it in her big red truck, you know, driving around in California. And we're just so excited that we get to talk to you today.

RUSH: I'm glad you made it through. Your grandmother drives a big red truck?

CALLER: Yes, she does.

RUSH: Cool. Very, very cool. Where in California do you live?

CALLER: I live in Bakersfield, California.

RUSH: Oh, yeah, Bakersfield. I've been there. Bakersfield Business Conference. Got kicked out of it one year. I did. They gave me the hook. Do you like Florida?

CALLER: Oh, yeah, I love Florida. It's beautiful here. Yeah.

RUSH: Thinking of moving here, Logan?

CALLER: Maybe.

RUSH: Yeah. Yeah. Well, we'd love to have you. We'd love to have you. Thank you very much for calling. I appreciate it. It's great to have you with us out there.

CALLER: I just wanted to thank you. Thank you for just being you and inspiring us.

RUSH: Well, I appreciate that very, very much. That's very, very nice of you to say.

CALLER: Yeah.

RUSH: I love standing up for people. I love standing up for people who can't stand up for themselves or who don't have a voice. I'm not talking about cowards, people that just can't go beyond their little limited group. I love standing up for people. I love letting people know that they're not alone in things. So I appreciate that very much.

      . . .

I'll tell you this: This goes for any and all of you, not just the young people in this massive audience. Do not let the never-ending drumbeat of catastrophe, apocalypse, [and] doom and gloom that is on virtually every media outlet and in way too many movies—don't let that affect you. You are an American. You live in the United States of America. You live in the most prosperous country the human race has ever produced and known. —Rush Limbaugh

      . . .

IT'S NEVER TIME TO PANIC!
The Rush Limbaugh Show, November 6, 2020

All right, full disclosure: A number of people have called today, and Mr. Snerdley has put them up there. "You said that you would tell us when it's time to panic. You said that you thought the election was over. You said this and you said that," and so let me try to answer all of these challenging questions that you have.

Yes, I've told you that I'll tell you when it's time to panic. I've said over and over again that I'll tell you when it's time to panic. It isn't time to panic, because I'm never gonna panic. I'm never gonna give up. So, no, it's not time to panic. It's not time to run away. It's not time to walk away. It's never gonna be time to run away or walk away from the country.

I'm never gonna run away from the United States of America.

You know, life goes on. American politics, the business of the country goes on. Younger people feed into the system all the time. They bring with it their enthusiasm. The cynics that get old, yeah, they may drift away, go by the wayside, but there's always enthusiasm, because there is always gonna be love for America. There's always going to be, in my estimation, a huge majority of people who love this country, who want the best for this country and the people who live in it. There will always be a majority of Americans who want that to be the case, no matter how depressing it looks in the aftermath of an election defeat. That will pass. Human beings are human beings. They will gravitate to the positive and the possible.

You and I, people like us, are never gonna give up on this country. We live here. Your kids live here, your grandkids. You're never gonna give up on this country. And because of that, that's why I have always had faith in the future. It's because of you. Because I know who you are and I know how you look at the country, and I know what your hopes and dreams for it are and I know what your own personal hopes and dreams are.

NOW THAT YOU'VE TAUGHT ME, RUSH, WHAT DO I DO WITH IT?

The Rush Limbaugh Show, September 6, 2019

RUSH: Jerry from Detroit, you're on next on the EIB Network. Hello.

CALLER: Hello, Mr. L., how are you?

RUSH: Good, sir. Thank you for calling.

CALLER: I'm going to come at you from a little different direction than you're used to. I'm going to give you about twenty seconds of context so you know how to answer this. I found you a little less than three years ago, driving in the car with my friend. I've been listening to you ever since. You have actually changed the way I think as a person. You have no idea the impact you have on some people. And I just wanted to get this point across to you: I never did homework as a kid, but I became a student of yours. I take notes every single day. I actually spend time on weekends going over the stuff of how you come up with the stuff you do, and then I don't know what to do with all this information. So my question is, what do you want us to do with all this stuff that we learn from you? You know?

RUSH: This is such a great question! By golly, you have zeroed in on something. Let me do something first for you. I appreciate your taking notes. And I will tell you this: Taking notes and writing down what you've heard helps you remember it exponentially. So you're doing something really right there. But I want to offer you a subscription to my website, RushLimbaugh.com. You don't have to take notes anymore if you don't want to. Every transcript is reprinted. Every monologue, you can watch it, you can listen to it. And it's right there on the web. You can print out what you need and carry it around with you. I'd like to offer you that, because you're into this, and I cannot emphasize that writing down will facilitate how much you remember. It's the primary way that I studied when I did.

CALLER: I appreciate it. I accept.

RUSH: Okay. So when the call is over, don't hang up. Somebody will pick up the phone and get the information necessary from you to give you a lifetime username and password. This is a fifty-dollar-a-year subscription that you're gonna get for life because you have qualified here. Now, what do you do with all that you're learning? You're essentially asking me why am I doing this, in one sense. I don't mean that in an attack way. What you're to do with this is to share it with others. You are to become an extension of me. You are to become a confident expert in whatever it is that happens here that interests you, that you have therefore taken a special amount of time to learn. You are to use it to spread it to others. You are to use it to continue to shape your life and to have it affect the way you live, the decisions that you make. And you become a role model, and then you find other like-minded people and keep doing the same thing. This is how— I don't want to equate this to a classroom, because this is a radio show. But it's a learning process. I can't tell you how flattered I am to get your reaction to this show and what it means to you. You're to use what you know when you vote. You're to use what you know when you make decisions on issues as you follow them. You're to use what you know to become the go-to guy in your circle of friends who has the answers. You don't say, "Well, Rush said it." It's because *you* said it. You say it with confidence, because you know it and believe it. And that's what you do with it. You help others. You spread the word. That's going way beyond voting. That's a classic question. It's exactly why I'm doing this, to expand the universe of knowledge out there in a usable way by people.

• • •

It's never time to panic, folks. It's never, ever gonna be time to give up on our country. It will never be time to give up on the United States. It will never be time to give up on yourself. Trust me. —Rush Limbaugh

• • •

WHAT WOULD I DO IF I DIDN'T DO THIS?
The Rush Limbaugh Show, June 20, 2014

The Official Program Observer has a question. What is it? *[Interruption]* Mmm-hmm. Oh, wow. If I . . . ? El Snerdbo has asked me what I would be passionate about if I, what, retired, or just was not doing this at all? If I was not doing radio, what would I have done? Well, that was the problem.

You know, when I got fired for the fifth time and left radio, I was twenty-eight and went to work for the Kansas City Royals. I thought I was finished in radio. I'd given it my best shot. Being a deejay didn't work out, and I was not passionate about working for a baseball team. It's just what was available. I tried to make the most of it, but I found out that I wasn't cut out for corporate conformity.

[Interruption] No, I never wanted to be a pilot. I didn't want to do anything else. Well, I always said that I would run an airport if I weren't doing this. I'm fascinated by how that all works. But this has been my one passion. I don't know. *[Interruption]* Oh. Snerdley has said he can see me running a tech company. No, no, I like being a customer too much.

One thing I learned about working for the baseball team: Once something that is a hobby or a vocational passion becomes your job, it totally changes. I got to the point where in year five, I was hoping the team didn't make the playoffs because I was ready for eighteen-hour days to end. Well, I couldn't tell anybody that. Making the playoffs, going on the World Series *[chuckles]*, that's what it's all about.

But that had happened in the first year. Well, second year for me. So it was grueling, and it wasn't a whole lot of money, either. But this has been the only real passion that I've had. One of those times I got fired, I thought about going into radio sales, until I had an interview with a sales manager at a station in Kansas City, and the guy was a genuine lunatic.

I'm interviewing for the job, and he's yelling and screaming at me about what his demands will be and what they are. I'm saying, "Geez, I have to face this every day?" He was a genuine shouting, maniacal guy. It's like sometimes I think people behave in front of me just to see what I will do or how I will react to, say, what they think is outrageous. When I met Shimon Peres in his office in Israel . . .

On my famed trip to Israel in the summer of 1993, Rabbi Nate Siegel was one of my hosts, along with Malcolm Hoenlein of the American Conference of Presidents of Major American Jewish Organizations. It was five days that was worth a college semester. It was five jam-packed days. By the way, Nate Siegel just had a birthday. I sent a video. Did you ever get an acknowledgment on that video? I didn't either, so I don't know if he got it, but I sent him a Dittocam birthday greeting. Anyway, we had meetings with Yitzhak Rabin and with Shimon Peres in his office, and in the meeting with Peres, he kept undoing his belt. He's sitting there and he kept undoing his belt and then rebuckling it. He'd look at the holes in his belt while we're talking.

His first topic of conversation with me was the importance of trees and greenery to everything. It's like somebody had given him a briefing and he thought that I was some extreme, wacko right-winger walking in there and he was trying to taunt me. So this sales manager, who knows what this guy thought. The guy was shouting and screaming and throwing things off of his desk, and showing me what he was going to be demanding every day in terms of sales.

This guy every day in a sales meeting? No way.

This is the long version here of telling you that this is why I'm so fortunate. I was able to end up doing what I think I was born to do. I've never had passion for anything else—I mean, career-wise—like I've got for this. *[Interruption]* Thought about being an actor? I've never thought about being an actor. By the way, you have to temper all of these thoughts with: If I ever did, what are the odds?

There's no way, unless I became a liberal first.

You know, folks, let me tell you. I'm watching some things happen in the media. There are a lot of . . . I shouldn't say "a lot." There are some noteworthy supposed conservatives in the media who are all of a sudden gaining a lot of praise from the Drive-by Media. I'm going to tell you, that is highly seductive. When you start getting universal accolades and praise from those people, it's tough to resist.

"The Big Clique wants you," is the way it works, and I'm starting to sense that happen to some in the media that you have always thought to be conservative. I can't ever imagine something like that happening to me. So, being an actor? No way. I've never wanted to be. I mean, that's not actually true. To be honest, there's a whole lot of stuff I would like to try. Just tons of it. But in terms of making careers out of them? No.

We are forever grateful to the entire Trump family for their continued support.

EVERYONE REMEMBERS THE FIRST TIME THEY HEARD RUSH
The Rush Limbaugh Show, February 19, 2021

MARK STEYN (Guest Host): You know, before Rush, things were grim. You could be a right-wing guy, you could be modestly center right, but you lived in a center-left or far-left world. Basically, when you switched on the TV, when you switched on the radio, it was Dan Rather, it was Peter Jennings, it was Oprah, it was Phil Donahue, and there wasn't a lot of talk stations because of the Fairness Doctrine. It wasn't just that you had to balance out the left-wing talk with the right-wing talk so you could find a really great left-wing guy to give a two-hour show to but then you had to find a right-wing guy to give a two-hour show to. That was all incredibly difficult for most radio station owners. So it was easier just to program soft-and-easy favorites twenty-four hours a day, or top forty, or country, or whatever, than actually trying to run a talk station because of the Fairness Doctrine. So the Fairness Doctrine didn't mean there was left-wing talk or right-wing talk. It actually meant there was hardly any talk at all. I think when Rush started there were only two hundred talk stations in the United States of America. Now it is the dominant form of AM radio, and there are thousands and thousands and thousands. And, as you know, this show is carried on over six hundred of them. So, it was completely new.

BRIT HUME: Along comes this guy. You know, I was a reporter working for ABC News at the time, and I remember people saying, "Have you heard about this guy, Rush Limbaugh?" And I started listening to his radio show, and it was tremendously fun to listen to. . . .

SEAN HANNITY: 1987 or '88, and I remember I was in a radio studio, and somebody told me, "You gotta hear this guy on the radio."

DAN BONGINO: We accidentally flipped on the radio and heard "talent on loan from God." You heard that, and you said, "Who's this guy?" That's the first time, was sitting outside of Queens College and flipping on the dial and hearing the incredible voice of Rush Limbaugh—and it changed my life.

BEVERLY HALLBERG: My dad, who picked me up from school every day, always had Rush on the radio.

MARK STEYN: The first time I heard him, we were driving through the North Maine Woods, and suddenly this voice comes in—'cause the radio is, like, automatically scanning for stations—and we hear Rush for the first time, and we're agog. We all stopped talking. It was amazing. There was nothing like that. *[Chuckles]* That was me right at the end there, and I will never forget that. We were very, very deep into the North Maine Woods, where no radio station comes through, and the only one that kind of really sort of does is 94.9. I think it's off Portland, Maine. But they got a big trans-mitter on the top of Mount Washington and they're playing that, you know, bland, insipid adult contemporary, which you wouldn't really want to listen to except [when] there is nothing else. So we're all just talking and the radio is scanning around the dial, around the dial, around the dial. We drive for whatever it is, forty-five minutes, and eventually—and suddenly, out of nowhere, as I said there—Rush's voice comes on, and he starts talking about what happens when the Arts and Croissant Crowd descends on your small town, and he's playing "Born Free," punctuated by gunfire. We don't talk about anything else except this incredible guy we just heard doing politics in a way that no one had ever done before and none of us had after heard before. I will never forget that. It just . . . Rush basically just opened up the possibilities.

* * *

CALLER: Mega Rush dittos, Mark.

MARK: And the same to you. Mega dittos into eternity.

CALLER: Agreed. Totally agreed. The last two days have been hell. I can tell you that from my personal life and my friends. But I want to focus on the good things, and the best thing that Rush ever did for me—even though I've been listening for thirty years, so God only knows the impact he had on my life—was the last two years of my father's life he was in poor health, very fragile. His faculties were totally intact. You know, he was still Dad. But every day that I could, which was about six out of seven days a week, I would bring lunch, and I always timed it for Rush because him and I both love Rush. And we would eat our lunch listening to Rush, and that was the only time in those two years where he would buckle over belly laughing—I mean, a laugh that I haven't heard in my life. I'm his son and I never heard this laugh before, and he listened to Rush literally 'til the day he passed away. It meant so much to him, and so much to me. When Rush passed away, all of a sudden, it hit me. I was like, boy, I was blessed to have those moments. Blessed. And Rush made it possible, and that's something I will remember for the rest of my life, Mark.

* * *

MARK: I asked for stories of when you first heard Rush, and Marie said that she first heard him when she was a child. She grew up on a farm, and as soon as she started driving the tractor at the age of twelve, Rush was tuned in. Marie says, "And for the longest time I thought he broadcasted from the middle of our field." You know, he loved being on the radio, and he would have broadcast from the middle of your field and just put a little transmitter on the back of your tractor. But that's Marie, who has been listening to Rush as soon as she started driving the tractor on the family farm at the age of twelve, and Rush was tuned in every day.

LIFELONG LISTENER ON HOW RUSH'S VOICE CONNECTS THREE GENERATIONS
The Rush Limbaugh Show, December 22, 2020

RUSH: Adam in Lancaster County, Pennsylvania. Hello.
CALLER: Hello, Rush. Thank you so much for taking my call. Merry Christmas—and, sir, you are definitely family to me. No, it's not Open Line Friday, but I need to tell you what I mean by family. I grew up a lifelong listener, thanks to my father, Jeffrey, and my grandfather, Monroe. We've always listened to you, and my grandfather was fortunate enough to go see you live in your studio. He passed away when I was in high school, and when I think of him, I can picture him clearly. I picture him in your studio. Three years ago,

I was driving with my wife after a particularly rough year, turned on the radio, and you were there. I started to tear up, and my wife said, "What's going on?" I said, "It's because when I listen to Rush," when I listen to you, "I remember my grandfather, and I remember my father," who lives in South Carolina. Every time I hear you, it's all three together. Your voice, sir, transcends time and space.

RUSH: Wow.

CALLER: Whether you're listening in heaven or you're listening on this earth, we all thank you.

RUSH: That is heart-stopping. That's incredible—and, you know, I happen to know what you mean, which is why it's so meaningful. I've had similar things happen. Just a short example here. I remember . . . One of the things I like [about] Mannheim Steamroller, I was in an airplane around Christmastime, and I was flying out to California. I had a Rush to Excellence Tour stop I had to do. My father had recently passed away. I was thinking about him, and I'm looking out the window. I've got a window seat, and it's a crystal-clear night, with the moon just as visible as it can be. And Mannheim Steamroller is on my tape deck. That's what we used back then to listen to music. There were no such things as iPods or things like that. So, I had marvelous remembrances of my dad while I'm listening to Mannheim Steamroller. And it made me . . . Every time I heard Mannheim Steamroller, it's what made me think of my dad. We all have these connections. I am so honored and flattered to be yours that I . . . I'm . . . I don't know what to say. I just have this profound appreciation. I'm glad you got through, and I really, really do appreciate very much all of that.

WHAT THESE THIRTY-YEAR LISTENERS LEARNED FROM RUSH
The Rush Limbaugh Show, November 22, 2019

RUSH: Bernie in Elkhorn, Nebraska. Great to have you with us today, sir. Hello.

CALLER: Hi, Rush. My wife and I are thirty-year-long listeners of yours. And we recently took some time to compile a list of the top ten things we learned from you, and within the top ten we have a top three. Number one is what we learned from you about the true meaning of Thanksgiving and how William Bradford dumped socialism in favor of incentives and letting the Pilgrims all work their own land. Number two, we learned from you about the American Dream. And number three, we've heard you all these decades making reference to your talent on loan from God. We believe and we've observed that you should say instead that you've been touched by God to play a role in saving this country.

RUSH: Well, now, I have enough trouble with talent on loan from God; people think I'm saying I *am* God. You'd be amazed the number of people that don't understand that. They have a knee-jerk reaction to it, Bernie, and they think, this guy, he really thinks he's God. And of course I don't. It's the ultimate statement of humility. "Touched by God" would be—I like that. I like that.

CALLER: You play a role in saving this country, Rush.

RUSH: Well, I don't know about that. This country's gonna be around. The people of this country are gonna be the ones that save it, and have constantly saved it. That is the greatest unstated aspect of this country. Despite all the brilliant bureaucrats and the think tanks, media people, it's the people of this country who make it work every day. And most of them do so in anonymity. Most of them are not seeking fame. They just get up and do what they do every day. And they, in the process, make all this work. And they use everything God-given that they have that is fueled by their freedom. And that's what sets this country apart. It's what's always set this country apart. It's the route of American exceptionalism. So that's very kind of you, Bernie, you and your wife sitting around thinking about it.

• • •

Rush is irreplaceable, unique. He had an audience that
was massive. He was a fantastic man, a fantastic talent.
People, whether they loved him or not, they respected him.
They really did.
—President Donald J. Trump, Tribute to Rush, 2021

• • •

MERRY CHRISTMAS, EVERYBODY—I LOVE YOU ALL
The Rush Limbaugh Show, December 23, 2020

A yearly tradition. We wrap up with Mannheim Steamroller and "Silent Night," and my ongoing attempts to thank everybody in the audience—all of you—for everything you mean to me. That last call—that reminds me how much I love all of you, how much I so appreciate everything you've meant to me and my family.

You don't have any idea how . . . I know so many people think this program has changed their lives for the better. You have no idea what you all have meant to me and my family. The day's gonna come, folks, where I'm not gonna be able to do this. I don't know when that is. I want to be able to do it for as long as I want to do it.

I want to, but the day will come where I'm not going to be able to, and I want you to understand that even when the day comes, I'd like to be here. 'Cause I have this sense of needing to constantly show my appreciation for all that you have done and meant to me. I hope you all have a great Christmas, and a great New Year. . . . Again, folks, thank you so much. I wish there were a way to say it other than "thank you." You're just the best. My family is just the best.

*I'm never going to be able to adequately thank
the people who are responsible for one of the
greatest lives anybody could have. I am doing
what I was born to do. It was what I wanted to
do since I was eight years old. I have met the
goals I set for myself. I've maintained them.
And I have been able to do it all, for the most
part, on my terms. It cannot get any better.
I have been so thankful for the blessings that I
have, and to be able to share all of this with you
and tell you how grateful I am, how gratified
I am that you have made this possible.*

CONCLUSION
David Limbaugh

Rush will forever be Radio's Greatest of All Time: the GOAT. His timeless words and passion for our country will always fill our hearts with pride. He dedicated his life to challenging us all to think about the vital issues that affect the future of our country and how we must never let go of the principles enshrined in our Declaration of Independence, Constitution, and Bill of Rights. We must always remember our country is miraculous, regardless of our shortcomings.

Rush was truly an irreplaceable pioneer who paved the way for so many future broadcasters and conservative talk programs. He was also a life coach of sorts for countless Americans. Over the years, he encouraged his audience to find their personal passions and to never let obstacles hold them back. He pushed each of them to be the best they could be—to dream, discover what they love, pursue it with passion, and reject naysayers in their lives. He inspired them to open small businesses, engage in politics, and support their communities. We've received thousands of messages from grateful fans, sharing that he changed their lives. What a blessing to read these stories.

Rush was an extraordinary man with the greatest gift in broadcasting the world has ever known. As a fearless champion of liberty, he changed America forever. He was taken from us too soon, and we miss him profoundly, but his legacy lives on. We will carry on the Rush Limbaugh legacy through many efforts, including the Rush and Kathryn Adams Limbaugh Family Foundation, where scholarships will be provided to young patriots to continue their education and to families facing hardship brought on by a medical crisis. We will also continue to support owners of small businesses and the United States military through a new website, www.OfficialRushLimbaugh.com.

Let's honor Rush by remaining committed to this great nation and doing everything we can to preserve our God-given rights and our precious liberties. Let's carry his torch in this never-ending struggle, and do all we can to ensure that the miracle of our founding is never forgotten.

Until we all meet again, may Rush remain our guiding light as Heaven's Anchorman. Remember: It is never time to panic. Life will go on, and our best days are ahead.

--- ✦ ---

This special boy, born on our wedding day, was named after Rush Hudson. A true honor!

ACKNOWLEDGMENTS

We are forever grateful to David Limbaugh for being there for Rush as a brother and trusted confidant throughout their lives. Rush admired David tremendously and always appreciated how supportive he was of all endeavors, including this collection. Rush loved his family with all of his heart.

We would like to thank Jonathan Adams Rogers for his true devotion to this project and for the countless hours he spent on historical research. This book simply could not have been completed without him.

Thank you sincerely to Spero Mehallis and Luke Mathisen for their exceptional work over many years. Both contributed significantly to the cover design, overall production, and layout of this beautiful book.

Over the years, we have received the most special letters, emails, gifts, and photos from all over the world. Please know how much your kindness means to us. Rush was honored in so many wonderful ways.

The inspiration for this book came in part from our dear friend the late Vince Flynn, bestselling novelist, who encouraged us to put together a collection of Rush's favorite shows. Vince always said that Rush was the Greatest of All Time and his commentary timeless.

We know without hesitation that Rush is watching from heaven with tremendous pride.

With love,

Kathryn

May the road rise to meet you.
May the wind always be at your back.
May the sunshine be warm upon your face,
and rains fall softly upon your fields.
And until we meet again,
May God hold you
in the palm of His hand.

—Irish Blessing

PHOTO CREDITS

Pages x–xi: Rush and Kathryn Limbaugh Archives

Page xii: Rush and Kathryn Limbaugh Archives

Page 4: Rush and Kathryn Limbaugh Archives

Page 11: Rush and Kathryn Limbaugh Archives

Page 15: Rush and Kathryn Limbaugh Archives

Page 22: President Ronald Reagan and William F. Buckley, Jr. (Bettmann, Getty Images, February 21, 1983)

Page 25: Rush speech at *National Review* event (Photo by @LilaPhoto)

Pages 30–31: President Ronald Reagan with Prime Minister Margaret Thatcher during a working luncheon at Camp David (Wikimedia Commons, December 22, 1984)

Page 35: President Ronald Reagan walks with Prime Minister Margaret Thatcher, Camp David (Wikimedia Commons, November 6, 1986)

Page 38: Rush and Kathryn Limbaugh Archives

Page 46: Rush and Kathryn Limbaugh Archives

Page 52: Rush and Kathryn Limbaugh Archives

Page 53: President Ronald and First Lady Nancy Reagan (Bettman, Getty Images, August 15, 1988)

Page 59: Rush and Kathryn Limbaugh Archives

Page 62: *New York Times Magazine* cover, July 6, 2008 (*New York Times*)

Page 68: Justices Antonin Scalia and Ruth Bader Ginsburg (Photo by Alex Wong, Getty Images, April 17, 2014)

Page 74: *Limbaugh Letter,* September 2020 (Estate of Rush Limbaugh—Legacy)

Page 80: Rush and Kathryn Limbaugh Archives

Page 87: Bob S., Wilmington, CA (Kathryn Limbaugh, KARHL Holdings, LLC)

Page 92: Rush and Kathryn Limbaugh Archives

Page 94: Rush and Kathryn Limbaugh Archives

Page 99: Rush and Kathryn Limbaugh Archives

Pages 100–101: Rush and Kathryn Limbaugh Archives

Page 104: Rush and Kathryn Limbaugh Archives

Page 106: Rush and Kathryn Limbaugh Archives

Page 109: Rush and Kathryn Limbaugh Archives

Page 111: Rush and Kathryn Limbaugh Archives

Page 112: Harmony, 8 years old (Kathryn Limbaugh, KARHL Holdings, LLC)

Page 114: Rush and Kathryn Limbaugh Archives

Page 122: Rush and Kathryn Limbaugh Archives

Page 125: Rush and Kathryn Limbaugh Archives

Page 128: Rush and Kathryn Limbaugh Archives

Page 131: Rush and Kathryn Limbaugh Archives

Page 132: Rush and Kathryn Limbaugh Archives

Page 135: Mark L., (Kathryn Limbaugh, KARHL Holdings, LLC)

Pages 138–39: Rush and Kathryn Limbaugh Archives

Page 141: Rudolph Giuliani, George H. W. Bush, and Barbara Bush at Republican National Convention (Photo by Carley Margolis/FilmMagic, Getty Images, 2004)

Page 142: President Trump with Rush and Kathryn Limbaugh at the White House (White House Photographer, Rush and Kathryn Limbaugh Archives)

Page 151: Photo by Donna Newman, Rush and Kathryn Limbaugh Archives

Page 160: Rush and Kathryn Limbaugh Archives

Page 163: Rush and Kathryn Limbaugh Archives

Page 165: Rush and Kathryn Limbaugh Archives

Page 168: Rush Limbaugh speaks at the rally for President Bush's reelection campaign (Photo © Wally McNamee/CORBIS/Corbis, Getty Images)

Pages 172–73: Rush and Kathryn Limbaugh Archives

Pages 176–77: Rush and Kathryn Limbaugh Archives

Page 182: Rush and Kathryn Limbaugh Archives

Page 186: Rush Limbaugh appeared on a number of television shows highlighting his sense of humor, including this *Family Guy* episode that aired October 3, 2010, titled *Excellence in Broadcasting.*

Page 188: Rush Limbaugh at his studio at WABC Radio in New York City on December 14, 1988 (Photo by Bruce Gilbert, Jr./Newsday RM via Getty Images)

Page 195: Dr. Ben Carson sworn in as the Housing and Urban Development (HUD) Secretary for the Trump Administration, with Candy Carson, and granddaughter Tesora Carson, March 2, 2017 (Photo by Alex Wong/ Getty Images)

Page 200: Rush Limbaugh appeared on many news and political television shows, including *20/20* with Barbara Walters.

Page 204: Leif W. (Kathryn Limbaugh, KARHL Holdings, LLC)

Page 207: *Limbaugh Letter*, June 2020 (Estate of Rush Limbaugh—Legacy)

Pages 218–19: Rush Limbaugh sits at his desk at Talk Radio 700 KSEV during the Republican National Convention in Houston. (Photo © Shepard Sherbell/CORBIS SABA/Corbis via Getty Images, January 1, 1992)

Page 224: Rush and Kathryn Limbaugh Archives

Page 228: Rush and Kathryn Limbaugh Archives

Pages 244–45: Newly elected Senator Fred Thompson (R-Tenn.) and talk-show host Rush Limbaugh after a Saturday night dinner at Camden Yards in 1994. (Photo Maureen Keating/ CQ Roll Call via Getty Images)

Page 247: Rush Limbaugh talks on a phone as House Speaker Newt Gingrich gestures during a break in taping of NBC's *Meet the Press,* Sunday November 12, 1995, in Washington. (AP Photo/ Doug Mills)

Page 248: *National Review* cover depicting Rush Limbaugh as Leader of the Opposition, September 6, 1993

Page 251: Rush and Kathryn Limbaugh Archives

Page 254: Rush Limbaugh is congratulated by Larry King at the Radio Hall of Fame induction ceremony at the Museum of Broadcast Communications in Chicago, Ill., November 7, 1993. (AP Photo/Mike Fisher)

Page 259: Rush and Kathryn Limbaugh Archives

Pages 262–63: Vice President Mike Pence participates in a live interview on *The Rush Limbaugh Show,* Friday, February 28, 2020, at the EIB Network in Palm Beach, Fla. (Storms Media Group/Alamy Live News)

Page 267: Rush and Kathryn Limbaugh Archives

Page 270: Rush and Kathryn Limbaugh Archives

Pages 274–75: Rush and Kathryn Limbaugh Archives

Pages 278–79: Rush and Kathryn Limbaugh Archives

Page 282: Rush and Kathryn Limbaugh Archives

Page 288: Rush and Kathryn Limbaugh Archives

Page 292: Rush and Kathryn Limbaugh Archives

Page 298: Photo by Donna Newman, Rush and Kathryn Limbaugh Archives

Page 304: Rush and Kathryn Limbaugh Archives

Pages 308–9: Rush and Kathryn Limbaugh Archives

Page 317: *The Tonight Show with Jay Leno*— Episode 408—Pictured (l-r): Talk show host Rush Limbaugh during an interview with host Jay Leno on February 25, 1994 (Photo by Margaret Norton/NBCU Photo Bank/NBCUniversal via Getty Images via Getty Images)

Page 321: Rush and Kathryn Limbaugh Archives

Page 323: Rush and Kathryn Limbaugh Archives

Page 327: Photo by Donna Newman, Rush and Kathryn Limbaugh Archives

Page 329: Al Michaels and Rush Limbaugh talk on the field before the New York Jets face the New England Patriots for the last *Monday Night Football* game, on ABC, at Giants Stadium in East Rutherford, New Jersey, on December 26, 2005. (UPI Photo/John Angelillo via Alamy)

Page 332: Letter from Prime Minister Benjamin Netanyahu (Rush and Kathryn Limbaugh Archives)

Page 333: Witnessed by President Trump, Prime Minister Netanyahu signed a peace deal with the UAE and a declaration of intent to make peace with Bahrain. (Photo by Alex Wong via Getty Images)

Page 336: Rush and Kathryn Limbaugh Archives

Page 339: Rush and Kathryn Limbaugh Archives

Page 340: Rush and Kathryn Adams Limbaugh Archives

Page 345: Rush and Kathryn Limbaugh Archives

Page 348: The US Navy Blue Angels fly overhead at United States Naval Academy, 2021. (Photo by Alex Edelman/CNP/Bloomberg via Getty Images)

Page 350: Rush and Kathryn Limbaugh Archives

Page 353: President Trump with Rush and Kathryn Limbaugh (White House Photographer)

Page 365: Rush and Kathryn Limbaugh Archives

Page 370: Rush and Kathryn Limbaugh Archives

Page 374: Rush and Kathryn Limbaugh Archives

Page 379: Rush and Kathryn Limbaugh Archives

Page 382: Photo by Donna Newman, Rush and Kathryn Limbaugh Archives

Page 391: Photo by Donna Newman, Rush and Kathryn Limbaugh Archives

Page 396: *Limbaugh Letter,* November 2015 (Estate of Rush Limbaugh—Legacy)

Page 410: Photo by Donna Newman, Rush and Kathryn Limbaugh Archives

Page 413: Photo by Donna Newman, Rush and Kathryn Limbaugh Archives

Pages 414–15: Photo by Donna Newman, Rush and Kathryn Limbaugh Archives

Pages 416–17: Photo by Donna Newman, Rush and Kathryn Limbaugh Archives

Pages 418–19: Photo by Donna Newman, Rush and Kathryn Limbaugh Archives

Pages 420–21: Photo by Donna Newman, Rush and Kathryn Limbaugh Archives

Page 422: Rush and Kathryn Limbaugh Archives

Page 425: Rush and Kathryn Limbaugh Archives

Pages 426–27: Rush and Kathryn Limbaugh Archives

Page 428: Rush and Kathryn Limbaugh Archives

Page 438: Rush and Kathryn Limbaugh Archives

Page 441: Rush and Kathryn Limbaugh Archives

Page 442: Rush and Kathryn Limbaugh Archives

Page 449: Rush and Kathryn Limbaugh Archives

Pages 454–55: Photo by Drew Angerer, Getty Images, February 4, 2020, Washington, D.C.

Pages 458–59: Rush Limbaugh at State of the Union Address, February 4, 2020 (Photo by Mandel Ngan/AFP via Getty Images)

Page 461: Rush and Kathryn Limbaugh Archives

Page 464: Rush and Kathryn Limbaugh Archives

Page 468: Rush Limbaugh embraces his wife, Kathryn Adams Limbaugh, after First Lady Melania Trump gives him the Presidential Medal of Freedom during the State of the Union address in the chamber of the US House of Representatives on February 4, 2020, in Washington, DC. (Photo by Drew Angerer via Getty Images)

Pages 472–73: Rush and Kathryn Limbaugh Archives

Page 482: Ivanka Trump with Rush Limbaugh (Photo by Mario Tama via Getty Images, February 4, 2020)

Page 489: Rush and Kathryn Limbaugh Archives

Page 490: Rush and Kathryn Limbaugh Archives

Page 494: Baby Rush Hudson (Kathryn Limbaugh, KARHL Holdings, LLC)

Pages 496–97: Rush and Kathryn Limbaugh Archives